Nation Branding

Nation Branding

Concepts, Issues, Practice

Keith Dinnie

ELSEVIER

Amsterdam • Boston • Heidelberg • London • New York • Oxford
Paris • San Diego • San Francisco • Singapore • Sydney • Tokyo

Butterworth-Heinemann is an imprint of Elsevier

Butterworth-Heinemann is an imprint of Elsevier
Linacre House, Jordan Hill, Oxford OX2 8DP, UK
30 Corporate Drive, Suite 400, Burlington, MA 01803, USA

First edition 2008

Notice
No responsibility is assumed by the publisher for any injury and/or damage to persons
or property as a matter of products liability, negligence or otherwise, or from any use
or operation of any methods, products, instructions or ideas contained in the material
herein

British Library Cataloguing in Publication Data
A catalogue record for this book is available from the British Library

Library of Congress Cataloging-in-Publication Data
A catalog record for this book is available from the Library of Congress

ISBN: 978-0-7506-8349-4

For information on all Butterworth-Heinemann
publications visit our website at books.elsevier.com

Printed and bound in Great Britain

08 09 10   10 9 8 7 6 5 4 3 2 1

Contents

Preface

This book has been written to make a contribution to the small but rapidly growing literature on nation branding. It is designed to show not only the ways in which conventional brand management techniques can be applied to nations but also to provide some background depth on the context and nature of nation branding. Therefore, the scope of the book encompasses wider issues related to national identity, sustainable development and political awareness, in addition to the more familiar branding themes of brand identity, brand image, brand positioning, brand equity and so on. This approach is intended to ensure that the theory and practice of nation branding is covered in a rich, multi-dimensional manner.

The book is written for a number of audiences, each of whom will come to the field of nation branding with their own specific interests and agenda:

- MBA, Masters and upper level undergraduate students studying marketing, branding, international business, public diplomacy and tourism
- Government and policy-makers worldwide, particularly in economic development agencies, export promotion agencies and tourism organizations
- Individuals with an interest in how their country is perceived and the ways in which their country is (or is not) attempting to enhance its reputation

A key feature of the book is the provision of multiple perspectives on nation branding through the inclusion of over 20 contributions from a wide range of academics and practitioners. These contributions illuminate vividly the theories, concepts and frameworks that form the basis of the book. Country case insights are offered on the nation-branding activities and challenges of countries as diverse as France, Japan, South Africa, Egypt, Brazil and many more. It is a key contention of this book that the principles of nation branding can be applied successfully by any nation whether small or large, rich or poor, developed or emerging. The country case insights are designed to demonstrate this point.

Many people have contributed in different ways to this book. I hope that you will find it stimulating and thought-provoking to read. It is designed to act as a starting point for discussion and action, rather than as a final statement on the topic of nation branding.

Enjoy the book!

Keith Dinnie
Edinburgh
www.brandhorizons.com

Acknowledgements

First and foremost, my thanks go to Anna Fabrizio, Commissioning Editor at Elsevier Butterworth-Heinemann, whose enthusiasm for this book was key to making it happen. Thanks also to Tim Goodfellow and Liz Burton, and all the other people at publishers Elsevier Butterworth-Heinemann for their hard work in bringing this book to fruition.

I express many thanks to all the individuals and organizations who contributed to this book in the form of country case insights, academic perspectives and practitioner insights. Your contributions have immeasurably enriched this book.

Many thanks also to colleagues and students at Edinburgh University, Glasgow Caledonian University, and Strathclyde University for numerous interesting discussions and insights into the theory and practice of nation branding.

Finally, my thanks go to my parents and my wife for their unending support during the writing of this book.

About the author

Dr Keith Dinnie teaches at Temple University Japan (TUJ), Tokyo. He has delivered Masters and Honours level courses in various aspects of marketing and branding at the University of Edinburgh. He has also taught on the world class Strathclyde MBA programme, delivering seminars on marketing management and brand management & strategy in the UK as well as in international centres such as Athens, Hong Kong and Shanghai. He has lectured on a visiting basis at the University of Hanover and the University of Koblenz, Germany, as well as conducting research and consultancy in several countries worldwide.

He has published in various journals including the *Journal of Customer Behaviour*, *The Marketing Review*, *Journal of Brand Management*, *Journal of General Management* and *Corporate Communications: An International Review*. As Book Review Editor for the *Journal of Brand Management*, he has reviewed over 25 books on branding over the past 6 years. He was invited to act as Guest Editor for the *Journal of Brand Management* special editions on Global Branding (2005) and Nordic Brands (2008). His research and consultancy work includes projects conducted on behalf of market-leading consultancies Landor Associates and Burson-Marsteller, as well as innovative research conducted into the emerging field of nation branding amongst senior decision-makers and brand consultants on a worldwide basis. He is the founder of Brand Horizons consultancy.

Email: keithdinnie@brandhorizons.com

About the contributors

Ximena Alvarez Aguirre

Ximena Alvarez Aguirre is former Vice-President of CABOTUR – Cámara Boliviana de Turismo (Bolivian Tourism Chamber 2002–2004) and former Vice-Minister of Tourism in Bolivia (2004–2005). Wide experience in the tourism sector of the country. Teaching experience in the Tourism area in the CEMLA – Centro Empresarial Latino Americano (Latin American Entrepreneurial Center) in Cochabamba, Bolivia. Currently, she is the General Director and owner of Discover the World Marketing in Bolivia, which represents several airlines from different parts of the world. First degree in Economic Science from the Bolivian Catholic University. Diploma in Tourism from CETT – Centro de Estudios Técnicos Turísticos (Technical Tourism Study Center) in Barcelona, Spain.

Satoshi Akutsu

Satoshi Akutsu is an Associate Professor at Graduate School of International Corporate Strategy, Hitotsubashi University in Tokyo. He received his Ph.D. from the Haas School of Business at the University of California, Berkeley. He has published more than a dozen books/articles on marketing and brand management in Japanese. He is the co-author of 'A Mentality Theory of Knowledge Creation and Transfer' in Managing Industrial Knowledge (Nonaka and Teece, eds.) and 'Branding Capability' in Hitotsubashi on Knowledge Management (Takeuchi and Nonaka, eds.). Professor Akutsu is an advisor to a number of companies and has been a speaker at management conferences, seminars and workshops throughout the world. He is a member of the Task Force on Contents in the Intellectual Property Policy Headquarters and a judge of Japan PR Award by the Japan PR Association.

Simon Anholt

Simon Anholt is the leading authority on managing and measuring national identity and reputation. He is a member of the British Government's Public Diplomacy Board and has advised the governments of the Netherlands, Jamaica, Tanzania, Iceland, Latvia, Sweden, Botswana, Germany, South Korea, Romania, Scotland, Croatia, Mongolia, the Baltic Sea Region, Bhutan, Ecuador, New Zealand, Switzerland and Slovenia, as well as organizations including the United Nations, the World Economic Forum and the World Bank. He is Founding Editor of the quarterly journal, *Place Branding* and *Public Diplomacy*. His books include

Brand New Justice, *Brand America* and *Competitive Identity – The New Brand Management for Nations, Cities and Regions*. He publishes three major global surveys, the Anholt Nation Brands Index, City Brands Index and State Brands Index. For further information, please see www.earthspeak.com.

Stephen Brown

Stephen Brown is Professor of Marketing Research at the University of Ulster, Northern Ireland. Best known for Postmodern Marketing, he has written numerous books ranging from *The Marketing Code* and *Free Gift Inside* to *Wizard: Harry Potter's Brand Magic*. He is currently working on *Agents & Dealers*, a prequel to *The Marketing Code*.

Francis Buttle

Dr Francis Buttle is Director of two Australian-based organizations – Francis Buttle & Associates (www.buttleassociates.com) and Listening Post (www.listeningpost.com.au). He was formerly full Professor of Marketing and Customer Relationship Management at three of the world's top 40 graduate schools of management. He is author of the book *Customer Relationship Management: Concepts and Tools* and over 300 other publications. He can be reached at francis@buttleassociates.com.

Leslie de Chernatony

Leslie de Chernatony is Professor of Brand Marketing and Director of the Centre for Research in Brand Marketing at Birmingham University Business School. With a doctorate in brand marketing, he has a substantial number of publications in American and European journals and is a regular presenter at international conferences. He has several books on brand marketing, the two most recent being *Creating Powerful Brands* and *From Brand Vision* to *Brand Evaluation*. A winner of several research grants, his two most recent grants have supported research into factors associated with high-performance brands and research into services branding. He was Visiting Professor at Madrid Business School and is currently Visiting Professor at Thammasat University, Bangkok, and University of Lugano, Switzerland. Leslie is a Fellow of the Chartered Institute of Marketing and Fellow of the Market Research Society. He acts as an international consultant to organizations seeking more effective brand strategies and has run acclaimed branding seminars throughout Europe, Asia, America and the Far East. He is an experienced expert witness in legal cases involving branding issues in commercial and competition cases.

Philippe Favre

Philippe Favre was appointed French Ambassador for international investment, Chairman and CEO of Invest in France Agency on August 24, 2006. Before this nomination, Philippe Favre, 45, was Chief of Staff to the French Trade Minister and Deputy Chief of Staff to the Finance Minister. He also worked as Director of Human Resources, Budget and Information Technology at the Ministry of Trade. From 1993 to 2001,

Mr Favre was the French Trade Commissioner in Hong Kong, and later in Taipei, Taiwan. Between these postings, he was a personal adviser for international affairs at the finance and trade ministries in Paris. Mr Favre was a counselor at the French Embassy in Washington, D.C., from 1990 to 1993. Earlier in his career, he worked at the Ministry of Finance in Paris in charge of economic relations with the former USSR and Eastern Europe. Mr Favre has degrees from the Institut d'Etudes Politiques de Paris and Paris University. He is also a graduate of L'Ecole Nationale d'Administration (ENA). In April 2007, he was appointed 'Chevalier' of the Legion of Honour.

Christian Felzensztein

Dr Christian Felzensztein, B.Com. (Honors), M.B.A., Universidad Austral de Chile. Post-graduate diploma on Local Economic Development, Weitz Center for Development Studies, Rehovot, Israel. M.Sc. and Ph.D. in International Marketing, University of Strathclyde, Glasgow, Scotland. He is founder and Managing Director of STEIN Business Center, specialized solutions in International Marketing Strategy and Professor of International Marketing in the Faculty of Management and Economics at Universidad Austral de Chile, Valdivia, Chile. He has researched and published in the subjects of country of origin effect in agricultural and aquaculture products as well as regional clusters and innovation. Currently, he is leading a major international research project on natural resource-based clusters. Email: cfelzens@uach.cl

João R. Freire

João R. Freire is a Brand Consultant for MMG Worldwide (mmgworldwide.com), a global marketing communications firm specializing in the travel, hospitality and entertainment industry. João has recently completed his Ph.D. in Place Branding at London Metropolitan University, where he is also a guest lecturer in Marketing. His Ph.D. focused on the analysis of the interaction between place-brands and consumers. The main objective of his investigation was to provide a deeper understanding of the different dimensions that compose a place-brand. He is also the founder of Ecoterra (ecoterra.co.uk), a company specializing in the branding and marketing of natural food products. João is an economist by trade, who has worked in the fields of finance and marketing for several multinational companies in Brazil, Portugal and the UK. João is a frequent speaker and author on Branding topics. His articles have appeared in well-respected international publications such as *Place Branding* and *Journal of Brand Management*.

Anthony E. Gortzis

Anthony E. Gortzis was born in Athens, where he studied Economics and Law in the University of Athens. He completed his postgraduate studies in England, concentrating in Business Administration (M.B.A.), Marketing and Econometrics. He also attended a crash course M.B.A. in

Harvard University. In 1973, he was hired in the Marketing Department of Unilever. He worked in the Marketing Department of Unilever in London, as Marketing Specialist on detergents for Europe and North America. In 1982, he became Marketing Director for Unilever detergents in Greece. In 1986, he became Marketing Director of Elais-Unilever Foods Division, and in 1998, he became Public Affairs, Media and Research Director for all Unilever companies in Greece. He has also been President of the Greek Institute of Marketing. Since 1994, he has been a member of the Board of the Greek Advertisers Association, and since March 1996, he has held the presidency. In 2000, he was elected President of the World Federation of Advertisers (WFA). In 2003, he was elected as the General Secretary of the Board of the Chambers of Commerce for Piraeus. Since the beginning of 2003, he has been active as a consultant in the area of Media, Marketing and Public Relations, Public Affairs, CSR, Crisis Management, and he is the Chairman of One-Team, a CSR, marketing and communication company. In April 2005, he was elected as Vice-President of the Hellenic Management Association and also as a member of the board of the Action-Aid. Since May 2005, he has acted as the President of the EBEN.GR (Business Ethics Institute).

Interbrand

Interbrand are a leading international branding consultancy. Interbrand's brand professionals serve clients globally with over 30 offices in over 20 countries. Working in partnership with its clients, Interbrand combine rigorous strategy and analysis with world-class design and creativity. Interbrand's services include brand analytics, brand valuation, strategy, naming and verbal identity, corporate identity, packaging design, retail design, integrated brand communications and digital branding tools.

Daniel M. Jackson

Daniel M. Jackson has worked in film and music theatre production, media planning, advertising and commercial radio. He is the author of the groundbreaking book, *Sonic Branding* (Palgrave Macmillan, 2004).

Yvonne Johnston

Yvonne Johnston is the Chief Executive Officer of the International Marketing Council of South Africa (IMC), an organization that aims to create a positive, united image for South Africa to give the country a strategic advantage in an increasingly competitive marketplace. This, it does through the promotion of Brand South Africa. Its mission – to articulate a brand for South Africa, which positions the country in order to attract tourism, trade and investment, as well as realize international relations objectives; to establish an integrated approach within government and the private sector towards the international marketing of South Africa and to build national support for Brand South Africa. Pivotal to the success of the work of the IMC is the realization of its mission as this will help the country deal with its socio-economic issues. The IMC has been in existence since 2000, and in her 4 years at the helm of the organization, Yvonne is credited with raising the profile of Brand South Africa to the point where it was voted amongst the Top 5 Hot Brands for 2004 by Intelligence Total Business (formerly Business 2.0), an authoritative publication that offers information on next generation business trends, processes and insights. Another highlight was being selected as one of five finalists for the 2005 Business Woman of the Year. She is widely respected as a leading communications strategist and has played a major role in the training and teaching of strategic media skills in the industry and is a much sought-after public speaker locally and abroad on Brands, as well as the current mood of our nation. Previously, she has worked in the Advertising and Marketing industry in a career spanning over 20 years as a Media Director of leading ad agencies. For 5 years, she was Group Media Director of Ogilvy and Mather. This was followed by a stint in marketing, including running her own marketing consultancy, refreshing marketing, specializing in experiential marketing and marketing to women. She currently sits on the boards of SA Tourism, The African Hall of Fame and The Valued Citizens.

Vladimir Lebedenko

Vladimir Lebedenko is Deputy Director of Department for Relations with the Subjects of the Federation, the Parliament, Public and Political Organizations, Ministry of Foreign Affairs of the Russian Federation. Graduated from the Moscow State Institute of International Relations (MGIMO – University). Occupied diplomatic positions in Russian missions to Togo (Africa), France (Marseilles and Paris). In Russian Permanent Representation to the Council of Europe (Strasbourg). The author of a number of articles in periodicals, as well as in *International Life* magazine, published by the Ministry of Foreign Affairs of Russia. Participated in international conferences and seminars.

Chris Macrae

Chris Macrae (chris.macrae@yahoo.co.uk) has, over a 30-year career, researched intangibles of marketing and organizational systems in ways inspired by his father's Entrepreneurial Revolution trilogy published in *The Economist and Offensive Marketing Principles* of Thedore Levitt and Hugh Davidson. His work includes

- projects in 30 countries and hundreds of markets directed at database modelling of what innovation societies wanted next
- working in Japan, which provided insights into corporate branding of founders built to last visions
- articles (since 1980s) on nation brands as a new arena of world class brands
- innovating genre of living and learning how to charter brand architecture

- senior consultant on value of branding at coopers & lybrand
- hosting brandknowledge.com for corporate identity enterprises of WPP

Chris concludes that media and global markets have lost exponential sustainability and the transparency needed to integrate societies into globalization. Mathematically, sustainability investment is missing a hi-trust audit of flows and goodwill. Open-sourcing communal maps of empowerment economics is his passion at leadership portals: http://economistclub.tv and http://www.valuetrue.com.

T.C. Melewar

T.C. Melewar is a Professor of Marketing and Strategy at Brunel University London. He has previous experience at Warwick Business School, University of Warwick, MARA Institute of Technology in Malaysia, Loughborough University, UK, and De Montfort University, UK. T.C. teaches Marketing Management, Marketing Communications and International Marketing on a range of undergraduate, M.B.A. and executive courses with companies such as Nestlè, Safeway, Corus and Sony. He is a Visiting Professor at Groupe ECS Grenoble, France and Humboldt University, Berlin, Germany. His research interests are global corporate identity, corporate branding, corporate reputation, marketing communications and international marketing strategy.

Olutayo B. Otubanjo

Olutayo B. Otubanjo is a Marketing Communications and Consumer Behaviour tutor at Brunel University, London, where he is completing a Ph.D. focusing on 'Organisational Construction of Corporate Identity'. He has given a number of papers on corporate identity and corporate reputation at international conferences in England and was for a few years an Account Executive at CMC Connect Lagos (Nigeria) where he carried out numerous corporate identity and corporate branding assignments for leading multinational brands such as Coca-Cola, Microsoft, UPS, Peugeot, Shell, Peugeot, Accenture and many more. He holds an M.Sc. in Marketing (with emphasis on corporate identity communications), a postgraduate diploma in Marketing, another postgraduate diploma in Journalism and a B.Sc. in Accounting.

Inga Hlín Pálsdóttir

Inga Hlín Pálsdóttir is a Project Manager in consultancy and training with the Trade Council of Iceland. She obtained her M.Sc. in International Marketing in 2005 from the University of Strathclyde, Glasgow. Before that, she graduated with a B.Sc. in Business Administration in 2003 from Bifröst School of Business in Iceland, completing part of her studies in Fachochschule Nordostniedersachsen in Lüneburg, Germany. Before she started working for the Trade Council of Iceland, she worked as a Project Manager for Educate – Iceland and Atlantik Tours (DMS).

Dipak R. Pant

Dipak R. Pant, B.A., M.Phil., Ph.D., is Professor of Anthropology and Economics, founder and head of the Interdisciplinary Unit for Sustainable Economy, Università Carlo Cattaneo, Italy. Field surveyor and sustainable development-planning advisor in Italy and abroad. Visiting professor in various European, Asian, South American and US universities. Senior Fellow, Society for Applied Anthropology, USA. Member, editorial board of Place Branding, London (UK). Born and schooled in Nepal; military training and higher education in India; post-graduate studies in Europe.

Formerly: Associate Professor of Human Ecology and Anthropology, Tribhuvan University, Kathmandu (Nepal); Professor of International Studies, University of Trieste (Italy) and Professor of Development Studies, University of Padua (Italy).

International Research Associate, Environmental Health and Social Policy Center, Seattle (USA).

Martial Pasquier

Martial Pasquier is Professor for Public Management and Marketing at the Swiss Graduate School of Public Administration IDHEAP in Lausanne. Studies at the Universities of Fribourg/CH, Berne and Berkeley. From 1998 to 2003, Director of a consulting firm and lecturer at diverse Universities. Since 2003, Full Professor at the IDHEAP. Guest Professor at the Universities of Berne, Lugano, Strasbourg, Nancy II and Paris II. Member of the Board of the Swiss Marketing Association GFM. Member of the Swiss Competition Commission. Research interests: Nation's image, Marketing and Communication of Public Organizations, Transparency of the Public Organizations. Email: martial.pasquier@idheap.unil.ch

Ximena Siles Renjel

Ximena Siles Renjel has 5 years experience in the banking industry in Bolivia and Ecuador, acting as a risk analyst and relationship manager for different industries and sectors. M.Sc. in International Marketing with Distinction from the University of Strathclyde, Glasgow, Scotland. First degree in Business Administration from the Bolivian Catholic University, graduated with honors.

Renata Sanches

Renata Sanches has worked for 21 years in International Affairs, having held several positions in the Brazilian government and worked on several projects for the European Union and the United Nations, in Brazil and abroad. For the last 7 years, Sanches has served as a senior-consultant and project unit coordinator of APEX-Brasil, Brazil's export agency. Sanches is a graduate of the University of Brasilia in International Affairs and has a masters in International Corporations and Globalization from the Université Libre de Bruxelles-ULB, where her thesis received the 'Grand Distinction – 1991' prize. Sanches has an MBA in Marketing and

E-Commerce from ESPM, teaches graduate and post-graduate classes in International Marketing and International Negotiations at Universidade Católica de Brasília since 1999.

Flavia Sekles

Flavia Sekles is the executive director of the Brazil Information Center, a non-profit trade association that promotes Brazil and Brazilian private sector interests in the USA, since 2000. With a BA in Journalism from Boston University, Sekles previously worked for 15 years as Washington Correspondent for *Veja* magazine, Brazil's largest circulation news-weekly, and *Jornal do Brasil*.

György Szondi

György Szondi is a Senior Lecturer in Public Relations at Leeds Business School, Leeds Metropolitan University. His Ph.D. at the University of Salzburg, Austria involves researching the concepts of Public Relations and Public Diplomacy for the European Union. His interest and publications include international public relations, public diplomacy, country branding, risk and crises communication. He has been a regular conference speaker and PR trainer throughout Eastern Europe, including Hungary, Poland, Estonia, Latvia. He has written on country branding in Eastern Europe for *Place Branding and Public Diplomacy* and also contributed to *The Public Diplomacy Handbook*. György worked for Hill and Knowlton, the international PR agency in Budapest, Hungary and in its international headquarters in London. He holds a Bachelor degree in Economics, a MA in Public Relations from the University of Stirling and an MSc in Physics. Besides his native Hungarian, he speaks English, Italian, German, French, Polish and Estonian.

Gianfranco Walsh

Dr Gianfranco Walsh was a Senior Lecturer in Marketing with a British university before joining the University of Koblenz-Landau in 2006 as a Professor of Marketing and Electronic Retailing. He is also a Visiting Professor in the University of Strathclyde Business School's Department of Marketing. From 2002 to 2004, Gianfranco Walsh was an Assistant Professor of Marketing at the University of Hanover's Department of Marketing. After graduating with a B.B.A. in marketing from the University of Applied Science, Lueneburg (now University of Lueneburg) in autumn 1996, Gianfranco Walsh earned an M.Phil. from Manchester School of Management, now Manchester Business School, in 1998. He received his Ph.D. in marketing from the University of Hanover in 2001 and his Habilitation degree in 2004. His Ph.D. thesis won two awards for academic excellence given by the Berufsverband Deutscher Markt- und Sozialforscher and Freundeskreis der Universität Hannover. In addition, Gianfranco Walsh actively consults companies in the fields of market research, customer marketing and E-Commerce.

Klaus-Peter Wiedmann

Dr. Klaus-Peter Wiedmann is Professor of Marketing at the Department of Marketing and Management, Leibniz University of Hanover. He is the Reputation Institute Country Director for Germany. Professor Klaus-Peter Wiedmann, Ph.D., studied business, psychology and sociology at the University of Stuttgart and the University of Mannheim (he received his MBA from the University of Mannheim). Following this he was an assistant to Professor Hans Raffée (Chair for General Business Economics and Marketing II) as well as a member of the Institute for Marketing at the University of Mannheim. After receiving his Ph.D. in 1992, Klaus-Peter Wiedmann did his post-doctorate studies at the University of Mannheim's school of business. He has been a full professor at the University of Hanover, Institute for Business Research, Chair for General Business Economics and Marketing II (M 2) since August 1, 1994.

Elsa G. Wilkin-Armbrister

Elsa G. Wilkin-Armbrister is currently a Ph.D. candidate and Graduate Teaching Assistant at the University of Strathclyde in Glasgow. Her area of study is nation branding, with a sub-focus in E-Branding. She has an M.Sc. in International Marketing from the University of Strathclyde and a B.A. degree in Psychology from Alabama A&M University. Elsa's interest in nation branding stems from an innate belief that her native country Nevis can be successfully repositioned from a global perspective through this process. She is founder and director of Cellisvae Trust and Corporate Services Limited.

Jack Yan

Jack Yan, L.L.B., B.C.A. (Hons.), M.C.A., is CEO of Jack Yan & Associates (jya.net) and a director of the Medinge Group (medinge.org), a branding think-tank in Sweden. He is the co-author of *Beyond Branding: How the New Values of Transparency and Integrity Are Changing the World of Brands* (Kogan Page, 2003) and the author of *Typography and Branding* (Natcoll Publishing, 2004). He may be reached through his personal site at jackyan.com.

ZAD Group

ZAD Group is a group of service companies specialized in a long-term development for industries and organizations. ZAD offers high-quality alternative to both in-house and outsource resources for Business Development, Sales & Market Development, Recruitment and Export Management implementation. ZAD headquarters is based in Cairo, Egypt, owned by its principal investors. Another store for exporting Egyptian goods is based in Siralion – West Africa. ZAD's challenge is establishing itself as a Leading Service Firm that partners with its clients for a full integrated solutions starting from recruitment on the seniors' levels, capacity building through a high-quality facilitation workshops, passing by human resources and management consultation and till achieving maximum results in increasing the market share till exporting overseas through its export division. ZAD's goal is to become a development partner for its clients on a long-term basis. The company's founders are experts in the pharmaceutical, engineering, exporting and telecommunication fields, all in multinational companies in the Middle East. They are founding ZAD to formalize the various services they offer. ZAD is managed by those working partners. See the website www.zadgroup.org

PART 1

Scope and scale of nation branding

CHAPTER 1

The relevance, scope and evolution of nation branding

Country Case Insight – South Africa

Developing Brand South Africa

Yvonne Johnston
CEO, International Marketing Council of South Africa

■ 1. Background

The International Marketing Council of South Africa (IMC) was brought into being in August 2000 upon the realization that it was absolutely imperative to create a positive and compelling brand image for South Africa. At the time, there was a gap between the perception of the country and the reality of the country in the global marketplace. To exacerbate matters, there were many messages entering the international arena, and these messages were as varied as the sources and did very little to change the perceptions. They added to the confusion. For a democracy as young as ours, whose history was rooted in social injustice, there needed to be something that accelerated the world's correct understanding of South Africa that is so important for the much needed attraction of Trade, Tourism, and Investment. It was against this background that the IMC was established. Its mandate is to establish a compelling brand image for South Africa, which correctly positions the country in terms of its investment potential, credit worthiness, export opportunities, tourism potential and international relations.

■ 2. First steps

Because there were no strong country brands with major marketing drives behind them at the time, the IMC had to be quite innovative in approach in terms of putting together a process that ensured a very strong foundation for Brand South Africa.

This process was broken down as follows:

Phase 1: Developing a compelling brand proposition for South Africa (mother-brand)
Phase 2: Defining a Brand Architecture that defines the relationship between the mother-brand and the various sub-brands (Tourism and Business)

Phase 3: Defining the Strategy that the IMC will follow in realizing its objectives

Phase 4: Monitoring and Reviewing progress.

So, the IMC would become the custodian of the nation brand and other stakeholders will represent sub-brands.

Phase 1 – Developing a compelling brand proposition for South Africa

As can be imagined, this phase was the most research intensive, as it was important that we get the basics right. It was also important that whatever the outcome was, it was credible, believable and also differentiating.

Step 1 – Interrogation of all existing research on South Africa:
Over 25 000 people were interviewed in South Africa and all around the world as part of this research. In South Africa, the interviews and interactions took place in all 11 languages, involving all levels of society.

Step 2 – Consultation with local and international stakeholders:
A series of specialist focus groups and 'generator' workshops was conducted involving communities, targeted groups of stakeholders across the social, political, economic, media and business spectra.

Step 3 – Testing phase:
During the testing process, a number of positioning statements were tested for validation amongst influencers, the South African population, stakeholders and departing tourists.

The end result of this phase was essentially the development of the Brand South Africa essence: 'South Africa, Alive with Possibility'. The various elements supporting this essence are attached in the Brand key (Figure CS1.1).

When this was adopted by all, South Africans from all sectors of its society were engaged to live up to the brand Promise: 'Alive with Possibility'. To this end, IMC continuously seeks the cooperation of government departments, public entities, the private sector non-government entities and the media.

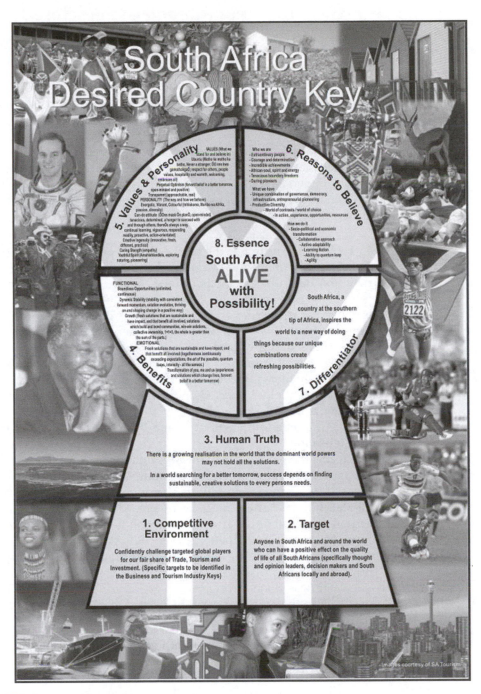

Figure CS1.1
South Africa Desired Country Key

Phase 2 – Defining a brand architecture that defines the relationship between the mother-brand and the various sub-brands (tourism and business)

The IMC needed to ensure that all messages about South Africa internationally are consistent. Constant alignment and checking then becomes the key.

The aligning of messaging was very challenging as some of the brands had already established their own brand platforms. But, because all involved understood the value of this type of collaboration from an impact and scale benefit perspectives, there was commitment to get this done as efficiently as possible:

Step 1 – Understanding of the mother-brand and how it was arrived at:
This step was about the various stakeholders understanding the richness and depth of the mother-brand. It was also about them buying into the various elements of the brand key so that they could start articulating at their level. Because of the extensive research that was done up-front, there was good stakeholder buy in.

Step 2 – Understanding what the sub-brand's mandate is:
The IMC brand team also needed to understand the business of the other stakeholders involved so that they could also understand how all of these potentially impacted on the mother-brand and how to exploit potential areas of synergy.

Step 3 – Understanding what the sub-brands could borrow from the mother-brand:
The teams then looked at all this information and decided that because the mother-brand is so rich and could not communicate everything, it could focus on certain aspects that would then make soil fertile for all stakeholders. These areas were agreed to because they also took certain responsibilities away from the sub-brands so that they could focus on their core competencies.

Step 4 – Understanding how the sub-brands could support the mother-brand:
The same was done during this stage, ensuring that certain elements pertinent to the core brand can be carried at sub-brand level.
At the end of this process, the following was in place:

- All stakeholders understood their focus areas.
- Whenever there was crossover into each other's area of responsibility, the messaging was consistent.
- All stakeholders cooperated for the bigger benefit.

This stage was important for IMC because we realized that this was not something we could achieve on our own.
This is an ongoing process because of the complexity of South Africa as a country, especially as the brand gears itself up for the FIFA Soccer

World Cup in 2010. The messaging needs to be continuously monitored to ensure that everyone is aligned.

Phase 3 – Defining the strategy that the IMC will follow to realize its objectives:

In taking responsibility for the mother-brand, the IMC then decided there will be two basic components to their operations:

1. **International portfolio**
   Develop campaigns and activities aimed at changing perceptions in the international arena:
   a. Niche media advertising to influential people
   b. Public relations – Thought leaders and journalists
   c. Outbound missions
   d. E-Marketing
   e. Support material
   f. Surveys and documentaries
   g. Web portal
2. **Domestic portfolio**
   Develop campaigns ensuring that South Africans live up to the brand promise. An extensive campaign was undertaken to ensure South Africans not only feel proud to be South Africans but live up to the brand promise through:
   a. Mass media advertising
   b. Public relations – Thought and community Leader engagements
   c. Brand ambassadors

Phase 4 – Monitoring and reviewing Brand SA progress

Because we are accountable for the mother-brand, we also monitor progress on how well we are doing on both the domestic and the international fronts. It is important to note that this work does not just exclusively measure progress made by the IMC but measures progress by the total effort in the country. We mainly conduct two studies:

1. **National perception audit**
   This study measures important attributes of the brand and how well South Africans are delivering on those. It also measures how entrenched 'SA Alive with Possibility' is amongst South Africans (see Figure CS1.2 below).
2. **International brand equity study**
   Because of the lack of comparable studies around the world about country branding and how South African compares to other markets, we commission our own study to measure the brand's health (see Figure CS1.3).

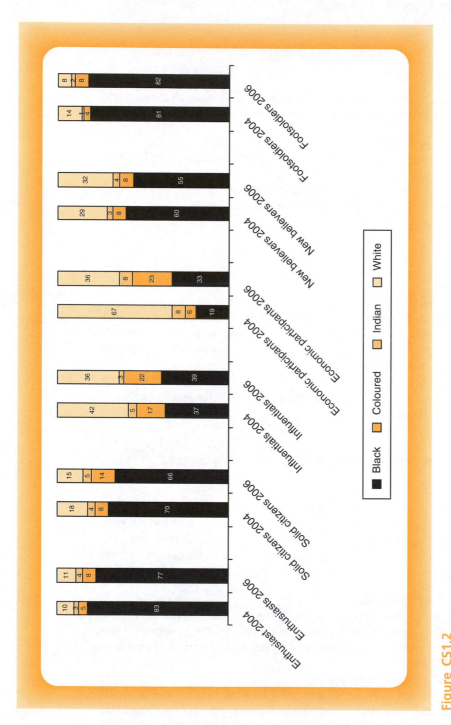

Figure CS1.2
National perception audit

SA's brand health benchmarked against the competitive set - *Equity scores*

n = 448

- The equity score represents the share of mind each country has in the minds of investors
- The sum of the equity scores for all potential investment countries is 100
- It is a one-number reflection of each country's brand health as calculated using CM^{TM}

	USA	UK	Germany	Netherlands	France
Brazil	7.2	5.5	6.9	4.4	6.6
Chile	5.1	3.7	3.5	3.0	3.5
China	14.7	10.7	11.1	8.8	10.1
Czech	3.5	9.2	11.2	8.6	11.2
India	6.0	7.8	5.2	4.8	6.2
Poland	4.1	10.7	12.8	11.5	12.2
SA	4.8	9.6	6.1	4.9	5.9

SA ranking	5th	3rd	5th	4th	6th

Best score	China	China & Poland	Poland	Poland	Poland

Source: CM^{TM}.

What are the top three countries investors are doing business with?

	USA (*n*=150) %	UK (*n*=61) %	Germany (*n*=38*) %	Netherlands (*n*=100) %	France (*n*=97) %
Germany	16	23	-	49	44
UK	24	7	24	38	26
China	38	16	16	14	13
USA	-	43	45	19	18
Canada	39	7	3	3	2
France	7	23	45	19	-
Spain	1	11	5	14	26
Italy	3	3	16	9	27
Belgium	1	7	8	31	10
Japan	15	7	24	-	9
Mexico	26	5	-	-	1

Source: Research Surveys 2006.

Figure CS1.3
International brand equity study

South Africa positive attribute score card – Total
In order of Jaccard importance

n = 448

	High assoc.	Different-iated	Winner
Most NB ↑ Growing economy		✕	China
Sizeable market for your goods/services		✕	China
Availability of suitable qualified labour			China/Poland/Czech
High productivity levels		✕	China
Low input costs		✕	China
Regional hub			China
Ease of doing business	✓		Czech
Stable currency			China
Innovation			China
Good infrastructure	✓	✓	Czech
Good corporate governance			Czech
Well-run country			Czech
Abundance of raw materials	✓	✓	China
Reliable energy supply	✓		Poland
Time zone compatibility	✓		Czech
Sophisticated financial systems		✓	China
Favourable tax incentives for investment	✓		China

Source: Research Surveys 2006.

South Africa negative attribute score card – Total
In order of Jaccard importance

n = 448

	High assoc.	Differe-ntiated	Loser
Most NB ↑ Unstable political environment	✓	✓	Brazil
High crime rate	✓	✓	Brazil
Rigid labour market			China
High inflation			Brazil
High levels of corruption	✓		China
Poor human rights record	✓	✓	China
Difficult to protect © and intellectual property			China

Note: **High association** is South Africa's association with the attributes indexed to South Africa's average attribute association. Indices of 1.3 or greater are ticked.

Note: **Differentiated** is ticked when South Africa is differentiated on a particular attribute.

Note: **Winner** is the country that has the highest association with a particular positive attribute.

Note: **Loser** is the country that has the highest association with a particular negative attribute.

Source: Research Surveys 2006.

Figure CS1.3
(Contiued)

■ 3. Conclusion

So far, anecdotal evidence and hard research suggest that our activities (albeit on a small scale) are breaking through, although more work still needs to be done.

Although our activities seem to be making a contribution towards altering South Africa's perceptual position, the brand, however, still suffers from limited familiarity and weak associations.

We will continue with efforts to sell South Africa to South Africans; the 2010 event makes the need to mobilize national support for the brand even more imperative.

Involving various government departments, public entities and the private sector will continue, as coordination of activities and messaging is a key success factor for our 2010 positioning effort.

*****

■ Introduction

Nation branding is an exciting, complex and controversial phenomenon. It is exciting, as it represents an area in which there is little existing theory but a huge amount of real world activity; complex, because it encompasses multiple disciplines beyond the limited realm of conventional brand strategy; and controversial, in that it is a highly politicized activity that generates passionately held and frequently conflicting viewpoints and opinions. Furthermore, nation branding is steadily gaining prominence, with more and more countries around the world committing resources to the development of their nation-brand. This chapter investigates the relevance of nation branding in terms of what value a nation-brand strategy can deliver to a country, as well as tracing the evolution of nation branding and outlining the prominence, which it has achieved in recent years.

The country case insight in this chapter illustrates how South Africa has set about developing its nation-brand through the activities of the International Marketing Council of South Africa, whose strategic objective is to establish a compelling brand image for the country and to position it favourably in order to attract trade, tourism and investment. In his academic perspective, Prof. Leslie de Chernatony discusses the ways in which brand theory needs to be adapted to the context of nation branding, whilst Simon Anholt offers a practitioner insight into the nature and essence of nation branding, suggesting that the term 'competitive identity' is more appropriate than 'nation branding' to describe much of the current activity in the field.

■ Defining 'brand' and 'nation-brand'

Before looking in detail at the concept of treating a nation as a brand, it is worthwhile to look at some definitions of what is meant by a 'brand'. Such definitions tend to fall into two camps. On the one hand are definitions that focus upon the visual manifestation of a brand. On the other hand, there are deeper definitions that go beyond the visual aspects of a brand and attempt to capture the essence of a brand.

A succinct and often quoted definition of a positive or successful brand is given by Doyle [1], who suggests that 'a successful brand is a name, symbol, design, or some combination, which identifies the 'product' of a particular organisation as having a sustainable differential advantage'. The American Marketing Association offers a similar definition of a brand as a 'name, term, sign, symbol, or design, or a combination of them intended to identify the goods and services of one seller or group of sellers and to differentiate them from those of competition'. A slightly richer definition of a brand, in that it incorporates a consumer rather than mainly producer perspective, is given by Macrae, Parkinson and Sheerman [2], who posit that a brand represents a unique combination of characteristics and added values, both functional and non-functional, which have taken on a relevant meaning that is inextricably linked to the brand, awareness of which might be conscious or intuitive. A similar perspective is taken by Lynch and de Chernatony [3], who define brands as clusters of functional and emotional values that promise a unique and welcome experience between a buyer and a seller.

Brands of course do not exist in a vacuum, and to be successful, they must co-exist effectively with the prevailing zeitgeist. Popular culture and trends in society drive and influence strong brands [4]. This theme is amplified and theorized by Holt [5], who analyses how brands become icons through creative interaction with their environment in a process that he terms 'cultural branding', a process that he considers particularly suitable for applying to nations. A similar culturally aware vision of brands is proposed by one of the UK's most creative and innovative thinkers on branding, who suggests that a brand is 'a cluster of strategic cultural ideas' [6]. Through the foundations of their national identity, nation-brands possess far richer and deeper cultural resources than any other type of brand, be it product, service, corporate or any other brandable entity. These cultural resources are explored in Chapter 5.

The practice of branding has been defined as the process by which companies distinguish their product offerings from those of the competition [7]. In an increasingly globalized economy, the challenge of distinguishing their product offerings from those of the competition has assumed critical importance for nations competing for both domestic and foreign consumers. Keller [8] suggests that the strategic brand management process involves the design and implementation of marketing programmes and activities to build, measure and manage brand equity. The concept of brand equity is explored in detail in Chapter 3.

A clarification regarding the role of branding is provided by de Chernatony and McDonald [9], who warn that it is imperative to recognize that while marketers instigate the branding process (branding as an input), it is the buyer or the user who forms a mental vision of the brand (branding as an output), which may be different from the intended marketing thrust. This point is particularly relevant to the branding of nations, where pre-existing national stereotypes may be entrenched in consumers' minds and therefore difficult to change. The notion that a brand is something that resides in the minds of consumers has been noted by some of the major writers on branding [10,11]. The brand-building process requires long-term commitment over a period of several years and in the short term only a small payoff may occur [12]. Nations need to acknowledge this reality and adopt a long-term strategic view when building their nation-brand, rather than aiming for a quick fix short-term advertising campaign whose effects may be ephemeral.

When applying the concept of a brand to nations rather than to mere products, there is an ethical obligation to do so in an honest, respectful manner and to acknowledge the limits of how appropriate it is to treat nations as brands. Nations do not belong to brand managers or corporations; indeed, if they 'belong' to anyone, it is to the nation's entire citizenry. Ethical considerations related to nation branding are examined in detail in Chapter 7.

To avoid confusion over terms, it may be helpful to distinguish between a *national brand*, defined as 'a brand available nationally as distinct from a regional or test-market brand' [13] and a *nation-brand*, where the brand is the country, state or nation in question. In this book, the nation-brand is defined as *the unique, multi-dimensional blend of elements that provide the nation with culturally grounded differentiation and relevance for all of its target audiences*. This definition acknowledges the multi-faceted nature of the nation-brand, together with the need to integrate national identity dimensions as discussed in Chapter 5. Moreover, the proposed definition of the nation-brand also recognizes the contention that brands exist in consumers' minds rather than being a totally controllable creation of the marketing function. The definition therefore incorporates reference to perceptual attributes and target markets.

In this chapter's academic insight, Prof. Leslie de Chernatony considers the adaptation of brand theory to the context of nation branding. The issues addressed by de Chernatony are discussed further in Chapter 8, focusing specifically on which stakeholders need to be involved in nation-brand development.

Academic Perspective

Adapting brand theory to the context of nation branding

Leslie de Chernatony
Professor of Brand Marketing
Birmingham University Business School

When considering the daunting challenge of nation branding, existing brand frameworks are available, but there needs to be some adaptation. There are various reasons for this. For example not one but numerous, powerful stakeholders seeking to influence the nature of the nation brand that has to appeal to diverse stakeholders.

The concept of 'brand' remains invariant, i.e. a cluster of values that enables a nation to make a promise about a unique and welcomed experience. Successful brands thrive because the people delivering the brand act in a manner that reflects the promised values. In nation branding, there would likewise be dominant values that define the behavioural characteristics of a population. The type of constitution governing the country, religions and social mores would enable the population to appreciate the boundary points defining the cluster of values. Through the social and economic interactions, individuals become more aware of the nation's core values.

Making explicit the values and promised experience of the nation brand should entail the collective involvement of the key stakeholders. This could start by first getting the key stakeholders to surface their vision for the nation brand. Various visions could emerge, but by using the Delphic brand-visioning technique, a process could be followed to arrive at a consensus vision.

The process necessitates identifying key stakeholders interested in shaping the nation brand. They might include representatives from government, commerce, not-for-profit organizations, tourism and the media. They would individually be sent a document explaining that a nation brand's vision is characterized by three components, i.e. desired long-term future, purpose and its values. They would be asked to write their vision for the nation brand. This would be sent to an impartial, objective co-ordinator who would identify the most common themes in the three components of the resulting visions. Each person would be sent back their vision, along with the most common themes. The individual is asked to reflect on their vision compared with the aggregate comments and to consider revising their original statement. The procedure is iterated until a consensus is reached, in broad terms.

The next stage entails the key stakeholders setting objectives to enable their group to work towards the nation brand vision. As this progresses, each stakeholder group begins to articulate how they conceive the nation brand. Meetings would ensue between the diverse stakeholders to exchange information about each stakeholder's brand objectives, the tasks they need to achieve their objectives and their assumptions about the values and experience they are seeking to support.

At these meetings, there would be reinforcing objectives. However, divergent objectives are also likely. Through a senior, impartial and respected chairperson, a process of dialogue would ensue to identify common ground about the way that stakeholders have supporting objectives for the nation brand. By getting each of the key stakeholders to surface their assumptions about the values and promised experience they are striving to support, each group can begin to appreciate how they can better work together to build a more coherent nation brand.

* * * * *

Why countries engage in nation branding

The application of branding techniques to nations is a relatively new phenomenon, but one which is growing in frequency given the increasingly global competition that nations now face in both their domestic and external markets. Nations are making increasingly conscious efforts to hone their country branding in recognition of the need to fulfil three major objectives: to attract tourists, to stimulate inward investment and to boost exports. A further objective for many nations is talent attraction, whereby countries compete to attract higher education students, and skilled workers. A wider set of potential rewards to be gained through nation branding has been proposed by Temporal [14], who suggests that in addition to the key goals of attracting tourists, stimulating inward investment and boosting exports, nation branding can also increase currency stability; help restore international credibility and investor confidence; reverse international ratings downgrades; increase international political influence; stimulate stronger international partnerships and enhance nation building (by nourishing confidence, pride, harmony, ambition, national resolve). A further objective that may be aspired to by transitional countries such as those in Central and Eastern Europe may be to distance the countries from the old economic and political system that existed before transition [15]. In this chapter's country case insight, Yvonne Johnston, CEO of the International Marketing Council of South Africa, describes how the South African brand has been developed in order to position the country in terms of its investment potential, credit worthiness, export opportunities, tourism potential and international relations.

The achievement of such goals requires countries to adopt conscious branding if they are to compete effectively on the global stage [16], a view also expressed by Olins [17], who asserts that within a few years, identity management will be seen as a key way of contributing to the nation's brand. It has also been suggested [18] that the unbranded state has a difficult time attracting economic and political attention, and that image and reputation are becoming essential parts of the state's strategic equity. A powerful and positive nation-brand can provide crucial competitive advantage in today's globalized economy (see country case insight on Egypt, Chapter 2). In his landmark text, *The Competitive Advantage of Nations* [19], Michael Porter emphasizes that nations and national character remain of prime importance, even in the age of globalization:

> My theory highlights and reinforces the importance of differences in nations and of differences in national character. Many contemporary discussions of international competition stress global homogenization and a diminished role for nations. But, in truth, national differences are at the heart of competitive success.

The realm of competitive advantage encompasses many sectors, including attracting tourists, investors, entrepreneurs, and foreign consumers of a country's products and services (see country case insight on Iceland, Chapter 8). Nation branding can also help erase misconceptions about a country and allow the country to reposition itself more favourably

Table 1.1 Key issues in treating nations as brands

Author	Themes and issues
Aldersey-Williams [20]	The branding or rebranding of a nation is a controversial and highly politicized activity
Wolff Olins [21]	Although historically brands are associated with products and corporations, the techniques of branding are applicable to every area of mass communications; political leaders, for example to inspire, need to become brand managers of their parties and preferably of the nation
O'Shaughnessy and Jackson [22]	The image of a nation is so complex and fluid as to deny the clarity implicit in a term such as brand image; different parts of a nation's identity come into focus on the international stage at different times, affected by current political events and even by the latest movie or news bulletin
Gilmore [23]	The importance of truthfulness when constructing the nation-brand; what is required is amplification of the existing values of the national culture rather than the fabrication of a false promise
Mihailovich [24]	The simplistic strapline approach to nation branding could be counter-productive; altruistic goals such as sustainable long-term employment and prosperity are objectives that may be met through emphasizing all forms of cluster and kinship alliances
Anholt [25]	The vocabulary of branding can appear cynical and arrogant; therefore, to some extent, politicians need to avoid the explicit use of such terminology

with regard to targeted audiences (see country case insight on France, Chapter 10), whilst the development of a strong nation-brand by Estonia was driven by key objectives including attracting FDI, expanding the country's tourist base beyond Sweden and Finland, and broadening European markets for its exports (see country case insight on Estonia, Chapter 9). In his academic perspective on the application of CRM to nation branding, Prof. Francis Buttle outlines how meeting different needs cost-effectively with the support of IT applies to the full range of a nation's 'customer portfolio', based on clear relationship management objectives and relevant customer insight (see academic perspective, Chapter 3).

Some central themes and issues in treating the nation as a brand are summarized in Table 1.1.

It has also been argued that thoughtful brand positioning gives a country a competitive advantage over other nations [26,27] and that active repositioning of a country through branding can be done successfully and holds great potential for countries, particularly in cases where a country's stereotype lags behind reality. In such cases, there exists great scope for country branding.

A further incentive for countries to embrace branding lies in the capacity of branding techniques to create meaningful differentiation. In the tourism sector, for instance, most destinations make almost identical claims regarding the beauty of their scenery, the purity of their beaches, the hospitable nature of the locals and so on, and therefore, the need for destinations to create a unique identity, to find a niche and differentiate themselves from their competitors, is more critical than ever [28]. This needs to be done on a long-term strategic basis and not as an *ad hoc* event if positive outcomes are to be sustained and not ephemeral. A note of caution is struck in this regard by Lodge [29], who cites the so-called 'Dallas experiment', where what was then called the New Zealand Market Development Board saturated the city of Dallas with New Zealand events, promotions and trade fairs. This intensive burst of marketing activity was sustained for 6 months during which sales increased sharply, but 1 year after the experiment had ended, the levels of awareness and purchase returned to the same levels as they had been before the experiment started. This kind of activity must be seen as a promotional exercise and not as a substitute for a long-term strategic branding campaign.

Nation branding, however, extends beyond the familiar realm of tourism marketing and encompasses a range of further objectives. Vanossi [30] states that it has never been clearer that in today's globalized world, countries and regions and cities suddenly have to compete with each other for tourism, for inward investment, for aid, for membership of supranational groups such as the European Union, for buyers of their products and services, and for talented people. Most places are, according to Vanossi, in need of clear and realistic strategies for communicating and promoting themselves, which leads to the question of which consultants or agencies will ultimately lead the field in managing and promoting these complex and often contradictory megabrands. Vanossi rhetorically asks whether promoting a country is more about policy, management consultancy, public relations, customer relationship management, advertising or brand strategy, or whether it is a combination of everything that working with companies has taught us in the last 50 years. This fascinating complexity is addressed in Chapters 8 and 9.

■ The evolution of nation branding

The evolution of nation branding is traced in Figure 1.1, in which the academic fields of national identity and country-of-origin are shown to interact within the context of economic globalization, whose contradictory effects consist of homogenization of markets and at the same time an increasing sense of national identity. The streams of knowledge embodied within the national identity literature on the one hand and within the country-of-origin literature on the other, have only recently converged. An early manifestation of this convergence could be observed in 2002 with the publication of a special issue devoted to nation branding by the *Journal of Brand Management* [31]. Although sporadic individual articles on nation branding had appeared in other publications in previous years, the JBM special issue for the first time provided a focused forum for the topic and contained papers from leading international scholars including Philip Kotler and David Gertner [16], Nicolas Papadopoulos and Louise Heslop [32], as well as papers from leading consultants in the field such as Wally Olins [33], Fiona Gilmore [27] and Creenagh Lodge [29]. Such was the level of interest generated by the special issue that the journal publishers went on to launch a new journal in November 2004 entitled *Place Branding*, dedicated to the branding of nations, cities and regions.

Probably the most significant earlier work in what has now become known as the emerging field of nation branding is the 1993 book *Marketing Places: Attracting Investment, Industry, and Tourism to Cities, States And Nations* [34]. Although this text takes a broad economic and marketing perspective rather than an explicit brand perspective, it sets the scene for much of the work that has followed in the field. To put the evolution of nation branding into yet wider historical perspective, it could be claimed that nations have always branded themselves – through their symbols, currency, anthems, names and so on – and that it is just the terminology of nation branding that is new, rather than the practice itself [33].

For better or worse, the use of branding techniques is now highly pervasive in most societies. From the most basic physical product to the most diverse nation, branding has steadily increased its scope of application. It could be argued that corporate branding is the closest type of branding to nation branding. The parallels between corporate branding and nation branding lie in the complex, multidimensional nature of the corporate/nation entity and also in the multiple stakeholder groups that

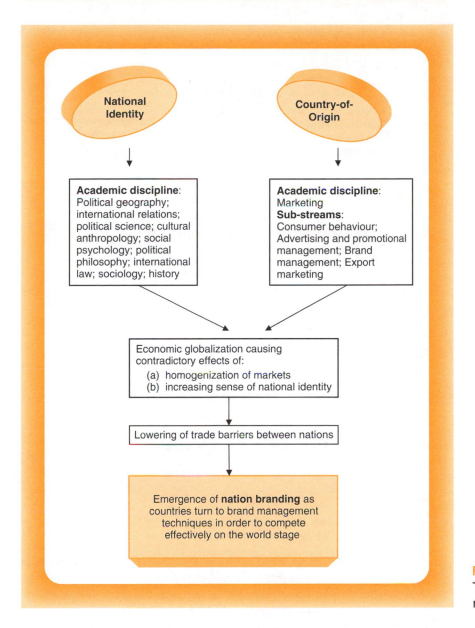

Figure 1.1
The evolution of
nation branding

must be acknowledged by both corporations and nations. Balmer and Gray [35] note that there is an increasing realization at organizational level that corporate brands serve as a powerful navigational tool to various stakeholders for a miscellany of purposes including employment, investment and, most importantly, consumer behaviour. The scope of branding has thus increased incrementally from its original application to simple products through to services, companies and organizations, and now nations. The product-nation brand continuum is depicted in Figure 1.2.

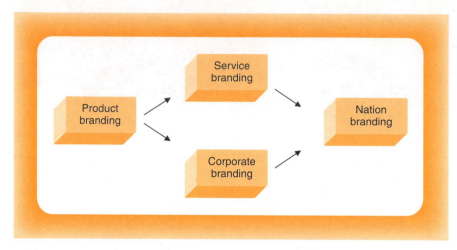

Figure 1.2
Evolution of the scope of branding: The product-nation brand continuum

The parallels between corporate branding and nation branding are explored further in the academic insight that appears in Chapter 8.

Practitioner Insight

From *nation branding* to *competitive identity* – the role of brand management as a component of national policy

Simon Anholt
Consultant and Author, Founding Editor of the quarterly journal, Place Branding

I first began to write about an idea I called *nation branding* in 1996. My original observation was a simple one: that the reputations of countries function like the brand images of companies and that they are equally critical to the progress and prosperity of those countries.

The notion of brand value is still an important part of my work, but I now call the approach *Competitive Identity*, because it has more to do with national identity and the politics and economics of competitiveness than with branding as it is usually understood in the commercial sector.

Today, almost every country wants to manage its reputation. Yet, we are still far from a widespread understanding of what this really means and how far commercial approaches can really apply to government. Many governments, consultants and scholars persist in a naïve and superficial interpretation of 'place branding' that is nothing more than product promotion, where the product happens to be a country rather than a running shoe.

Yet, what really seems to make a difference to the images of countries is when they become dedicated to developing new ideas, policies, laws, products, services, companies, buildings, art and science. When those innovations prove a few simple truths about the country they come from, reputation starts to move; the place produces a buzz, people pay attention and prepare to change their minds.

Not only is innovation more effective for enhancing reputation, it is also a wiser way of spending money. Innovation is good for the organizations that carry it out, so the money invested is also an investment in the economy, not simply frittered away on design or marketing.

Governments should never do things purely for brand-related reasons; no action should be dedicated to image management alone. But there should be something unmistakable about these innovations, the style of their conception and delivery and their alignment with each other, which will gradually drive the country from the image it has inherited towards the one it needs and deserves.

Where competitive identity differs from traditional calls for innovation is the idea of *aligning* the innovation to a strategy for enhancing national reputation. This makes the innovation more focused and more appropriate to the needs and resources of the country; and the improvement in image stimulates additional investment, creates new markets and increases interest in the changes taking place.

Brand management should be treated as a *component of national policy*, never as a 'campaign' that is separate from planning, governance or economic development. This is why my work now involves building and training teams consisting of head of state or government, cabinet ministers and CEOs of key corporations, in the principles of competitive identity, and coaching them through the process of strategy development and implementation.

If brand management is put into a silo of 'communications' or 'public affairs', there is little it can do. But when it informs policy-making and becomes implicit in the way the country is run, it can dramatically accelerate change.

*****

■ Nation-branding issues and initiatives

Different countries have adopted different strategies in order to confront the specific challenges they face. More and more countries around the world are embracing nation branding in order to differentiate themselves on the world stage and to strengthen their economic performance, primarily in terms of exporting, inward investment and tourism. Countries as culturally and geographically diverse as Germany, South Korea, New Zealand, Scotland, Egypt, Britain and Spain have judged it worthwhile to develop nation-branding strategies. We will now provide an overview of the issues impacting upon such countries and some of the initiatives they have taken as they confront the challenges of branding their respective nations.

Germany

Jaffe and Nebenzahl [36] recount how in 1999 ZDF, the German television network, approached identity consultant Wolff Olins to create a national brand for Germany. Although this was not an official campaign, the brand strategy suggested for Germany generated much public interest and debate within Germany. The campaign's main objective was to change consumer perceptions of Germany from what was found to be a nation of 'mechanical perfection', which lacks creativity, to a country that is also 'exciting and surprising'. The perception of Germany as cold and unemotional was attributed partly to German manufacturers such as Audi, whose famous slogan 'Vorsprung durch Technik' extolled German engineering prowess but lacked warmth and emotional depth.

The website of identity consultant Wolff Olins [37] gives details of the approach taken to fashioning a brand for Germany. The basis of their approach was founded upon the belief that Germany is the economic dynamo of Europe, but for historical reasons, it is often perceived in ways that are negative, even hostile. Wolff Olins suggested six practical steps to the German government and its agencies should they wish to address the issue of branding Germany: (1) Set up a national brand-steering committee under the leadership of the Chancellor or President of the Republic; (2) Create a research and development team responsible for reporting to the steering committee; (3) Begin a process of national consultation involving representatives of all the Lander as well as national figures in industry, commerce, education, media, culture and the arts; (4) Commission extensive research into perceptions of Germany overseas, benchmarking these studies against data on perceptions of other nations; (5) Carry out a thorough review of how and where the national brand could appropriately be utilized; (6) Draw up and submit for Bundestag approval a programme of implementation for the brand options adopted by the national steering committee.

Scotland

More and more countries around the world are consciously adopting nation-branding strategies. In Scotland, the organisation Scotland the Brand was set up in 1994 in order to promote Scottish tourism, culture and trade. The organisation's initial credo was as follows:

> As more and more countries focus and promote their national strengths, Scotland too must collectivise and synthesize its considerable virtues into appropriate persuasive messages. With Devolution, the European Union and the globalisation of world markets, now is a key time for Scotland to

build its identity and to exploit its history and heritage and contemporary values as a marketing tool to generate increased awareness of Scotland and drive commercial benefits for Scottish trade [38].

A driving force behind the creation of the Scotland the Brand organization was the growing conviction, based on empirical research, that Scotland has distinctive brand values that are recognized internationally. However, there was also concern that as a nation Scotland had not harnessed these values in its marketing efforts as effectively as it could have in order to derive commercial advantage. Consequently, Scotland the Brand was established in 1994 to promote the distinctive brand values of Scotland.

The organization aimed to provide a collective voice in the promotion of Scottish excellence in both domestic and international markets by combining the marketing efforts of Scottish business. Scotland the Brand Chairman Nick Kuenssberg [39] summed up the organization's goals as including the promotion of Scotland as a place to visit, a place to study, a place to invest in and a place to source knowledge from. This echoed the views expressed by the Scottish Executive [40] in their document 'A Smart, Successful Scotland', which emphasizes the need to promote Scotland as a world class business location for the globalization programmes of overseas and domestic companies.

To help achieve its objectives, Scotland the Brand commissioned a large-scale piece of international research into the brand equity of 'Scottishness'. The study comprised a survey of opinion inside Scotland and in the key export markets of England, France, Germany, Spain, Japan and the United States, and a comprehensive review of existing data. The outcome was used as the basis of efforts to construct a competitive positioning for Scotland, a persuasive proposition to buy Scottish products, services and facilities, and a strategy to help Scotland achieve long-term sustainable competitive advantage. An events/promotions plan covering the period 2002–2004 was drawn up, consisting of what the organizers termed an ambitious and expanding range of happenings in the form of a series of creative, effective and targeted campaigns. The events and promotions all had the common theme of identifying and fostering the core values of spirit, tenacity, integrity and inventiveness that had been elicited through the Scottish brand equity research referred to above.

Scotland the Brand's events/promotions plan 2002–2004 possessed both an internal and an external focus. Within Scotland, the organization intended to focus upon capitalizing on existing major events and calendar dates including Saint Andrew's Day, Burns Celebrations and regional events, as well as sporting events such as established golf, rugby and football occasions. An annual Scotland the Brand conference and awards dinner was also being developed as well as a series of monthly networking events. Externally, the most high profile event engaged in by Scotland the Brand was the Tartan Week celebrations held in Chicago, USA. The Chicago celebrations included tourism events, the finale of an international fashion competition, a ministerial event and a tartan ball. In addition to events in Chicago, a 3-month series of lectures on Scotland and a Scottish Folklife Festival were organized in Washington D.C. in participation with the Smithsonian Associates and Institute. Although open to criticism on the grounds that such events rely much on old-fashioned imagery such as tartan, kilts and bagpipes, there is no doubt that these events represented a major opportunity to raise Scotland's profile within the United States, the most lucrative consumer market in the world.

The visual aspect of Scotland's brand identity, as promoted by the Scotland the Brand organization, consisted of a logo known as the 'Scotland mark'. This logo was developed as a definitive mark for Scotland that would not only uniquely identify and authenticate Scottish products but would offer a guarantee of product quality. Although the creation of such a visual identity can be challenged as being purely superficial and cosmetic, the research process and design solution involved in this type of activity can help to articulate strategy with regard to corporate branding and communication [41]. The 'Scotland mark' could be found on a wide range of Scottish products, from the traditional such as food, drink, textiles and hotels, to more modern products/services such as electronics, software, financial services and transport. Research in the United Kingdom software sector has demonstrated that a quality assurance certificate benefits users by adding value to and confidence in a software product [42], and the logo provided by Scotland the Brand was intended to perform the same value-adding and confidence-providing role for consumers when purchasing products and services made in Scotland.

Ironically, however, there has been a trend in recent years away from explicitly using Scottishness in the branding of financial services. As part of a rebranding operation in 2003, Abbey National shortened its name to 'abbey' and simultaneously closed two famous Scottish names to new business – Scottish Mutual and Scottish Provident. Products for these two companies would henceforth be offered under the abbey brand. Scottish Amicable and Scottish Equitable are two other leading Scottish brands that have disappeared during the last decade [43]. The strategic imperatives inherent in merger and takeover activity have thus taken precedence over the use of country-of-origin as a marketing cue in the area of Scottish financial services.

Scotland the Brand's intention was for the Scotland mark to become an instantly recognizable symbol, conveying strong positive Scottish values and imagery that would add real value to Scottish products and services around the world. In 2003, the Scotland the Brand organization moved from the public to the private sector. Had the organization continued to exist, it would have been interesting to observe whether the organization could maintain its quality criteria for companies wishing to use the Scotland mark when public subsidy ceased and the organization was obliged to sustain itself from membership subscriptions. If quality criteria had been lowered in order to boost short-term subscriptions, that could have resulted in devaluation of the Scotland mark with consequent defection of current members who would not wish to be associated with products, services and brands of inferior quality to their own.

Events in 2003–2004 led to the demise of the Scotland the Brand organization. On Friday 28 March 2004, Scotland the Brand Chairman Nick Kuenssberg told an extraordinary general meeting that the board had voted to wind down the organization's operations [44]. Kuenssberg explained that this step was being taken in the light of the Scottish Executive's decision to set up its own unit for the promotion of Scotland. The board of Scotland the Brand felt that this duplication of effort in promoting the nation undermined the very existence of the Scotland the Brand organization, and therefore, the vote was taken to wind up the organization's operations. The subsequent emergence of a more coherent approach to building the nation's brand has become apparent in the past 2 or 3 years.

New Zealand

Parallels can be drawn between New Zealand and Scotland. Both are relatively small countries overshadowed by larger, more powerful neighbours in the shape of Australia and England. During the nineteenth century, emigration from Scotland to New Zealand occurred to such an extent that by 1861 almost a third of New Zealand's population were Scots [45]. This preponderance of Scottishness in New Zealand may not always prove to be a blessing. Lodge [29] explains that during her work on New Zealand's nation-branding strategy, a major problem was the self-deprecatory nature of the New Zealander. Lodge attributes this characteristic to the large amount of Scottish blood in their veins that makes them averse to 'showing off'. Both New Zealand and Scotland were seen to lack confidence in their national identity, but both had considerable if hidden potential to address their focal markets.

As Chairman of Corporate Edge consultancy, Lodge was involved in a brand definition and strategy exercise for New Zealand, a task that she defines as the identification of competitive positioning and a collectivized reason to buy across an economic spectrum comprising inward investment, culture, education, tourism and the export of produce and products. The process adopted in order to achieve a brand definition and strategy comprised the following series of steps. The first step was the gathering of data and opinion to produce a hypothesis as to how best the country can persuade the rest of the world to buy its collective offer. The data sought were information on the competitive set; the brand equity as ascertained through market research studies carried out by government bodies and exporting commercial bodies; the facts that constitute actual and potential 'pluses'; performance data and objectives on exports, tourism, inward investment and other relevant economic interests such as education; and the views of influential people about the internal issues that could make or break adoption and subsequent delivery of the strategy.

Existing perceptions of New Zealand were found to be negative amongst British consumers but more positive amongst French and German consumers. British consumers tended to believe that New Zealand was essentially an English suburb, mostly bungalows, and populated by rather sleepy people, whereas the French and Germans knew of fine wine, dramatic landscape and a fascinating Maori culture. To reverse British perceptions of New Zealand as the land of the bungalow, a proposition was developed to recast New Zealand as a dramatically exotic destination and source of produce, utilizing imagery based on the spectacular Southern Alps, the extraordinary birds and flowers, the live volcanoes and exotic fruits. Lodge emphasizes that a major factor in the success of the New Zealand nation-branding strategy was that the brand resonated as strongly for the people of New Zealand as it had been seen to motivate its prospective buyers. Further success factors included the fact that in New Zealand the nation-branding project was initiated and driven by acknowledged vested interest; by people with the authority and responsibility to make it work; who had clear economic goals from the outset, which could be used to guide and measure the work; who were unified in their goals and objectives; and who had committed monies for implementation before the work began.

South Korea

A huge amount of attention was focused upon South Korea through its co-hosting of the 2002 FIFA World Cup. Anholt [46] describes how, in an attempt to cash in on the publicity that would be generated by the co-hosting of the World Cup, the Ministry of Commerce, Industry and Energy announced an ambitious plan to raise the international recognition (and thereby boost the exports) of Korean brand-name products. Five strategies were worked out by the government – to internationalize Korean brand names; strengthen corporate brand management; reinforce electronic brand marketing; expand the infrastructure for brand marketing; and raise the nation's image abroad. To achieve the strategic objectives, a well-funded and coherent approach was adopted. The government announced that it would create a 100 billion won venture fund to help exporters improve the designs of their products and that it would also open 'industrial design renovation centres' in ten cities nationwide to help small- and medium-sized companies improve the design of their products as part of an integrated effort to boost the value and recognition of Korean brands.

Perhaps most visionary in the long term, according to Anholt, was the Korean government's plan to build up the nation's brand infrastructure by opening a 'Brand Academy' to train about 500 specialists every year in brand management, character design and industrial packaging. The internal education aspect of nation branding thus appears to have been grasped exceptionally well by Korea compared with the efforts of other nations.

Egypt

Egypt represents an interesting example of a country that has attempted to brand itself largely on the basis of one high-quality product, Egyptian cotton. Mucha [47] gives an account of how the Egyptian government is attempting to brand the country in extremely challenging times. Marketing the Middle East to Americans constitutes an enormous test and the Egyptian government is developing a campaign comprising global advertising, public relations, government relations, market research and event planning in order to raise the profile of Egyptian cotton. New York public relations agency Weber Shandwick has been hired to advise the Egyptian government as to how cotton as a product can help define the country.

However, the weakness of such a strategy is clear. By placing emphasis on a single product as a defining aspect of the nation, there is the risk of pursuing a strategy that is too narrowly focused and not fully representative of the nation as a whole. Also, if market conditions for cotton deteriorate then the risk is that the nation-brand will also be dragged down with it. The Egyptian government is aware of this risk and has initiated a further programme to promote its nation-brand, this time focusing on positioning Egypt as a business destination (see country case insight on Egypt, Chapter 2).

Spain

Spain is often held up as an example of successful nation branding. Preston [48], for instance, claims that Spain is among the best examples of modern, successful nation branding because it keeps on building on what truly exists and its branding efforts incorporate, absorb and embrace a wide variety of activities under one graphic identity to form and project a multifaceted yet coherent, interlocking and mutually supportive whole. The repositioning of Spain as a vibrant modern democracy throwing off the negative connotations of its recent past is also hailed as an exemplar in nation branding by Gilmore [49], who states that the core of a country's brand must capture the spirit of its people and how it can be developed into a brand positioning after consideration of four essential factors – macrotrends, target groups, competitors and core competencies. The positioning derived from such considerations should, according to Gilmore, be rich enough to translate into sub-positionings to target diverse groups, and it should also be substantiated in terms of what the country can actually offer.

An important point made by Gilmore is that exceptional individuals and their exceptional stories have the potential to bring a country's brand alive and make it more real to audiences worldwide for the simple fact that people relate to people. Long-distance runners from Kenya, gymnasts from Romania, musicians from Cuba or past explorers from Scotland represent the kind of exceptional individuals that may contribute to a nation's brand strategy. This issue is further examined in the context of nation-brand ambassadors (see Chapter 9).

Britain

The branding, or rebranding, of Britain in the late 1990s is perhaps the most controversial nation-branding campaign that has been seen to date. A report by the Demos public policy think tank, *Britain™: Renewing Our Identity* [50], formed the basis of the attempted rebranding of Britain instituted by the incoming Labour government under the new Prime Minister Tony Blair. The renewal of identity was deemed urgent because, although Britain had enjoyed many successes in creative industries and steady economic growth, a major problem was that around the world Britain continued to be seen as backward-looking and aloof. According to the British Council [51], British businesses had become wary of overtly marketing their national identity for fear of the more negative connotations associated with Britain – businesses did not want to be thought of as insular, old-fashioned and resistant to change.

The solution to this problem was considered by the New Labour government to be a modernization of Britain's image. 'Cool Britannia' replaced 'Rule Britannia', although it is important to note that it was the media and not the government who attached the 'Cool Britannia' label to the rebranding of Britain that was attempted in the late 1990s. McLaughlin [52] describes how the dawning of a new millennium, the sun finally setting on the last outposts of the British Empire, the working through of multi-ethnicization, a programme of radical constitutional reform and ongoing European integration required dynamic living colour images of national identity. However, from the outset of the branding of Britain campaign, there was overwhelmingly hostile reaction. Concerns were voiced about the viability and desirability of rebranding something as complex as national identity, as if the nation were just another supermarket product. Critics also asserted that it would not be so easy to airbrush out the myths, memories and rituals that underpinned the 'imagined community' of Britain. The concept of a nation as an 'imagined community' is well established in the national identity literature (see Chapter 5).

The rebranding of Britain campaign could be viewed as a salutary lesson for those engaged in nation-branding campaigns in the United Kingdom and elsewhere. Media reaction was almost hysterically hostile, and the campaign died before it could gain any momentum. The potential benefits of a nation-branding strategy did not appear to be communicated effectively to target audiences. There seemed to be insufficient integration of all the stakeholders in the nation-brand, and the perception arose of an exaggerated emphasis on the modern and cutting edge to the detriment of the traditional and established.

■ Summary

This chapter has provided an overview of the relevance, scope and evolution of nation branding. We have looked at the nature of brands and also at the way in which nations may be viewed as brands, however limited and imperfect the concept of nation-as-brand may be. The key objectives to be attained by nation branding centre upon the stimulation of inward investment, the promotion of a country's branded exports and the attraction of tourists. The country case insight on South Africa has illustrated such aspects of nation branding in action. The next chapter delves more deeply into brand theory, with a particular focus upon the concepts of nation-brand identity, image and positioning.

■ References

1. Doyle, P. (1992) Branding, in *The Marketing Book*, Second Edition (M.J. Baker, ed.). Butterworth-Heinemann, UK.
2. Macrae, C., Parkinson, S. and Sheerman, J. (1995) Managing marketing's DNA: The role of branding. *Irish Marketing Review*, 18, 13–20.
3. Lynch, J. and de Chernatony, L. (2004) The power of emotion: Brand communication in business-to-business markets. *Journal of Brand Management*, **11**, 5, 403–19.
4. Roll, M. (2006) *Asian Brand Strategy: How Asia Builds Strong Brands*, Palgrave Macmillan, USA.
5. Holt, D.B. (2004) *How Brands Become Icons: The Principles of Cultural Branding*, Harvard Business School Press, USA.
6. Grant, J. (2006) *The Brand Innovation Manifesto*, John Wiley & Sons, Ltd, UK.
7. Jobber, D. and Fahy, J. (2003) *Foundations of Marketing*, McGraw-Hill Education, UK.
8. Keller, K.L. (2003) *Strategic Brand Management: Building, Measuring, and Managing Brand Equity*, Second Edition. Prentice Hall, USA.
9. de Chernatony, L. and McDonald, M. (2003) *Creating Powerful Brands*, Third Edition. Elsevier Butterworth-Heinemann, UK.
10. Kotler, P. and Keller, K.L. (2006) *Marketing Management*, Twelfth Edition. Prentice Hall, USA, p. 275.
11. Temporal, P. (2002) *Advanced Brand Management: From Vision to Valuation*, John Wiley & Sons (Asia), Singapore.
12. Aaker, D.A. and Joachimsthaler, E. (2000) *Brand Leadership*. The Free Press, USA.
13. Bureau, J.R. (1998) in *The Westburn Dictionary of Marketing* (M.J. Baker, ed.). Westburn Publishers Ltd 2002, http://www.themarketingdictionary.com (accessed 05/02/03).
14. Temporal, P., http://www.asia-inc.com/index.php?articleID=2083 (accessed 23/06/06).
15. Szondi, G. (2007) The role and challenges of country branding in transition countries: The Central European and Eastern European experience. *Place Branding and Public Diplomacy*, **3**, 1, 8–20.
16. Kotler, P. and Gertner, D. (2002) Country as brand, product, and beyond: A place marketing and brand management perspective. *Journal of Brand Management*, **9**, 4–5, 249–61.

17. Olins, W. (1999) *Trading Identities: Why countries and companies are taking each others' roles*. The Foreign Policy Centre, London.
18. Van Ham, P. (2001) The rise of the brand state: The postmodern politics of image and reputation. *Foreign Affairs*, **80**, 5, 2–6.
19. Porter, M. (1998; first published 1990) *The Competitive Advantage of Nations*. Palgrave, UK.
20. Aldersey-Williams, H. (1998) Cool Britannia's big chill. *New Statesman*, 10 April, pp. 12–3.
21. Wolff Olins, *Branding Germany*, http://www.wolff-olins.com/germany (accessed 16/05/03).
22. O'Shaughnessy, J. and Jackson, N. (2000) Treating the nation as a brand: Some neglected issues. *Journal of Macromarketing*, **20**, 1, 56–64.
23. Gilmore, F. (2002) Branding for success, in *Destination Branding: Creating the unique destination proposition* (N. Morgan, A. Pritchard, and R. Price, eds.) Butterworth Heinemann, UK.
24. Mihailovich, P. (2006) Kinship branding: A concept of holism and evolution for the nation brand. *Place Branding*, **2**, 3, 229–47.
25. Anholt, S. (2007) *Competitive Identity: The New Brand Management for Nations, Cities and Regions*. Palgrave Macmillan, UK.
26. Anholt, S. (1998) Nation-brands of the twenty-first century. *Journal of Brand Management*, **5**, 6, 395–406.
27. Gilmore, F. (2002) A country – Can it be repositioned? Spain – the success story of country branding. *Journal of Brand Management*, **9**, 4–5, 281–93.
28. Morgan, N., Pritchard, A. and Piggott, R. (2002) New Zealand, 100% pure. The creation of a powerful niche destination brand. *Journal of Brand Management*, **9**, 4–5, 335–54.
29. Lodge, C. (2002) Success and failure: The brand stories of two countries. *Journal of Brand Management*, **9**, 4–5, 372–84.
30. Vanossi, P., *Country as Brand: Nation Branding*, http://www.affisch.org/web log/archives/00000187.html (accessed 14/01/06).
31. *Journal of Brand Management*, Special Issue: Nation Branding, **9**, 4–5, April 2002.
32. Papadopoulos, N. and Heslop, L. (2002) Country equity and country branding: Problems and prospects. *Journal of Brand Management*, **9**, 4–5, 294–314.
33. Olins, W. (2002) Branding the nation – the historical context. *Journal of Brand Management*, **9**, 4–5, 241–8.
34. Kotler, P., Haider, D.H. and Rein, I. (1993) *Marketing Places: Attracting Investment, Industry, and Tourism to Cities, States And Nations*, Free Press, USA.
35. Balmer, J.M.T. and Gray, E.R. (2003) Corporate brands: What are they? What of them? *European Journal of Marketing*, **37**, 7/8, 972–97.
36. Jaffe, E.D. and Nebenzahl, I.D. (2001) *National Image & Competitive Advantage: The Theory and Practice of Country-of-Origin Effect*. Copenhagen Business School Press.
37. Wolff Olins, *Branding Germany*, http://www.wolff-olins.com/germany (accessed 02/07/05).
38. http://www.scotbrand.com/about-branding.asp (accessed 26/03/02).
39. Ian Fraser (2003) Scotland the Brand ready to go private. *Sunday Herald*, 9 March, p. 8.
40. Scottish Executive (2001) *A Smart Successful Scotland*, 30 January, http://www.scotland.gov.uk/publications (accessed 08/01/02).
41. Baker, M.J. and Balmer, J.M.T. (1997) Visual identity: trappings or substance? *European Journal of Marketing*, **31**, 5/6, 366–75.

42. Jobber, D., Saunders, J., Gilding, B., *et al.* (1989) Assessing the value of a quality assurance certificate for software: An exploratory investigation. *MIS Quarterly*, **13**, 1, 19–31.
43. Flanagan, M. (2003) Abbey rebrand sees Scottish names consigned to history. *The Scotsman*, 25 September, 27.
44. *Sunday Herald* (2004) Scotland the Brand votes to wind up, 30 May, 1.
45. Herman, A. (2001) *The Scottish Enlightenment: The Scots' Invention of the Modern World*. Fourth Estate, London.
46. Anholt, S. (2003) *Brand New Justice: The Upside of Global Branding*. Butterworth-Heinemann, UK.
47. Mucha, T. No Terrorism Here – Just Fine Cotton: Egypt weaves a softer, gentler image, http://www.business2.com/articles (accessed 10/09/05).
48. Preston, P. (1999) Branding is cool. *The Guardian*, 15 November, 22.
49. Gilmore, F. (2002) A country – Can it be repositioned? Spain – the success story of country branding. *Journal of Brand Management*, **9**, 4–5, 281–93.
50. Leonard, M. (1997) *Britain™: Renewing Our Identity*, Demos, London.
51. British Council, The evolution of the traditional British brand, http://www.britcoun.org/arts/design/posh.htm, accessed 2003
52. McLaughlin, E. (2003) Rebranding Britain: The life and times of cool britannia, http://www.open2.net/newbrit/pages/features/coolbritannia.doc (accessed 18/12/03).

CHAPTER 2

Nation-brand identity, image and positioning

Country Case Insight – Egypt

Egypt – An aspiring modern state

ZAD Group

Nation branding is an important concept in today's world. Globalization means that countries compete with each other to attract the attention, respect and trust of investors, tourists, consumers, donors, immigrants, media and the governments of other nations. In such a context, a powerful and positive nation-brand provides crucial competitive advantage. It is essential for countries to understand how they are seen by other publics around the world, how their achievements and their failures, their assets and their liabilities, their people and their products are reflected in their brand images.

■ 1. Egypt's image

Egypt as a country has a key objective to improve its corporate business image (how it is perceived) through a unified consistent message to enhance and maintain its identity (how it wants to be perceived) by the relevant stakeholders. Awareness of its identity and image is a first step on the path towards building the new image. The second step is awareness of the role played by the various communication media such as public relations events, conferences, seminars, workshops and also TV, radio, brochures, folders, product sheets, catalogues, newsletters, CD-ROMs, websites and so on. Effective promotion is all about repetition and recognition of the same identity and message on a long-term basis. Egypt is recreating its identity, and its future image will follow provided that the content of its identity is properly communicated to the outside world.

The country's effort to build its positive image will be conditioned by its own factors such as campaigning, trade promotions, industry associations and national policies, and by the local companies' behaviour when dealing with the outside world. A positive image of Egypt will reflect on its economy. It will help the economy through direct and indirect sales as well as direct and indirect investments. A positive image of Egypt allows us to say 'Destination EGYPT'.

■ 2. Vision, mission, values, key strategies

The vision of Egypt is to be perceived as a business destination and to be placed on the world business map.

Highlighting this desire to build a modern Egypt based on flexible administrative, productive and economic bodies that are capable of reacting to successive international challenges, the Egyptian government has established strong links between production and exportation to form a harmonious scheme within the state-policy aiming at changing the image of Egypt abroad, boosting exports and upgrading national industry through modern international technology and expertise in order to produce high-quality, competitive and market-accessible products.

The objective of branding Egypt as a business destination is essential. Egypt has been a 'must see' destination for generations of visitors and tourism remains its dominant industry, accounting for 20% of its annual GDP. Although Egypt is now a vibrant emerging economy, its image has not developed beyond tourism to include other essential elements of a modern open economy. Specifically, it has not transmitted its openness to investment and trade or its desire for a greater awareness of its products. As a consequence, the world's business community does not think of Egypt first when expanding into new territory. And the consumer does not search out Egyptian products when shopping. But because of budget deficiency, a branding campaign is not achievable. A public relation campaign is a substitute for the branding campaign, aiming at reaching the required goal.

The implementation of the recommended plan is intended to create a new image for Egypt to be perceived as a business destination. It is achievable through a mission involving erasing the old negative image and replacing it with the new image. Egypt has to create and build a new image of Egypt's business environment to erase the old image and replace it with the new image highlighting reform and transparency. This mission involves creating awareness amongst international investors, business associations, importers and all other potential stakeholders so that they consider Egypt to be a land of opportunities either for trade or for investment. This will lead to the inclusion of Egypt in the world economy, which is coherent with the new policy of the government.

Key success factors for the image campaign are

- ownership;
- availability of information;
- acquiring a set of values;
- a comprehensive efficient communication campaign.

The components of Egypt's business image and its influencing factors are illustrated in Figure CS2.1.

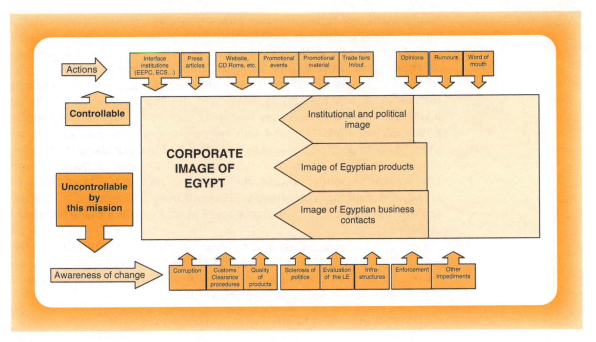

Figure CS2.1
Egypt's business image – components and influencing factors

3. Values

According to international markets and standards, there are certain values that affect the decisions of business decision makers and the business community. After research studies and recommendations by specialists and advisors on international marketing strategies, it is recommended to enhance the win–win situation values. The values that all agreed upon are integrity, guardianship, inclusion, initiative, teamwork and accountability. These values underpin the elements of the action plan devised by Egypt's Business Image Unit as described below.

4. Action plan for Egypt's business image unit

Branding, whether of a product, a service or the country, requires the fulfilment of several basic elements including trust, consistency and a long-term undertaking regarding trans-sectoral transformation. The branding of business Egypt requires a building up of trust in its products, services, people, promises, decisions, etc. It is an ongoing long-term undertaking that requires consistency in delivering the message on the communication level abroad and full ownership, support and awareness of the message on a public and business level locally.

A strong image of 'Business Egypt' can only be successful if it forms alliances with other Ministries within the Government, namely the Ministry of Tourism and the Ministry of Investment as they have a vested interest in improving Egypt's image and the implementation of related activities. An action plan is key to staying competitive. By plotting strategies ahead of time, business will run more smoothly and efforts are more likely to pay off. Ownership, an efficient business image campaign, appropriate information, communication and training of business and government personnel both inside Egypt and abroad, a budget that will sustain the campaign, together with monitoring and evaluation are the key success factors for building a credible and positive business image of Egypt.

Having a positive image is of the utmost importance not only for the success in contacts with partners and stakeholders in Egypt, but even more so with partners and stakeholders abroad. Thus, the objectives of Egypt's business image branding are as follows:

- Attract importers to buy Egyptian products.
- Attract foreign leaders and businesspeople to consider Egypt open for business for foreign trade and industry.
- Attract Foreign Investment and international private investors to invest in Egypt (direct, indirect, portfolio investment).

The strategic plan addresses the identified key strengths, weaknesses, opportunities and threats that apply to Egypt's business image now and in the foreseeable future (see Table CS2.1).

Table CS2.1 SWOT analysis of Egypt's business image

Strengths:	Weaknesses:
1. Attractive products	1. Unaware of buyers' needs
2. Rich in raw materials	2. Do not deliver on time
3. Cheap labour	3. Lack of training
4. Excellent location between continents	4. Lack of information for buyers
5. Easy to establish business	
6. Transparency	
7. Political reform	

Threats:	Opportunities:
1. Lack of finance	1. Open markets
2. No database of exporters or export services available	2. Implementing free trade agreements

In the light of the foregoing SWOT analysis, the strategy of Egypt's Business Image Unit involves

1. creation of a team to support the unit,
2. creation of an identity through a logo,
3. creation of digital media for communication and promotion,
4. creation of digital promotional tools,
5. use of internet as an interactive media maximizing the chances of outreach of overseas stakeholders,
6. arrangement of events abroad through working with public relation firms for extensive professional media coverage,
7. arrangement of press tours to Egypt and allowing them to see for real what they will write about and
8. upgradation of business-to-business communication to international standards.

On the basis of extensive research, and pursued with energy and commitment, Egypt's Business Image Unit seeks to achieve a key objective of positioning Egypt as an aspiring modern state ready to play a full role in the global economy.

*****

■ Introduction

In this chapter, we explore three of the key elements of branding theory – brand identity, brand image and brand positioning – and look at ways in which these concepts apply to the context of nation branding. This chapter's country case insight focuses on Egypt's strategy to enhance its brand image as a country for business and investment, whilst the academic perspective looks at Nepal's efforts to reposition itself in global public opinion and markets.

■ Identity versus image

Identity is an enthralling concept. It possesses an enduring fascination that can be the catalyst for supremely insightful discussion and negotiation, whether the identity in question is individual, group or national. Debates on identity can, however, also degenerate into unproductive navel-gazing, and such introspection needs to be tempered by an awareness of external perceptions of identity, particularly in the context of nation branding, where the audience of the nation-brand is not limited to the domestic population but extends to whichever international arenas the nation wishes to be present in. When discussing notions of *identity*, there often arises confusion regarding the related but distinct concept of *image*. Therefore, it is worth spending some time clarifying these terms and assessing their relevance to nation branding.

Identity is defined by the Concise Oxford Dictionary [1] as 'the fact of being who or what a person or thing is', with a sub-sense definition 'the characteristics determining this'. On the other hand, image is defined by the same dictionary in various ways including 'the general impression that a person, organization, or product presents to the public' and 'a mental representation'. Of course, there are numerous other dictionaries that could be consulted for alternative definitions, and there will never be universal consensus on the precise meanings of the terms. For our purposes, we shall take the following simple but robust perspective – *identity* refers to what something truly is, its essence, whereas *image* refers to how something is perceived. Evidently, there is frequently a gap between these two states. The identity–image gap tends to be a negative factor, with many nations struggling with the frustration of not being perceived by the rest of the world for what they truly are. Stereotypes, clichés and outright racism can dominate perceptions of certain nations. It is a prime objective of nation branding to identify such prejudices and assist nations to dismantle and oppose the negative forces that might otherwise hold back the nation's economic development and standing in the world.

The nature and importance of brand identity and brand image has been highlighted by many leading writers on brand management and strategy. Usually, this has been done in the context of products, services or corporations rather than in the context of nations. However, the core concepts of brand identity and brand image are eminently transferable to the context of nation branding. An analysis of the components of brand identity and brand image is therefore a useful starting point to develop an understanding of nation-brand identity and image. In his excellent book *Asian Brand Strategy* [2], Martin Roll proposes the following five important factors that companies should consider when developing a brand identity. First, brand vision – an internal document clearly describing the future direction for the brand and the desired role and status that the brand hopes to achieve in the stated time. Second, brand scope – a subset of the brand vision document, outlining the market segments and product categories the brand can enter into. Third, brand positioning – the place that the brand strives to occupy in customers' minds. Fourth, brand personality – a brand can take on a personality that helps the customer connect emotionally with the brand. Fifth, brand essence – the heart and soul of the brand, what it stands for and what makes it unique.

Roll's analysis of the key factors underpinning brand identity development requires only minor modification in order to be effectively applied to nation-brand identity development. Brand vision, brand scope, brand positioning and brand personality are clearly as applicable to nation-brands as to product brands. However, when it comes to brand essence, Roll contends that this can be stated in two or three words. Whilst this may be valid for many product or service brands, it would be rash to apply such a minimalist approach to nation-brands, whose multidimensional nature defies such brisk categorization. This is a central challenge in nation branding – the dilemma of encapsulation. How can the infinite cultural richness of nations be reduced to the soundbite-sized chunks of high-impact brandspeak favoured by fast-moving consumer goods (FMCG) marketers? The answer, of course, is that nations transcend such efforts at encapsulation. This is a theme that we will revisit in later chapters, as it represents one of the fundamental issues that those engaged in nation branding must grapple with.

Whereas Roll suggests five key factors in developing a brand identity, French professor Jean-Marc Lehu [3] suggests that brand identity comprises twelve components, all of which need to be taken into consideration when planning branding activities. The twelve components identified by Lehu are the name of the brand – without which no clear and unambiguous clear and unambiguous identification is possible; heritage – every brand has a past, a narration of former events; codes of expression – graphical characteristics such as a logo, font size and type, colours, etc.; positioning – the space occupied by the product in the minds of its target market; status – the necessity of making a clear statement of status, e.g. market leader, challenger brand; personality – the brand's character, creativity, dynamism, independence, etc.; everyday behaviour – brands are much more in the public eye now than in previous times; beliefs – the emotional, descriptive and qualitative components an individual will associate with the brand; values – the increasing importance of social awareness credentials; projected image – the image that the brand desires and that it presents to consumers; attitude of the brand's consumers towards it – the relationship between brand and consumer is now an interactive one; and finally, attitude of the brand towards its consumers – the need for brands to study, include and respect their consumers.

Lehu's detailed and insightful deconstruction offers multiple opportunities for analysis of brand identity. It could be argued that 'projected image' should not appear as a component of identity on the grounds that image resides in the mind of the consumer and is thus beyond the control of the brand owners. As Nandan [4] has pointed out, brand identity originates from the company whereas brand image refers to consumer perceptions, and identity and image are thus distinct but related concepts. However, the remaining eleven components are manipulable by brand managers and capable of application to nation-brands. Ways in which existing concepts of brand identity may be transferred to the context of nation branding are illustrated in Table 2.1.

It has been argued by one of the leading writers on corporate communications that the notion of identity is central to stakeholder management, in that a sense of identity and the core values that underpin it provide an anchor around which all activities and communications can be structured and carried out; additionally, inside the organization, a strong sense of identity can help raise motivation and morale among employees by allowing people to identify with their organizations [5]. This latter point relates to the field of internal branding, which represents another key challenge in nation branding, namely how do you generate buy-in to the nation-brand from a country's own population? The notion of identity

Table 2.1 Brand identity components and nation-brand manifestation

Brand identity component	Nation-brand manifestation
Brand vision	Strategy document agreed upon by the various members of the nation-brand development team – the team should comprise representatives of the government, public and private sectors, and civil society
Brand scope	Outline of the industry sectors and target markets in which the nation-brand can effectively compete. Will include segmentation strategies for sectors such as tourism, inward investment, education, etc.
Name of the brand	Some countries are known by more than one name – Holland/Netherlands, Greece/Hellas, etc. Nations should monitor whether such a duality in naming represents a potential asset or liability
Codes of expression	National flags, language, icons
Everyday behaviour	Political/military behaviour, diplomatic initiatives, conduct of international relations
What makes the brand different?	The uniqueness of the nation – embodied in its culture, history, people
Narrative identity	National myths and heroes, stories of emerging independence
Advocate an ideology	Human rights, sustainable development, the pursuit of happiness, etc.

Adapted from Roll [2], Lehu [3], Kapferer [6], Elliott and Percy [7], and Buchholz and Wordemann [8].

as an anchor around which brand communications may be planned, as outlined above, is also addressed by Madhavaram *et al.* [9] who describe how brand identity plays a key role in informing, guiding and helping to develop, nurture and implement a firm's IMC strategy. A coordinated approach needs to be taken so that countries understand how they are perceived by other publics around the world and to ascertain how the country's achievements, people, products and so on are reflected in their brand images (see country case insight on Egypt, this chapter).

Jean-Noel Kapferer, a world authority on strategic brand management, states that the following questions have to be answered in order to define brand identity clearly [6]: What is the brand's particular vision and aim? What makes it different? What need is the brand fulfilling? What is its permanent nature? What are its value or values? What is its field of competence? Of legitimacy? What are the signs that make the brand recognizable? This perspective on brand identity encompasses both the internal elements of the brand (its permanent nature, values and so on) and the external elements of the brand (the visual signs of the brand). Such a blend of internal and external brand components is also advanced by Aaker [10] who contrasts a brand's core identity – the central, timeless essence of the brand – with a brand's extended identity where various brand identity elements may be combined when the brand enters new markets. In some ways, nation-brand development teams are constrained by existing national iconography as regards the visual manifestation of the nation-brand. As the late French President Francois Mitterand warned, 'On ne touche pas aux symboles'. On the other hand, the internal, enduring essence of nations provides infinitely fertile potential for constructing nation-branding campaigns.

Identity-building activities for brands need not be limited to merely ticking boxes on identity criteria lists. There is considerable scope for imaginative and creative input in brand identity development. Narrative identity theory, for example, suggests that in order to make time human and socially shared, we require a narrative identity for our self and this is done by the stories we can or cannot tell [7]. Nations are clearly in an excellent position to construct such identity-building narratives, given the historical and cultural foundations upon which nations are built. Branding and marketing professionals are not generally renowned for their narrative skills, and therefore, it would make sense for nations to invite their 'real' writers to be involved in constructing the nation's narrative – poets, playwrights, novelists and other creative writers could potentially play a significant role in enhancing their nation's reputation. This already happens in an unplanned way, but nation-brand campaigns can benefit from a planned approach to integrating the country's creative community. This issue is addressed further in Chapter 5.

A further creative approach to identity-building lies in the possibility for brands to advocate an ideology, by standing up for what the consumer believes in and visibly sharing their convictions [8]. Human rights, sustainable development and respect for the environment potentially represent some ideologies that nation-brands could advocate, although the political nature of such ideologies throws into doubt whether such a tactic could withstand a change of political regime within a country. An incoming government, for example, may be less favourable to sustainable development policies than the outgoing government and therefore would not embrace or advocate the same ideology. Changes in political leadership can thus affect the direction of a nation-brand in the same way that the arrival of a new CEO or marketing director can affect the direction of a product, service or corporate (hereafter PSC) brand.

■ The facets of nation-brand identity

Nation-brand identity is a multifaceted concept. The principles of brand identity explored in the previous section provide a useful grounding in understanding the complex nature of nation-brand identity. To navigate from the infinite and irreducible concept of national identity towards the more manageable concept of nation-brand identity, it is necessary to acknowledge that nation-brand identity is built upon a limited range of all the constituent parts of national identity. It would be impossible to effectively develop a nation-brand identity that drew upon every strand of a country's national identity. External audiences – potential tourists, investors, students, workers, etc. – are not going to be willing to receive gargantuan amounts of information about a country's history, culture and people. Therefore, a key task of those engaged in constructing a nation-brand identity is to be selective in identifying which elements of national identity can usefully serve the stated objectives of the nation-branding campaign. In Chapter 5, we analyse in more detail the rich and fascinating area of national identity. In this section, we look at some ways in which nation-brand identity may be constructed.

In a paper on the creation of a country brand for Poland, Florek [11] describes the development of a potential core brand identity for Brand Poland and the possibilities over which the brand could be extended. The core value proposed by Florek for Poland's brand is 'nature', based on the country's relatively low level of industrialization. This core value is extended to relevant areas such as nature reserves, agrotourism, nature trails, natural foods, resorts and spas, extreme sports and so on. This view fits closely with Grant's perspective on brand-as-a-molecule [31]; however, it could be argued that such a nature-based positioning would be too limiting for an overall nation-brand and would not be useful in attracting inward investment or boosting exports of non-natural brands. The nature-based proposition could be more effective as a sub-brand of the overall nation-brand rather than as the overall nation-brand itself.

In addition to the natural environment, which for many nations is obviously a major component of nation-brand identity, there are many other facets of nation-brand identity. The commercial brands produced by a country, for example, can represent an important facet of nation-brand identity. Damjan highlights this point by expressing the hope that Slovenian brands can conquer a niche in the global market and thereby stand as symbols of the strength of the Slovenian economy [12]. A similar point is made by Jaworski and Fosher [13] who describe how the nation-brand identity of Germany has been largely built upon the global success of brands such as BMW, Mercedes and Daimler. The implication of this for nation-brand identity development is that the country's exporters need to be included in, or at least consulted on, the export brand facet of the country's nation-brand identity.

■ Deconstructing nation-brand image

So far, we have looked mainly at brand identity and by extension, nation-brand identity. We will now turn to the issue of nation-brand image and examine how this complex concept may be deconstructed. The mental representations that people may have of different countries can derive from various influencing factors. Firsthand, personal experience of a country through working or holidaying there can play a key role in the image an individual holds of a country. When one does not have any first-hand experience of a country, word-of-mouth can influence country image as can numerous other inputs in the image formation process. Other such inputs include pre-existing national stereotypes, the performance of national sporting teams, political events, portrayals of the country in film, television or other media, the quality of brands emanating from the country, the behaviour of individuals associated with a certain country and so on. These inputs can all determine to a greater or lesser extent a country's nation-brand image, even before one considers the potential effects of nation-brand advertising, promotion and development.

The most thorough examination of country image to date is provided by Jaffe and Nebenzahl [14], in whose book country image is defined as 'the impact that generalizations and perceptions about a country have on a person's evaluation of the country's products and/or brands'. Usunier and Lee [15] demonstrate how confusion regarding national images can arise because of the multiple levels on which such images operate, particularly relating to the combined influence of brand name and country-of-origin on product image where factors to be taken into consideration include the national image of the generic product; national image of the manufacturer; country evoked by the brand name label and country image diffused by the 'Made In' label. An example of the importance attached to the national image of the generic product can be seen in the strenuous and unrelenting efforts of the Scotch Whisky Association to pursue and prosecute any companies that attempt to pass off as 'Scotch' whisky a product that does not meet the rigorous criteria for Scotch whisky as a generic product [16].

When examining the concept of brand image and nation-brand image, it becomes clear that segmentation of target audiences needs to be carried out in order to both monitor and influence the image that is held by disparate groups of consumers. As Riezebos [17] explains, brand image is 'a subjective mental picture shared by a group of consumers'. Just as product brands segment their consumer base by whatever segmentation variables are appropriate to their specific circumstances, nation-brands must also segment their different audiences in order to understand existing nation-brand images and to develop targeted communications to counter negative perceptions and to reinforce positive perceptions. A deconstruction of the corporate image of Egypt reveals three components of the country's corporate image – first, institutional and political image; second, image of Egyptian products and third, image of Egyptian business contacts (see country case insight on Egypt, this chapter).

A commonly used technique by brand marketers who wish to assess their brand's image is brand personification. Brand personification is a qualitative research technique that invites consumers (and non-consumers) of a brand to treat the brand as if it were a person. At its simplest, the technique consists of asking consumers a question along the lines of 'If brand X were a person, what kind of person would it be?'. Product brands have been using this technique for years, and there is no reason why it could not be applied to nation-brands. Because brand personification is such an open-ended qualitative technique, the results can be both surprising and illuminating and at times disconcerting. As with any qualitative technique, the objective is not to provide statistically valid data but rather to produce insight and understanding into the mental associations that consumers hold regarding the brand. In the context of nation branding, the brand personification research technique can be used to gain insight into the degree to which the nation's image is bound up with its political leader or head of state. The image of Russia, for example, may be closely associated with the image of Russian President Vladimir Putin (see country case insight on Russia, Chapter 5).

The findings from brand personification research can provide useful pointers for areas in which the brand personality is weak, strong, desirable or undesirable. It has been suggested that when a brand has a well-defined personality, consumers interact with it and develop a relationship in much the same way as people do in life [18]. With ever increasing use of the internet, the consumer–brand relationship now frequently occurs online as well as offline. However, as Okazaki [19] indicates, although there is an abundant literature on brand personality in general, little attention has been paid to how companies attempt to formulate brand personality on the internet. In nation-branding terms, particularly for smaller or emerging nations with limited promotional budgets, online offers a relatively affordable means to attempt to establish a clearly defined nation-brand personality.

As with any PSC brand, nation-brand image may decay over time. The recent deterioration of Brand USA, for example, has been well documented [20]. If a nation-brand finds itself in such a situation, then a brand revitalization programme will need to be put in place. Product brands that have gone into decline need to display certain characteristics if a brand revitalization programme is to succeed. These characteristics include a long-held heritage, a distinct point-of-differentiation, and to be under-advertised and under-promoted [21]. All nation-brands can fulfil the first two criteria, and given the relatively recent embracing of nation branding by governments around the world, it could be argued that the vast majority of nations are also under-advertised and under-promoted, and thus capable of undergoing successful revitalization programmes. Sjodin and Torn [22] describe how consumers react when a piece of brand communication is incongruent with established brand associations, and the authors go on to maintain that sometimes it may be essential to challenge consumer perceptions if the brand is to remain relevant and vigorous.

However, challenging consumer perceptions can be a high-risk strategy given that existing consumers may be alienated or alarmed by brand communications that are incongruent with their mental associations of the brand. Additionally, as the gurus of positioning Ries and Trout [23] have stated, '...the average person cannot tolerate being told he or she is wrong. Mind-changing is the road to advertising disaster'. Whilst advertising may be limited in its mind-changing power, this does not imply that nation-brands should adopt a defeatist attitude. As we shall see in Chapters 9 and 10, there exists a wide and powerful range of tools available to nation-brands beyond just the conventional advertising route.

■ Conceptual model of nation-brand identity and image

The conceptual model of nation-brand identity and image shown in Figure 2.1 displays the multidimensional nature of the identity and image constructs in a nation-brand context. In the construction of their nation-brands, different nations will selectively focus upon those components and communicators of identity that are most appropriate for attaining their specific nation-brand objectives. For example, some countries may benefit from a range of successful branded exports and therefore seek to integrate branded exports as a communicator of their nation-brand identity; other countries may focus more on notable sporting achievements, their tourism offering, the activation of their diaspora and so on. Whatever route is chosen, countries are becoming increasingly aware that in today's globalized economy, the sphere of country image is assuming great importance (see country case insight on Russia, Chapter 5).

The conceptual model of the nation-brand demonstrates and acknowledges the multi-faceted nature of the nation-brand construct. Key

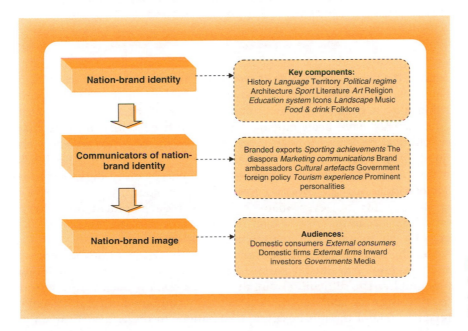

Figure 2.1
Conceptual model of nation-brand identity and image

components of nation-brand identity such as history, territory, sport, icons, folklore and so on represent the enduring essence of the nation. From these enduring characteristics are derived the communicators of nation-brand identity – these may be tangible or intangible. The model shows how nation-brand image is derived as a consequence of nation-brand identity as communicated through means such as cultural artefacts, the diaspora, brand ambassadors, marketing communications and so on. For example, branded exports may play an important role in the nation-brand image held by external consumers; but the market reaction of external consumers will partly determine the types of branded exports that are commercially sustainable. This is an important dimension of the nation-brand construct, as it demonstrates that the nation-brand may aspire to a certain brand image but the uncontrollability of external agents limits the precision with which the nation-brand image can be managed. The conceptual model also illustrates the diverse range of audiences that the nation-brand must address.

Academic Perspective

Re-positioning Nepal in global public opinion and markets: Place-branding for sustainable economic development

Dipak R. Pant
Professor of Anthropology and Economics, founder and head of the Interdisciplinary Unit for Sustainable Economy, Universita Carlo Cattaneo, Italy

Among the poorest agro-pastoral countries in the world, with more than half of its population below the poverty line, Nepal is in a painful transition after a decade-long communist insurgency and instability. Past governments have been moving forward with economic reforms that encouraged trade and foreign investment, but the result so far has been quite meagre. Hydropower, the main source of electricity in Nepal, has huge potential as a cheap and clean source of energy given the great number of Himalayan torrents and rivers that flow speedily down Nepal's ravines. So far, however, many hydropower development plans have only been accumulating dust on the government's shelves. Nepal has been largely unsuccessful in attracting investors.

Nepal is landlocked, isolated from most of the world's transport routes and severely constrained in surface transport because of the mountainous topography. The difficult terrain, the remoteness, the backwardness and the beauty of the landscape have produced a combined effect on Nepal's image as one of the most exciting destinations in the world. Tourism, a chief source of foreign currency (along with migrants' remittances and international aid), has been hurt by the conflict and poor law-and-order situation. Besides tourism, many high-quality agro-food products and large quantities of medicinal herbs, grown on the Himalayan slopes, are available. But a full development of their economic potential is hampered, as Nepal's products have neither competitive price (economy of scale, cost of transport) nor easy access to world markets because of the lack of investment in production processes, infrastructure, facilities and market services. Reaching out to the world market is difficult, if not impossible; so, pulling in buyers is more likely to have some success given Nepal's already well-known tourism destination status. Nepal needs a quality tourism strategy aimed at attracting long-haul travellers, holidaymakers and rest-seekers rather than hit-and-run and short-haul visitors. So, the top priority of Nepal's planners should be 'quality of context' (place-system). In Nepal's case, the 'quality of context' is the combination of safety with the beauty of natural ecosystems and historical (pre-industrial/pre-modern) landscapes. That means law and order, proper sanitation facilities and hygiene, minimalist non-invasive infrastructures and high socio-environmental standards – all well communicated and propagated within and outside the country in order to create a *place-brand*.

The place-brand strategy, based on the 'quality of context', makes good business sense for the place-systems that suffer from certain in-built disadvantages (rugged terrain, landlocked, etc.) and have a legacy of backwardness and instability, like Nepal. Nepal may have good chances with such a place-brand strategy. Enforceable and verifiable environmental and social quality standards may prove to be crucial in order to draw visitors, buyers and investors. Even without a significant growth in trade of goods and services with the outside world, this strategy may, at least, serve the basic purpose of improving the place-system, and hence collective well-being. As a consequence, a human capital of high quality in a happier place-system is built up. The place-brand strategy is probably a win/win strategy for Nepal.

*****

Positioning the nation-brand

The concept of positioning is a key issue in brand management and strategy. The literature on the topic is copious. A good understanding of what positioning entails is a key requisite for anyone involved in nation-brand development. This is particularly so when it comes to dealing with advertising agencies or branding consultancies, whose work rests largely on establishing effective positioning platforms and then designing appropriate creative executions to achieve successful implementation of the desired positioning.

A clear and concise definition of positioning is given by Kotler and Keller [24], who state that 'positioning is the act of designing the company's offering and image to occupy a distinctive place in the mind of the target market'. Jobber [25] builds on this definition and suggests that the keys to successful positioning are clarity, consistency, competitiveness and credibility. Whilst clarity, competitiveness and credibility are evidently useful criteria for successful positioning, the notion of consistency needs to be nuanced. If consistency is elevated to a high status in brand positioning, it could lead to excessively predictable and uninspiring brand communications.

Establishing points of difference is a key task in brand positioning. From a consumer perspective, a brand's points of difference must be relevant, distinctive and believable [26]. National tourism advertising campaigns can often be criticized for scoring very poorly on the 'distinctive' criteria regarding effective points of difference. Many tourism campaigns make generic, undifferentiated claims for their sandy beaches, sunny climate, laidback lifestyle and so on. Competing in this unimaginative way represents a step on the slippery slope towards commoditization. Hence, the recent efforts of many countries to refocus on more precise segmentation strategies promote higher-end cultural tourism, where it is indeed possible for countries to stake a claim to utterly distinctive and unique points of difference.

Meeting the criteria of distinctiveness does, however, bring with it one notable drawback or challenge. To make a strong and compelling appeal to any one particular consumer segment, the brand is likely to alienate other consumer segments; however, an acceptance of such a sacrifice is a characteristic of highly distinctive brands [27]. This kind of sacrifice may often be fairly easy for a PSC brand to accept – the company behind Bacardi Breezers, for example, is unlikely to be overly troubled by its brand's lack of acceptance from the 65 years and older male demographic. But for nation-brands it is a different matter. It is much more daunting for a nation-brand to actively consider alienating a potential consumer segment or audience, given that the nation-brand's remit extends to all areas of the nation's economic life. Therefore, the potential pitfall for nation-brands is that they select bland, inoffensive positioning platforms that offend nobody but at the same time are relatively meaningless and thus inspire nobody either. Table 2.2 illustrates some positioning platforms that have been used by nations across the world in recent years.

An ever-present complicating factor in nation branding in general, and in nation-brand positioning specifically, resides in the political sensitivities of the various stakeholders that must be accommodated. How, for example, should a highly diverse Britain be cohesively positioned [28]? This is not merely an abstract question, as some of the constituent parts of the United Kingdom are already establishing their own, distinct nation-brands. Scotland, for instance, developed a nation-brand positioning based on the key values of integrity, inventiveness, quality and independence of spirit [29]. This positioning platform is quite distinct

Table 2.2 Nation-brand positioning platforms	
Nation-brand	**Positioning platform**
South Africa	Alive with possibility
Bolivia	The authentic still exists
Scotland	The best small country in the world
India	India shining
Thailand	Amazing Thailand
Malaysia	Truly Asia

from any United Kingdom umbrella branding. On the other hand, a clear political statement may be used as the basis for a clear, positive positioning platform as can be seen in the case of Costa Rica, whose commitment to democracy and rejection of a standing army has allowed the country to position itself as a peaceful ecotourism destination [30]. Positioning strategies used by other nation-brands can be seen in the country case insights on Estonia (Chapter 9), Egypt (this chapter), Brazil (Chapter 6), Chile (Chapter 3), Switzerland (Chapter 4) as well as in the academic perspectives focusing on Nepal (Chapter 2) and Northern Ireland (Chapter 10).

■ Liberation through modularity

We have argued above that when it comes to brand positioning and brand communications, consistency may be an overrated virtue. Obviously, wild and random fluctuations in brand positioning will lead to consumer confusion and erode brand equity and are not to be recommended. However, an imaginative approach to the consistency dilemma is advocated by John Grant [31], who expresses his standpoint as follows:

> 'The way to manage brands is coherence, not consistency. Consistency is the idea that you need to make your marketing all look the same. But the most interesting brands, like people, are authentic (true to themselves) and can afford to be freer in their range of activities.'

There may be lessons to be learnt in this regard from *modularity*, a technique practised in the field of innovation and new product development. Modularity has been described as building a complex product from smaller subsystems that can be designed independently yet function together as a whole [32]. Transferring this concept to the domain of nation branding, the overall umbrella nation-brand may be viewed as the 'complex product' whilst entities such as inward investment agencies, tourism boards, export promotion agencies, etc. may be viewed as the 'smaller subsystems that can be designed independently yet function together as a whole'. When utilizing the technique of modularity, different companies take responsibility for each of the modules in the knowledge that their collective efforts will create value for customers [33]. By adopting a modularity approach, nation-brands may be able to liberate themselves from the straitjacket of consistent but bland, indistinct positioning and communications. The nation-brand development team will need to act as the architect company, ensuring that brand design rules are clearly set out to the different national agencies, each of whom are tasked with creating their own 'module' or sub-system to be integrated into the overall nation-brand.

■ Summary

This chapter has discussed the key branding concepts of brand identity, brand image and brand positioning. A distinction has been made between the two frequently confused concepts of identity and image. The components of nation-brand identity and nation-brand image have been analyzed, and the issues involved in positioning the nation-brand have been discussed, with the repositioning of Nepal covered in Prof. Dipak Pant's academic perspective. Basic principles of branding have been shown to apply to whole nations, despite the increased complexity inherent in a nation-brand as compared with a PSC brand.

■ References

1. *Concise Oxford Dictionary* (1999), Tenth Edition. Oxford University Press, UK.
2. Roll, M. (2006) *Asian Brand Strategy: How Asia Builds Strong Brands*. Palgrave Macmillan, UK.
3. Lehu, J.-M. (2006) *Brand Rejuvenation: How to Protect, Strengthen and Add Value to your Brand to Prevent it from Ageing*. Kogan Page, UK.
4. Nandan, S. (2005) An exploration of the brand identity-brand image linkage: A communications perspective. *Journal of Brand Management*, **12**, 4, 264–78.
5. Cornelissen, J. (2004) *Corporate Communications: Theory and Practice*. Sage Publications, UK.
6. Kapferer, J.-K. (2004) *The New Strategic Brand Management: Creating and Sustaining Brand Equity Long Term*. Kogan Page, UK.
7. Elliott, R. and Percy, L. (2007) *Strategic Brand Management*. Oxford University Press, UK.
8. Buchholz, A. and Wordemann, W. (2000) *What Makes Winning Brands Different: The Hidden Method Behind The World's Most Successful Brands*. Wiley, UK.
9. Madhavaram, S., Badrinarayanan, V., and McDonald, R.E. (2005) Integrated marketing communication (IMC) and brand identity as critical components of brand equity strategy: A conceptual framework and research propositions. *Journal of Advertising*, **34**, 69–80.
10. Aaker, D.A. (1996) *Building Strong Brands*. Free Press, USA.
11. Florek, M. (2005) The country brand as a new challenge for Poland. *Place Branding*, **1**, 2, 205–14.
12. Damjan, J. (2005) Development of Slovenian brands: Oldest are the best. *Place Branding*, **1**, 4, 363–72.

13. Jaworski, S.P. and Fosher, D. (2003) National brand identity & its effect on corporate brands: The nation brand effect (NBE). *Multinational Business Review*, **11**, 2, 99–113.

14. Jaffe, E.D. and Nebenzahl, I.D. (2001) *National Image & Competitive Advantage: The Theory and Practice of Country-of-Origin Effect*. Copenhagen Business School Press, Denmark.

15. Usunier, J.-C. and Lee, J.A. (2005) *Marketing Across Cultures*, Fourth Edition. FT Prentice Hall, UK, 287.

16. Scotch Whisky Association website: http://www.scotch-whisky.org.uk

17. Riezebos, R. (2003) *Brand Management: A Theoretical and Practical Approach*. FT Prentice Hall, UK.

18. De Chernatony, L. and McDonald, M. (2003) *Creating Powerful Brands in Consumer, Service and Industrial Markets*, Third Edition. Elsevier Butterworth-Heinemann, UK.

19. Okazaki, S. (2006) Excitement or sophistication? A preliminary exploration of online brand personality. *International Marketing Review*, **23**, 3, 279–303.

20. Anholt, S. and Hildreth, J. (2004) *Brand America: The Mother of All Brands*. Cyan Books, UK.

21. Wansink, B. and Huffman, C. (2001) Revitalizing mature packaged goods. *Journal of Product & Brand Management*, **10**, 4, 228–42.

22. Sjodin, H. and Torn, F. (2006) When communication challenges brand associations: A framework for understanding consumer responses to brand image incongruity. *Journal of Consumer Behaviour*, **5**, 1, 32–42.

23. Ries, A. and Trout, J. (2001) *Positioning: How to be Seen and Heard in the Overcrowded Marketplace*. McGraw-Hill, USA.

24. Kotler, P. and Keller, K.L. (2006) *Marketing Management*, Twelfth Edition. Pearson Prentice Hall, USA.

25. Jobber, D. (2004) *Principles and Practice of Marketing*, Fourth Edition. McGraw-Hill, UK.

26. Keller, K.L. (2003) *Strategic Brand Management: Building, Measuring, and Managing Brand Equity*, Second Edition. Prentice Hall, USA.

27. Bauer, A., Bloching, B., Howaldt, K., *et al.* (2006) *Moment of Truth: Redefining the CEO's Brand Management Agenda*. Palgrave Macmillan, UK.

28. Hall, J. (2004) Branding Britain. *Journal of Vacation Marketing*, **10**, 2, 171–85.

29. Lodge, C. (2002) Branding countries: A new field for branding or an ancient truth? *Journal of the Chartered Institute of Marketing*, Feb, 21–25.

30. Quelch, J. and Jocz, K. (2005) Positioning the nation-state. *Place Branding*, **1**, 3, 229–37.

31. Grant, J. (2006) *The Brand Innovation Manifesto: How to Build Brands, Redefine Markets & Defy Conventions*. Wiley, UK.

32. Baldwin, C.Y. and Clark, K.B. (1997) Managing in an Age of Modularity. *Harvard Business Review*, Sept–Oct, 84–93.

33. Mohr, J., Sengupta, S., and Slater, S. (2005) *Marketing of High-Technology Products and Innovations*, Second Edition. Pearson Prentice Hall, USA.

CHAPTER 3

Nation-brand equity

Country Case Insight – Chile

Chile – 'All Ways Surprising'

Christian Felzensztein
Professor of International Marketing
Faculty of Management and Economics, Universidad Austral de
Chile, Valdivia, Chile

Chile 'All Ways Surprising' or Chile 'Always Surprising' are the main slogans used for the new country brand of Chile, which wants to position itself as unique in the continent. The new logo and slogan were designed by ProChile, the Export Promotion Bureau, which is responsible for implementing and enhancing Chile's trade policy and promoting of the country in international markets.

Located in the Southern part of Latin America, Chile has become a regional leader thanks to its democratic stability that offers a secure business environment. Chile extends over a surface more than 4000 km long with an average width of 180 km. It is the longest South American country. It has developed a robust economy, based on a diversified production structure coupled with a low inflation rate, stable external accounts and strong international reserves. Chile has a vast network of free trade agreements with other countries, including the USA, EU and Korea among others, which have placed it in a privileged position as a leading world trader and a strategic business base in the region. However, the main export products are still largely limited to copper and traditional products such as fresh fruit.

The country is positioning itself through ProChile as 'Chile, all in one country', which can produce and sell a more diversified range of products because of its geographical locations. The objective is to develop an array of export products ranging from exquisite salmon to world-class wine to fresh fruit and to award-winning extra virgin olive oil. For instance, 'We have it!' was the theme of recent advertising appearing in the Chilean airline LAN's in-flight magazine. International focus groups in London, New York and other key capitals around the world formed part of an independent study, as well as the development of a new brand strategy, led by Interbrand the specialist brand agency selected by ProChile to carry out the country brand strategy in 2005.

Certainly, there have been two key industries that have helped to create a clear positioning of Chile in international markets. These are the wine industry and the salmon industry. This case is going to focus on Chile's wine industry and discuss the effect of nation branding and country-of-origin on this crucial sector of the Chilean economy.

■ 1. The Chilean wine industry

The Chilean wine industry operates in a highly competitive international environment, exporting more than 50% of local wine production. In 1990, Chilean wines represented less than 1% of the global wine market; by 2005, this figure had risen to nearly 10%. Exports to Europe, the USA and Asia grew most markedly, registering a total of US $600 million in 2002. Chilean wine producers now export more than 50% of their produce to 90 countries in five continents around the world.

According to the previous figures, traditional European wine producers have faced unprecedented competitive challenges over the last decade as so-called 'new world' wines (e.g. from the USA, Australia, Chile, South Africa, New Zealand) have become ever more prominent in the marketplace. The reputation of wine-producing countries and regions has previously been relied upon as a core feature of differential advantage. Studies carried out by different researchers have suggested that geographic origin or country-of-origin effect (COO) does matter in this industry. Wine tends to be perceived as a national product with companies from a single country sometimes cooperating in generic advertising campaigns. This reflects the notion that wine has a fairly strong COO effect and can readily be promoted in this way.

In the new competitive environment, Chile has continued working to position itself as a wine country by creating links between its culture, tradition, singular geographic position and tourism as other wine producer countries have done with relative success. This combination of cultural and geographic characteristics constitutes an important dimension of Chile's nation-brand equity (NBEQ).

As an early step in this positioning strategy, in 2002, Viñas de Chile and Chile Vid[1] introduced their project for the international marketing of Chilean wines by re-launching, after 2 years of inactivity, the 'Wines of Chile' brand. Target markets for the campaign include Germany, the USA, Japan and the United Kingdom. This entity is responsible for handling development plans and the promotion of Chilean wines' image abroad. This means that the Wines of Chile challenge is to take charge of putting into practice the international development strategy of the wine industry, giving it a unified vision abroad and also a development plan that allows it to create a trustworthy marque for consumers through which Chile is presented as a single country showing its best attributes – friendship, emotions, lifestyle, naturalism, magic realism and sensuality.

Although Chilean wines have successfully penetrated international markets, Chile is still recognized as a small production country compared with the big worldwide wine producers of France, Australia, Italy and Spain. Until now, the international competitiveness of the Chilean wine industry has been based on its good quality–price relationship or *value for money*. On the other hand, the international competitiveness of other wine producers such as California and Australia has been based on products with a range of higher prices and excellent quality. International

---

[1] Chilean wines export associations

wine experts and international reports have illustrated an opinion that, although Chilean wines have clear competitive advantages in terms of agricultural and climate conditions for wine production, there remains a huge gap in the coordination of international marketing strategies compared with competitors such as Australia, France and the USA.

For example, although Chilean wines are well known in the specialist media, average consumers are not fully aware of the importance of Chile as a wine producer. This situation may be explained by the fact that Chile has only established its reputation and gained recognized market share in the past 10 years within worldwide wine markets. According to ProChile, the Chilean governmental export promotion office, countries such as Australia and South Africa have shown in the UK market the huge potential of campaigns aimed at introducing their wines into the collective consciousness of British consumers. However, in the case of Chile, many of these consumers are aware of this South American country but not in terms of a precise geographical location. In addition to this, during 2002, other wine-producing competitors also started generic campaigns based on regions and countries of origin, e.g. Bordeaux, or 'Wines from Spain' using posters and magazines with their slogan 'Spanish wine – Body and Soul'. It is therefore becoming ever more important for Chile to enhance its COO effect through effective nation branding, as well as actively promoting its wine sector in particular.

In this evolving competitive environment, what should the Chilean wine industry do next in terms of positioning and branding using the new Chile slogan and brand strategy? This is a question that most wine companies, wine export associations and the Chilean export promotion office are looking to answer. Wines of Chile should become an organization that represents the interests of Chilean wineries abroad and be fully coordinated with other key industries that the Chilean Government wants to engage as part of the 'All Ways Surprising' campaign.

It remains to be seen whether Chile 'All Ways Surprising' is the best and right slogan for the country. Some believe that a unique positioning based on one specific industry should be the solution. Others argue that the Chilean country brand should not benefit any one industry in particular. But what is the key element of Chile? Its wines, the salmon, the Andes mountains, the Pacific Ocean, the desert, the glaciers. . . ? Or maybe none of these comes clear to the top of mind of our potential international consumers? As its says, Chile is all ways surprising!

*****

■ Introduction

This chapter focuses on the concept of brand equity. We first look at the two major perspectives on brand equity, the consumer perspective and the financial perspective. We then apply the brand equity concept to nation-brands and examine the range of potential sources and dimensions of NBEQ. The country case insight in this chapter demonstrates how

Chile's NBEQ derives to a considerable extent from its cultural and geographic characteristics, whilst the academic perspective by Prof. Francis Buttle provides insights into the applicability of customer relationship management (CRM) techniques to nation branding.

■ Alternative perspectives on brand equity

The term 'brand equity' is a prominent one in the theory and practice of branding. Fundamentally, brand equity refers to the value of a brand. The notion of equity is borrowed from the field of finance; although, when the term is transposed to the field of branding, it loses any precise, universally accepted meaning. As we shall see, there are two distinct approaches to viewing the concept of brand equity. One approach may be characterized as the *consumer perspective*, wherein brand equity may be evaluated in terms of consumer awareness of the brand in question, consumer judgements regarding brand quality, uniqueness, prestige and so on. The alternative approach to viewing brand equity is the *financial perspective*, which involves attempts of various kinds to attach a financial value to specific brands. Within both the consumer perspective and the financial perspective, there exist several different viewpoints with regard to what brand equity means. These different viewpoints will now be examined.

Consumer perspective

One of the leading proponents of the consumer perspective on brand equity, Kevin Lane Keller, uses the term customer-based brand equity (hereafter CBBE) which he defines as 'the differential effect that brand knowledge has on consumer response to the marketing of that brand'; Keller elaborates upon this concise definition by suggesting that 'customer-based brand equity occurs when the consumer has a high level of awareness and familiarity with the brand and holds some strong, favourable, and unique brand associations in memory' [1]. In a study by other researchers, the following four dimensions of CBBE were proposed – brand awareness, brand associations, perceived quality and brand loyalty [2]. It is important for nations to conduct research to gain insight into such dimensions of their NBEQ, rather than relying on gut instinct. Many nations might assume, for example, that they are suffering from negative brand associations, when in reality there might be an almost complete lack of awareness of their nation-brand in the minds of external audiences. The need to conduct ongoing research into a nation's brand equity is highlighted by Prof. Akutsu, who notes that 'just like a company brand, the equity of a nation resides in the minds of its audiences' (see country case insight on Japan, Chapter 9).

Still grounded in the consumer perspective on brand equity, although utilizing the vocabulary of accounting, Aaker states that brand equity represents 'a set of brand assets and liabilities linked to a brand, its name and symbol, that add to or subtract from the value provided by a product or service to a firm and/or that firm's customers' [3]. The idea of adding value is also referred to by Farquhar [4], who defines brand equity as 'the added value to the firm, the trade, or the consumer with which a given brand endows a product'. Farquhar's inclusion of 'the trade' is a useful indication that the consumer perspective on brand equity should take a broad-based view of who the 'consumer' or the 'customer' is. Stakeholder models suggest that a brand must appeal to and communicate with multiple constituencies, rather than take a myopic uni-dimensional view of the customer. The stakeholder theory of brand equity is articulated by Jones [5], who argues that brand value is co-created through interaction with multiple strategic stakeholders, and therefore, it would be erroneous to focus only on the customer when assessing brand equity. The country case insight on France provides a nation branding illustration of Jones' perspective on brand value being co-created with multiple strategic stakeholders (see Chapter 10).

Temporal [6] describes how the term brand equity is often used in referring to the descriptive aspects of a brand, whether symbols, imagery or consumer associations, and to reflect the strength of a brand in terms of consumer perceptions. Nations are particularly rich in terms of symbols and imagery, with every nation possessing its own unique and distinctive iconography. These, and other components of national identity, underpin nation-brand development and ensure that nation branding remains an encapsulation and expression of a nation's true essence, rather than a mere PR exercise.

Brand equity can create a relationship and a strong bond between brand and consumer, which grows over time, involving trust and an emotional connection [7]. Baker [8] defines brand equity as the value imputed to a brand that recognizes its worth as an asset; this value reflects the market share held by the brand, the degree of loyalty and recognition it enjoys, its perceived quality and any other attributes that distinguish it positively from competitive offerings, e.g., patent protection, trademark and so on. Baker's perspective on brand equity is echoed closely by Riezebos [9] who identifies four sources of brand equity: the size of the market share; the stability of the market share; the price margin of the brand for the organization and the rights of ownership (patents, trademarks) linked to the brand. Kapferer [10] in his discussion of brand equity also proposes four indicators of brand assets: aided brand awareness; spontaneous brand awareness; membership of the consumer's evoked set and whether the brand has already been consumed. A similar view is taken by De Chernatony and McDonald [11], whose view is that brand equity describes the perceptions consumers have about a brand, and this in turn leads to the value of a brand.

Consumer loyalty is a key element in brand equity. Brand-building efforts typically revolve around creating differentiation and value for consumers, and achieving high levels of customer loyalty is a useful metric for assessing the success of a brand's strategy. Whereas PSC brands have for many years dedicated considerable resources to developing loyalty programmes, nation-brands have taken relatively few initiatives in this area. In his academic perspective in this chapter, Prof. Francis Buttle explores the potential application of CRM principles to nation-brands. An enlightened view on building customer loyalty acknowledges that loyalty programmes must aim to build consumers' emotional attachment to the brand rather than aiming solely at engendering repeat buying, because the correlation between emotional loyalty and brand purchase is exponential rather than linear – at the highest level of emotional loyalty to a brand, consumers will buy at least twice as much as consumers just slightly less attached to the brand, and often three to four times more [12]. As rich repositories of cultural meanings, possessing deep emotional and experiential qualities, nation-brands should be well-placed to develop such emotional attachment to their brands.

In the context of product brands, it has been shown that regular permission-based e-mail marketing can have various positive effects on brand loyalty: e-mail-activated consumers go on to visit retail stores, recommend the brand to their friends, and loyal customers appear to appreciate regular communication and various other information content from the brand more than mere offers [13]. If a brand fails to develop customer loyalty, then there is the risk of what Perrin-Martinenq [14] has termed 'brand detachment', where the affective or emotional bond between a brand and a consumer dissolves in a similar way to the dissolution of other types of relationships. One way in which nation-brands can avoid the negative consequences of such 'brand detachment' is through the application of CRM principles to the nation's full range of audiences and stakeholders (see academic perspective, Chapter 3).

The visual manifestations of a brand clearly play an important role in contributing to overall brand equity. For many consumers, a brand's logo, name, symbols, typeface, colour scheme and so on will represent a prime trigger of and contributor to brand awareness. It has been claimed that there is a significant relationship between visual design and positive brand responses in terms of positive affect, perceptions of quality, recognition and consensus of meaning [15]. Nations need to actively manage their visual identity to ensure maximum impact and synergy across different target audiences and stakeholders – this has been done through campaigns such as Iceland Naturally (see country case insight, Chapter 8) and Brazil IT (see country case insight, Chapter 6).

Financial perspective

As we have seen, the *consumer perspective* on brand equity has clear relevance to nation-brands, particularly in the light of stakeholder theory's concept of multiple audiences, which for nation-brands include potential tourists, investors, employees, students and consumers both domestic and international. The relevance to nation branding of the *financial perspective* on brand equity is less obvious. In this section, we briefly overview the financial perspective on brand equity before discussing one specific attempt that has been made to place a financial valuation upon nation-brands.

To date, there is no universal consensus on accounting methods and procedures for the financial valuation of brands. There are, however, certain techniques available to companies and analysts who wish to make an estimate of a brand's financial value. Such techniques include valuation by historic costs, valuation by replacement costs and valuation by future earnings. Valuation by historic costs treats a brand as an asset whose value is derived from investments over a period of time; valuation by replacement costs centres upon estimating how much it would cost to create an equivalent brand, and valuation by future earnings aims to estimate future cash flows associated with the brand [16].

Probably the most high profile and widely known exercise in brand valuation is the annual 100 Top Brands survey conducted by branding consultancy Interbrand and published by Business Week magazine. To qualify for the top 100 list, each brand must have a value greater than $1 billion, derive about one-third of its earnings outside its home country and have publicly available marketing and financial data. Interbrand's methodology is based on the future cash flow technique. A detailed description of this method can be accessed at Interbrand's website [17]. Interbrand's top six global brands in 2005, along with their estimated financial valuations, were as follows: Coca-Cola ($67.5 billion), Microsoft ($59.9 billion), IBM ($53.3 billion), GE ($46.9 billion), Intel ($35.5 billion) and Nokia ($26.4 billion). From a corporate point of view, brand valuation can be a useful tool in that it can allow a company to use a brand to raise credits, determine potential revenue streams from licencing agreements and gain an insight into the value of a possible future brand acquisition [18]. Whilst the potential benefits of conducting brand valuation are thus clear, at least in the case of most PSC brands, what, if any, relevance does financial valuation of brands hold for nation-brands?

In his book *Competitive Identity* [19], nation-branding expert Simon Anholt explains that he has incorporated a financial valuation of nation-brands into his Nation Brands Index (NBI) in order to give 'a sense of the real contribution of the brand to the nation's economy'. This view is in line with the perspectives on brands as assets discussed above. Anholt uses 'royalty relief' methodology in order to calculate the financial valuation of nation-brands, and in the last quarter of the 2005 NBI survey, this resulted in the following valuations for the top five nation-brands: USA ($17.9 billion), Japan ($6.2 billion), Germany ($4.6 billion), UK ($3.5 billion) and France ($2.9 billion). Whilst there will always be debate within accounting and financial circles as to the validity of the various brand valuation techniques currently in use, Anholt's innovative attempts at financial valuation of nation-brands may help to focus governments' attention on the need to cultivate their nation-brands in an increasingly globalized economy.

Academic Perspective

A CRM perspective on nation branding

Francis Buttle
Former Professor of Marketing and Customer Relationship Management at Macquarie Graduate School of Management (MGSM), Sydney, Australia

Although CRM entered the management lexicon in the early 1990s, it is still a disputed territory. There is no firm consensus on the meaning of the term. This is in part because a number of different types of CRM have been identified – operational, analytic, collaborative and strategic – and although these are related, they are in some senses quite different. My view of CRM is that it involves the application of technology to help manage interactions and transactions with customers, so that organizations can optimize their returns across their customer portfolio. Not all customers want or value the same experiences, products, services, information, interactions or benefits. Neither are all customers equally valuable. CRM lets organizations identify and respond to these differences in a cost-effective manner.

At a macro level, a nation's 'customer' portfolio might include its own citizens, nation-trading partners, foreign consumers of the nation's goods and services, international organizations, political allies, political opponents, tourists and inward investors.

Drilling down into each of these categories yields more differentiation. The citizen group is not homogenous. Different subsets of citizens want and value different services and information from government. Consider the case of Knowsley Metropolitan Borough Council. This Merseyside metropolitan district has a population of approximately 150 000 people with a relatively young age profile. Knowsley has implemented citizen relationship management, investing in Onyx CRM. The council produces over 1000 services for its citizens through nine operational departments. It not only uses CRM to ensure greater consistency and performance in service delivery but also to make certain that citizens are aware of and get access to the services to which they are entitled. It is striving to develop a 360° view of its citizens so that it knows the history of service provision to each citizen. This will enable it performs trend and cluster analysis, improves service provision to different groups of citizens and tracks inbound and outbound communications across departmental silos. Knowsley reports that CRM has delivered annual savings of well over £250 000, which can be diverted to service enhancement.

This same principle of meeting different needs cost-effectively with the support of IT extends into all other groups of a nation's customers. The key is to have clear relationship management objectives and relevant customer insight. Consider foreign direct investment (FDI). Australia's share of FDI fell from 1.6 to 0.6% between 1996 and 2001, sparking serious government concern about the country's ability to understand the needs of, and satisfy the requirements of, investors. The 2002 report from Invest Australia entitled 'Global Returns: The National Strategic Framework for Attracting Foreign Direct' was quite clear about the need for customer (investor) insight.

'Understanding the drivers of investment location decisions is important in determining Australia's competitive advantages, formulating generic marketing messages and developing targeted campaigns for priority industry sectors. In addition, insight into the investment decision-making process and the operating methods of investors helps to target potential investors effectively.'

CRM systems not only store this information at a unique customer level, and make it available to users when and where they want, but are also able to perform analysis to identify trends and patterns, and predict decisions. They can be used for lead and opportunity management, contact management, proposal generation, campaign management and knowledge management. Essentially, any functionality that marketing, sales and service personnel want to enable them to understand, service and satisfy a nation's many customers effectively and efficiently is available in today's CRM systems.

*****

■ Sources and dimensions of NBEQ

In this section, we identify the major sources of NBEQ that potentially form the basis for developing strategic nation-branding campaigns. These sources are presented in the form of an asset-based model of NBEQ (see Figure 3.1) in which the internal and external assets comprising NBEQ are conceptualized in terms of innate, nurtured, vicarious and disseminated assets. We build on the preceding discussion and definitions of brand equity and apply them to the context of nation branding. We define NBEQ as *the tangible and intangible, internal and external assets (or liabilities) of the nation*. These internal and external assets (or liabilities) represent the sources of NBEQ. Internal assets are conceptualized as *innate* (iconography, landscape and culture) or *nurtured* (internal buy-in, support for the arts). External assets are conceptualized as *vicarious* (country image perceptions, external portrayal in popular culture) or *disseminated* (brand ambassadors, the diaspora, branded exports). These sources will now be discussed in terms of their contribution to overall nation-brand equity.

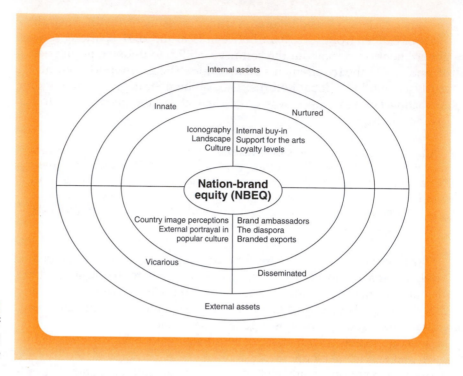

Figure 3.1
Model of
asset-based
nation-brand equity

Internal assets

We view a nation-brand's internal assets as being either innate or nurtured. *Innate assets* are enduring elements of national identity, those aspects of the essence of the nation that can be viewed as assets in attempts to build nation-brand equity. Such assets include a nation's iconography, landscape and culture. *Nurtured assets*, on the other hand, derive from conscious contemporary efforts to create a healthy environment for nation-brand equity development. Internal buy-in and support for the arts represent such nurtured assets.

Innate assets: Iconography, landscape, culture

The distinguishing features of a nation include its iconography, landscape and culture, and these provide a powerful and authentic means of differentiation for the nation-brand. A nation's iconography comprises visual images, symbols and other unique representational elements associated with the nation. National flags are the most obvious element of a nation's iconography, although the modern meaning of the word 'icon' now extends to cover places, individuals and even products that have attained the status of symbolically representing something with wider connotations in society. In this light, for example Nelson Mandela may be regarded as an icon of South Africa, the Acropolis as an icon of Greece and whisky as an icon of Scotland. As with the other innate assets possessed by nations, these elements are unique and cannot be copied – the kind of distinctive attributes that any type of brand is built upon.

Landscape, including cities, plays a prominent role in helping define the essence of a nation and thus may be regarded as a key component of nation-brand equity. Landscape is one of the great equalizers in nation branding – even if a nation is economically poor or disadvantaged in other ways, it may possess landscape that is sufficiently distinctive to represent a powerful asset. The coloured lagoons, exotic rock formations and volcanic craters that surround the Uyuni Salt Flats in Bolivia, for instance, represent a key asset for that nation (see country case insight on Bolivia, Chapter 7). Another nation that is economically deprived yet rich in unique and dramatic landscape is Nepal, where the beauty of the landscape has contributed to that country's image as one of the most exciting destinations in the world (see academic perspective on the repositioning of Nepal, Chapter 2).

As with iconography and landscape, a nation's culture represents a truly unique and authentic facet of national identity. These assets are not contrived artificialities devised by marketers; on the contrary, they are authentic manifestations of what the nation truly is. Culture, in particular, offers an infinitely rich source for nations attempting to fashion their nation-brand. Russia, for example, has been increasingly active in modernizing its cultural centres abroad as part of a wider attempt to develop a more positive image for its nation (see country case insight on Russia, Chapter 5). For smaller or emerging nations with limited financial resources, highlighting their national culture through music, film, literature, art, and food and drink represents a far more attractive and feasible means to build nation-brand equity rather than potentially expensive and superficial advertising campaigns.

Traditional forms of culture may play a critical role in terms of external recognition of the nation, but these must not be allowed to position the country as backward-looking as this would act counter to attempts to portray the country as a vibrant modern economy. The fast-growing sector of ecotourism provides a contemporary context within which a focus on the past, in terms of promoting a nation's traditional culture, represents a potentially key aspect of sustainable development. The true identity of Bolivia, for example, lies largely in its ancestral cultures manifested in folklore, clothing, food and ancestral traditions, and these aspects of culture form a core part of the country's 'The authentic still exists' positioning (see country case insight on Bolivia, Chapter 7).

Music, film, literature, language and sport represent some of the expressions of contemporary culture that can play a significant role in determining country image perceptions and that therefore should be integrated into nation-branding strategy. Negative perceptions connected with a country's political regime or military profile may be offset by more positive associations with the same country's contemporary culture. The worldwide appetite for American films, for example to some extent counterbalances the hostility in many parts of the world to perceived

American dominance of world affairs. Organizations such as the British Council are charged with the task of actively promoting British culture abroad, thus implicitly acknowledging the economic importance of culture. For smaller countries with a low or invisible political profile, culture can compensate through enabling a perceptual niche to be occupied on the global stage through association with the nation's unique and distinctive cultural figures.

Nurtured assets: Internal buy-in, support for the arts, loyalty levels

One source of nation-brand equity that has to some extent be overlooked both by nations and also by researchers is the issue of securing internal buy-in to the nation-brand. This represents a communications challenge for those organizations whose role is to promote a nation abroad. If the domestic population and other domestic stakeholders are not aware of the images and reputations that are being projected of their own country, they cannot be expected to 'live the brand'. The result can be a gap between reality and the projected image, which will create dissonance when tourists, foreign investors and so on discover that the nation's projected image is not rooted in reality. There needs to be internal buy-in to the nation-brand by both the public sector (see country case insight on Estonia, Chapter 9) and also by private sector companies in their behaviour with foreign companies (see country case insight on Egypt, Chapter 2). In terms of generating internal buy-in from the country's citizens, Taiwan invited the public to vote online to choose the set of iconic images that would be used in the country's future branding. It may therefore be argued that rather than expecting the population of a country to 'live the brand', the nation-brand should be reflective of the people and the culture.

Another key nurtured asset is support for the arts. Support may come from the state through organizations tasked with fostering the nation's cultural life; alternatively, support may be more overtly commercially driven through sponsorship of the arts by private companies. Management of the commerce–culture interface can be problematic. Traditionally, suspicion abounds between the worlds of commerce and culture. Although patronage of the arts by wealthy business people dates back several centuries and continues in varied forms in the present day, many individuals and organizations from the cultural sector harbour serious reservations about using culture as part of a branding strategy. The word 'brand' in particular alienates many people. On the other hand, business people often appear to lack a sense of cultural awareness and reject any initiative that is not easily or immediately quantifiable, a common view being that culture is either a luxury or an irrelevance.

Loyalty is an important component of brand equity. In the context of nation-brands, programmes need to be put in place to enhance loyalty levels amongst a very diverse range of 'customers', including the country's own citizens, trading partners, foreign consumers of the nation's goods and services, international organizations, political allies, tourists and inward investors (see academic perspective on CRM and nation branding in this chapter).

External assets

The external assets that constitute nation-brand equity are either *vicarious*, in that they are experienced second-hand rather than through direct personal contact, or they are *disseminated*, tangible projections of the nation-brand existing beyond the nation's homeland and throughout the wider world. As with the nation-brand's internal assets, these external assets need to be strategically managed if they are to deliver maximum benefits to the nation.

Vicarious assets: Country image perceptions, external portrayal in popular culture

Country image perceptions may not always in accord with reality, and where this occurs, a conscious strategy needs to be implemented in order to ensure that negative or outdated perceptions do not damage overall nation-brand equity. On the other hand, a negative image may be an accurate reflection of underlying problems such as high crime levels, government corruption and so on. In this case, remedial action to tackle the real problems needs to occur before any branding work can be undertaken.

It is important to monitor and evaluate existing country image perceptions and to manage these effectively. Such perceptions can be a powerful asset or a severe liability. If image tracking is not done, then historically skewed and stereotypical imagery may obscure the present-day reality of the nation. This issue is addressed further in Chapter 9 in terms of nation-brand tracking studies. Sometimes, a country's image is strongly positive but only in one dimension, and this can be problematical in that it limits that nation's potential scope of activity. For example, Egypt is currently addressing the challenge of being perceived solely as a tourism destination rather than also as a business destination (see country case insight on Egypt, Chapter 2). A similar challenge is being successfully addressed by the Brazilian information technology sector, where a lack of knowledge about the existence of Brazil's IT sector was hampering the country's efforts to compete effectively on the global stage (see country case insight on Brazil, Chapter 6). As Prof. Stephen Brown notes in his academic perspective (Chapter 10), 'there is more to Brazil than carnival'.

There are many sources of nation-brand equity that are beyond the control of those responsible for orchestrating nation-branding campaigns. For example, national sporting teams may perform poorly, government may prove to be blatantly corrupt and companies producing branded exports may be caught behaving in an unethical and anti-social way. In the same way, little control can be exerted over external portrayals of a country in popular culture. Positive or negative national stereotypes may be endlessly repeated in books and on film. Although these phenomena cannot be controlled, it is important to manage their effects and consequences by forefronting that which is positive and helpful to the nation-brand, and downplaying more negative portrayals. The film *Braveheart*, whilst of questionable historical accuracy, has raised the profile of Scotland and contributed to the country's positioning as heroic underdog. Other small countries that do not receive the same external portrayal in popular culture may struggle to establish themselves in the minds of consumers.

Cinema is not the only medium through which powerful images of contemporary culture can be expressed. Music can play a similarly powerful role, and this is acknowledged through the public funding of contemporary singers and bands to tour abroad, enhancing the country's reputation in a non-military, non-imperialistic way. This may be particularly important for nations such as Britain where the legacy of Empire may be viewed by many in a hostile manner.

Disseminated assets: Brand ambassadors, the diaspora, branded exports

A potentially cost-effective strategy for countries lacking the resources to undertake expensive promotional campaigns is to appoint a network of brand ambassadors whose role is to advance the nation-brand at every opportunity. In Scotland, the internationally known golfer Colin Montgomerie has been appointed as such a brand ambassador. Individual companies within Scotland, such as Scotch whisky company William Grant & Sons, employ brand ambassadors in order to enhance their corporate reputations, and it is likely that nations will in future also view the use of the concept of brand ambassadors as an integral component of their nation-brand equity. A key issue when appointing brand ambassadors is to ensure that as far as possible, the individuals selected truly reflect the personality of the country and the positive attributes that the nation wishes to project. Many sporting figures are *de facto* nation-brand ambassadors, even if they have not officially been appointed to such a role. For certain audiences, individuals such as tennis player Roger Federer could be regarded as a brand ambassador for Switzerland, footballer Ronaldo as a brand ambassador for Brazil and so on.

Closely linked to the concept of brand ambassadors is the diaspora that a nation may possess. The diaspora may be viewed as a pre-existing network of potential nation-brand ambassadors awaiting activation. Leautier [20] has stated the people within diaspora networks 'can be crucial bridges between state-of-the-art in policy, technological, and managerial expertise and local conditions in their homeland', a view that is shared by Kuznetsov and Sabel [21] who identify policy expertise and managerial and marketing knowledge as the most significant resources of diaspora networks. However, this intangible benefit of diaspora networks is complemented by the more tangible financial benefit offered by diaspora networks through the provision of FDI and individual remittances. China, for instance, has benefited hugely from its diaspora in terms of FDI – the Chinese diaspora has provided an estimated 70% of recent foreign investment [22]. For other countries, remittances play an equally crucial role in the home country's economy. Haiti and Jordan, for example, both receive about the equivalent of 20% of GDP from remittances [23].

The third type of disseminated asset is branded exports. Branded exports can play an important role in establishing a country's reputation abroad. Chilean wine producers, for example now export more than 50% of their produce to ninety countries in five continents around the world (see country case insight on Chile, Chapter 3). For many consumers, their only personal experience of Chile will be through consuming a brand of Chilean wine. Branded exports may be viewed as a key asset in a nation's brand equity; therefore, countries engaged in nation branding need to ensure that the nation's export promotion agency is adequately resourced.

■ Summary

In this chapter, the concept of brand equity has been applied to the context of nation branding through a focus on the sources and dimensions of nation-brand equity. Differing, though complementary, perspectives on brand equity have been analyzed in terms of the consumer perspective and the financial perspective on brand equity. Taking an asset-based perspective on nation-brand equity, we have seen how NBEQ comprises internal and external assets that can be considered as being innate, nurtured, vicarious or disseminated, whilst the country case insight in this chapter gives a view of some of the characteristics of Chile's NBEQ.

■ References

1. Keller, K.L. (2003) *Strategic Brand Management: Building, Measuring, and Managing Brand Equity*, Second Edition, Prentice Hall, USA.
2. Pappu, R., Quester, P.G. and Cooksey, R.W. (2005) Consumer-based brand equity: improving the measurement – empirical evidence. *Journal of Product and Brand Management*, **14**, 2/3, 143–154.
3. Aaker, D. (1991) *Managing Brand Equity*, The Free Press, USA.
4. Farquhar, P. (1989) Managing Brand Equity, *Marketing Research*, September, pp. 1–11.
5. Jones, R. (2005) Finding sources of brand value: Developing a stakeholder model of brand equity. *Journal of Brand Management*, **13**, 1, 10–32.
6. Temporal, P. (2002) *Advanced Brand Management: From Vision to Valuation*, John Wiley & Sons (Asia), Singapore.
7. VanAuken, B. (2002) *The Brand Management Checklist: Proven Tools and Techniques for Creating Winning Brands*, Kogan Page, London.
8. Baker, M.J. (2002) *The Westburn Dictionary of Marketing*, Westburn Publishers Ltd, www.themarketingdictionary.com

9. Riezebos, R. (2003) *Brand Management: A Theoretical and Practical Approach*, FT Prentice Hall, United Kingdom.

10. Kapferer, J.-N. (2004) *The New Strategic Brand Management: Creating and Sustaining Brand Equity Long Term*, Kogan Page, United Kingdom.

11. De Chernatony, L. and McDonald, M. (2003) *Creating Powerful Brands*, Third Edition, Butterworth-Heinemann, United Kingdom.

12. Hallberg, G. (2004) Is your loyalty programme really building loyalty? Why increasing emotional attachment, not just repeat buying, is key to maximising programme success. *Journal of Targeting, Measurement and Analysis for Marketing*, **12**, 3, 231–241.

13. Merisavo, M. and Raulas, M. (2004) The impact of e-mail marketing on brand loyalty. *Journal of Product and Brand Management*, **13**, 7, 498–505.

14. Perrin-Martinenq, D. (2004) The role of brand detachment on the dissolution of the relationship between the consumer and the brand. *Journal of Marketing Management*, **20**, 9–10, 1001–1023.

15. Henderson, P.W., Cote, J.A., Leong, S.M., and Schmitt, B. (2003) Building strong brands in Asia: Selecting the visual components of image to maximize brand strength. *International Journal of Research in Marketing*, **20**, 297–313.

16. Kapferer, J.-N. (2004) *The New Strategic Brand Management: Creating and Sustaining Brand Equity Long Term*, Kogan Page, United Kingdom.

17. Interbrand, http://www.interbrand.com

18. Riezebos, R. (2003) *Brand Management: A Theoretical and Practical Approach*, FT Prentice Hall, United Kingdom.

19. Anholt, S. (2007) *Competitive Identity: The New Brand Management for Nations, Cities and Regions*, Palgrave Macmillan, United Kingdom.

20. Leautier, F.A. (2006) Foreword, p v, *Diaspora Networks and the International Migration of Skills: How Countries Can Draw on Their Talent Abroad* (Y. Kuznetsov, ed.), WBI Development Studies.

21. Kuznetsov, Y. and Sabel, C. (2006) International migration of talent, diaspora networks, and development: Overview of main issues, in *Diaspora Networks and the International Migration of Skills: How Countries Can Draw on Their Talent Abroad* (Y. Kuznetsov, ed.), WBI Development Studies, pp. 3–19.

22. Devane, R. (2006) The dynamics of diaspora networks: Lessons of experience, in *Diaspora Networks and the International Migration of Skills: How Countries Can Draw on Their Talent Abroad* (Y. Kuznetsov, ed.), WBI Development Studies, pp. 59–67.

23. Torres, F. and Kuznetsov, Y. (2006) Mexico: Leveraging migrants' capital to develop hometown communities, in *Diaspora Networks and the International Migration of Skills: How Countries Can Draw on Their Talent Abroad* (Y. Kuznetsov, ed.), WBI Development, pp. 99–128.

PART 2

Conceptual roots of nation branding

CHAPTER 4

Nation branding and the country-of-origin effect

Country Case Insight – Switzerland

The image of Switzerland: Between clichés and realities[1]

Martial Pasquier
Professor of Public Management and Marketing,
Swiss Graduate School of Public Administration IDHEAP, Lausanne

In a world that has been largely globalized, the image of a country and its promotion assume an ever larger importance economically, politically, socially and culturally. Since 2000, Switzerland has enacted a law regarding the promotion of its image abroad and established an organization charged with the coordination of the various actors and activities in this field.

This contribution will first of all present the current situation in terms of image promotion in Switzerland. The various studies done of Switzerland's image abroad will then be briefly presented. These elements will allow for a discussion on the results obtained and on the measures taken to correct the image deficit and image problems encountered.

■ 1. An organization to coordinate the promotion of Switzerland's image

Always considered important, the promotion of Switzerland's image had previously been managed in a fragmented manner by various public and private sector organizations. A number of reasons explain this particular situation. On the one hand, Swiss federalism gives relatively few powers to the federal government on such issues. For example economic promotion, including lobbying for the relocation of industries, is still a power of the Cantons. On the other hand, the diversity of issues involved in the promotion of the country has led to the creation of a large number of agencies and organizations, each focusing on a particular aspect.

For a number of reasons, the most important being the Jewish World War II dormant accounts (1995–2000) – a crisis that has effectively stained the image of Switzerland, mainly in the United States – a law aimed at coordinating the image of Switzerland was enacted and institutions put in

[1] The content of this article engages the sole responsibility of the author and not that of the mandating organizations.

place. We should mention the creation, within the federal administration, of a new Office, Presence Switzerland, that assumes directly some of the promotional tasks but that, above all, coordinates the activities of other organizations active in that particular field (Pro Helvetia, Swiss info, Location Switzerland, OSEC Business Network Switzerland, Swiss Tourism).

The establishment of this coordination organ has allowed the establishment of priorities (what types of activities in what countries) and to move forward in a coordinated manner especially when dealing with large international events (Olympic Games, Universal Exhibitions, etc.).

■ 2. Studies on the image of Switzerland

To be able to define a strategy in terms of image promotion in the various countries identified as priorities, Presence Switzerland has systematically conducted studies on the image of Switzerland abroad. All these studies were done using the same research strategy and methodology, thus allowing for cross-study comparisons. Table CS4.1 shows the studies realized between 2001 and 2006.

Table CS4.1 Overview of studies on the image of Switzerland

Country	Year	Sample			Method
		General population	Opinion leaders	Students	
USA	2001	1004 (18 years old and up)	150 p; 150 j	–	Phone interviews: general population, opinion leaders
UK	2001	1000 (adults)	100 p; 121 j; 121 m	518	Phone interviews: general population, opinion leaders Face-to-face interviews: students
Spain	2002	1000 (16 up)	119 p; 116 j; 118 m	501	Phone interviews: general population, opinion leaders Face-to-face interviews: students
France	2002	1002 (15 up)	204 p; 103 j; 99 m	305	Phone interviews: general population, opinion leaders Face-to-face interviews: students
Germany	2003	1003 (15 up)	121 p; 120 j; 120 m	304	Phone interviews: general population, opinion leaders, students

(Continued)

Table CS4.1 (Continued)

Country	Year	Sample			Method
		General population	**Opinion leaders**	**Students**	
Japan	2003	1000 (18 up)	120 p; 120 j; 120 m	500	Phone interviews: general population, opinion leaders, students
China	2006	2000 (18 up)	120 p; 120 j; 120 m	500	Phone interviews: general population, opinion leaders
HK		400 (18 up)	25 p; 26 j; 50 m		Face-to-face interviews: students

P: politicians; J: journalists; M: managers.

The concept is based on a representative sample of the general population of the country under study as well as a limited (and thus non-representative) sample of opinion leaders chosen among politicians, journalists, managers and students. The studies are managed by a Swiss university but were conducted by research firms established in the country being studied. In each study, other countries such as the Netherlands, Austria or Germany have been chosen to allow greater comparability of results.

The key issue surrounding country image has long been envisaged as a relation between product and origin (Product-Country-Image or Country-of-Origin). Current research is taking place in a much wider framework (Place Branding) and is touching on all the characteristics of a country that might have an incidence on such diverse aspects as tourism, economic promotion, export development, promoting national values, etc. Such studies must therefore take into account the characteristics of both the product and the producer, but now also the geographic, political, economic and socio-cultural aspects of a country.

■ 3. Results and consequences on image promotion

The main results were published and can be downloaded from Presence Switzerland's website. We will therefore limit our analysis to a small number of integrated results that led to specific actions being taken.

One of the main aspects of these studies is the evaluation of the structure of the image of Switzerland.[2] From a methodological point of view, the respondents had to indicate the level of importance they attributed to various dimensions and then evaluate Switzerland and other countries on that same aspect. Figures CS4.1 and CS4.2 present the results. The horizontal axis corresponds to the level of importance given and the vertical axis the evaluation of Switzerland.

A first result, interesting and awaited by the authorities, is the evaluation for 'Top level education and research' (see Figure CS4.1). This dimension, important to attract the best students but also to attract businesses and so to promote characteristics such as reliability, precision, etc. is priority in terms of positioning for Switzerland.

The results for the dimension 'Innovative features' were surprising. Like numerous other countries, Switzerland tries to position itself internationally as a country promoting innovation. An objective evaluation proves the point: Switzerland is a leader in terms of patents and was

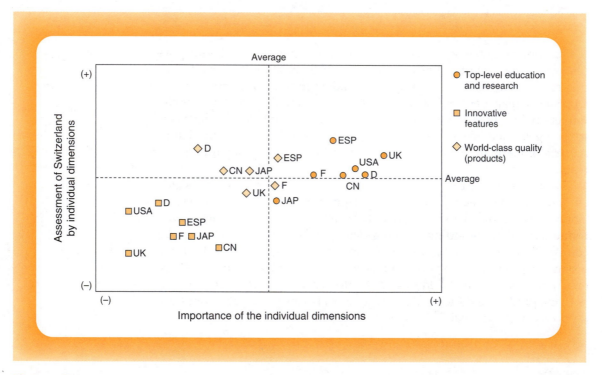

Figure CS4.1

Positioning of Switzerland in various countries for three dimensions linked to production and training. F, France; D, Germany; ESP, Spain; JAP, Japan; CN, China; UK, United Kingdom; USA, United States of America

---

[2] For various reasons, it has not been possible to include every single dimension in each study. In the case of China, for example items related to the promotion of human rights or the participation of citizens to political decisions were removed.

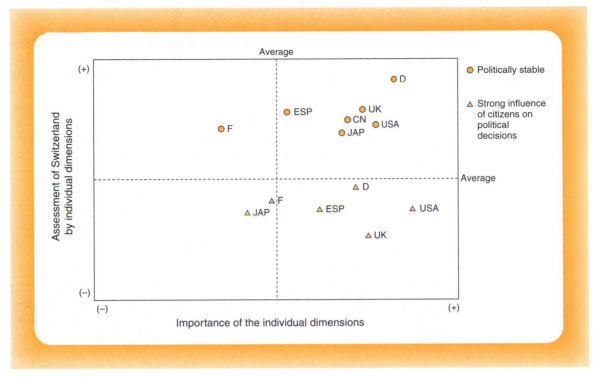

Figure CS4.2
Positioning of Switzerland in various countries for two dimensions linked to the characteristics of its political system. F, France; D, Germany; ESP, Spain; JAP, Japan; CN, China; UK, United Kingdom; USA, United States of America

ranked among 'Innovation leaders' in a recent European Union study.[3] Switzerland is also the European country with, proportionately to population, the highest number of Nobel Prize winners. These elements do not impact on the necessarily subjective evaluation of this dimension by the respondents. Even if this dimension is not considered very important, Switzerland systematically obtains poor evaluations. This has led to a modification of the activation mechanisms of this dimension in certain promotional activities. Instead of promoting and presenting this aspect directly, it will be communicated via other dimensions such as the protection of the environment that are evaluated strongly for Switzerland.

As indicated above, Figure CS4.2 presents two dimensions linked to the political system. If the 'politically stable' dimension receives the intuitively assumed answers, those linked to the particularities of the Swiss system 'Strong influence of citizens on political decisions' created a certain level of surprise. It is a dimension evaluated as important and where Switzerland obtains results that can be labelled as weak. This result is the more surprising given that Switzerland has a system whereby the

[3] www.proinno-europe.eu/inno-metrics.html

population is called on numerous occasions every year to give its opinion on various subjects through votations.[4] This perception of our system being probably linked to a lack of knowledge, the Swiss Confederation finances Research Chairs on federalism in foreign universities (notably at the European Institute in Florence) to explain and promote the Swiss federal system.

The knowledge linked to the dimensions characterizing the positioning of a country is very important if one wants to develop promotional activities that either allow to reinforce certain aspects deemed important for a country or correct image deficits that could eventually tarnish the image of a country.

*****

■ Introduction

In this chapter, we examine the concept of the country-of-origin (COO) effect and place the COO effect in the context of nation branding. We focus on issues including COO and brands, COO and demographics, COO and semiotic theory, as well as noting that COO perceptions are not necessarily static but can change over time. The relevance of COO to nation branding is illustrated in Prof. Pasquier's country case insight on Switzerland, where a coordinating body, 'Presence Switzerland', has been established to help ensure that COO perceptions of Switzerland are tracked and effectively managed.

■ Overview of COO research

The COO effect refers to the effect that a product or service's origin has on consumer attitudes and behaviour towards that product or service. There are many obvious product categories where COO plays an important role as a differentiator that is valued by consumers – French perfume, Scotch whisky, Swiss watches, Italian fashion, Japanese technology and Colombian coffee represent some of the best known product categories where a perceived fit between the product and its COO confers consumer value. In such cases, there is a positive association between the product and its COO, although it may not always be clear in which direction the positive perceptions flow – does a prestigious brand such as Sony enhance the nation-brand image of Japan or does the high credibility of Japan as a source country for high technology products enhance the Sony brand? Given this and other questions surrounding the COO effect, it is not surprising that there has been a vast and ever-expanding amount of COO research conducted by marketing academics.

[4] Semi-direct democracy with initiative rights and referendums.

However, there has been criticism levelled at much of the existing academic COO literature on the grounds that the methodology employed in the research to date has tended to exaggerate the influence of COO because of the use of single-cue designs (where the only attribute of the product given to respondents is its COO, rather than a multi-cue design where COO would be just one attribute alongside other relevant criteria such as price, brand name, design, etc.) and also because of the use of verbal descriptions rather than real, tangible products [1]. Other reviews of the COO literature have identified further weaknesses as being the small number of studies that have examined the impact of COO effects on the consumption and evaluation of services, and the tendency of those few studies on services and COO to focus upon services in the West rather than in the rest of the world [2]; an over-reliance on student samples that limits the generalizability of research findings to a wider population [3]; and it has also been suggested that there is a need for more research on the symbolic and emotional aspects of COO [4]. A brilliant exposition of how and why academic research on COO has sometimes tended to degenerate into self-serving careerism, rather than keeping up with and illuminating developments in international business, is provided by Prof. Jean-Claude Usunier of the University of Lausanne in an analysis of the growth of COO research over the period 1965–2002, a period during which over 400 peer-reviewed academic articles have been published [5].

Nonetheless, it would be mistaken to dismiss the entire COO literature as worthless and detached from reality. Much interesting work has been done that identifies and analyses important issues for products, services and whole nations with regard to how effective the use of COO can be. The symbiotic relationship between a nation-brand and the PSC brands that highlight (or downplay) their COO deserves attention not only because it is conceptually interesting but also because the nation-branding activities of a country will impact upon COO perceptions for that country's PSC brands. This represents another fundamental reason why a nation's public and private sectors must collaborate and communicate in order to fully support the economic welfare of the nation and its commercial organizations.

■ COO and brands

When Icelandic vodka brand Reyka launched in the United Kingdom market in 2005, it did so with advertising which proclaimed that 'In Iceland, vodka is a natural resource...Reyka vodka is made with arctic spring water in one of the purest countries in the world. We make Reyka in small batches and we use geothermal energy to make sure that our country stays as pure as our vodka'. This claim led to the brand being described by one journalist as 'probably the most environmentally friendly tipple you can get' [6]. The match, or fit, between the product and its COO appears seamless. The Reyka brand benefits from Iceland's association with environmental purity whilst Iceland the nation benefits from the emergence of a new high-quality brand that should add to the nation's existing brand equity. Such win–win scenarios testify to the potential power of COO as a brand-building tool. The Reyka brand is not actually owned by an Icelandic company – its owners are Scotch whisky firm William Grant and Sons – yet, the discreet foreign ownership is unlikely to impact upon consumer perceptions of the brand as being Icelandic.

The matching of product category and country image perceptions has been widely researched [7–11]. One such study [12] concluded that product–country match information should be used by managers to assess consumers' purchase intentions and to assist them in managing their product's COO. The term 'brand origin' has been coined in order to conceptualize cases where consumer perceptions of a brand's origin may not coincide with reality – in such cases, brand origin is 'the place, region or country to which the brand is perceived to belong by its target group' [13]. Consumers may hold misperceptions of a brand's COO simply through ignorance or through branding activity by companies designed to suggest a more positive COO than is actually the case. Table 4.1 lists some brands whose names may lead to consumer confusion regarding their COO.

The emergence of China as a global economic superpower, together with the opening up of the Chinese market to foreign firms, has created huge interest in how Chinese consumers view domestic Chinese brands as compared with imported foreign brands. Within Asia, Japanese brands such as Toshiba, Mitsubishi and Sony have for many years established premium quality perceptions, and more recently, South Korean brands such as Samsung and LG have done the same, and it is probably just a matter of time before Chinese brands join their Asian neighbours in the realm of positively perceived brand names. Traditionally, emerging

Table 4.1 Brand origin – potentially perceived origin versus actual origin

Brand	Product category	Potentially perceived origin	Actual origin
Haagen-Dazs	Ice cream	Scandinavia	United States
Matsui	Consumer electronics	Japan	United Kingdom
Lexus	Automotive	United States	Japan
Klarbrunn	Bottled water	Switzerland, Austria, Germany	United States

nations have suffered from low-quality perceptions for their products but the increasing confidence of the BRIC nations (Brazil, Russia, India, China) is set to galvanize those and other emerging nations to make the change from commodity suppliers to producers of sought-after branded goods. An investigation into COO effects and how these affect the attitudes and behaviour of urban Chinese consumers, conducted amongst a sample of 432 Shanghai consumers, produced results that support the growing view that Chinese consumers are not necessarily attracted to foreign brands; an implication drawn by the researchers involved in that study is that in order to capitalize on the stated preference for local brands, managers should highlight the Chinese origin of their brands and use this in their brand-positioning strategies [14]. The shoes, sportswear and sports accessories brand Li Ning is an example of a local Chinese brand that has successfully competed against the global might of brands such as Nike, Adidas and Reebok in the Chinese market, with a positioning based largely upon the brand's eponymous founder, the Olympic gold medal winner Li Ning [15].

Some countries find that their brands are disadvantaged because of an overpowering image of the nation as just a tourism destination and nothing more. Egypt has suffered from this phenomenon to the extent that 'the consumer does not search out Egyptian products when shopping' (see country case insight on Egypt, Chapter 2). Other countries may enjoy more favourable COO associations for their products but find themselves in fiercely competitive sectors, forcing the countries in question to redouble their nation-branding activities. Chile, for example, is actively striving to enhance its COO effect for the benefit of its wine sector (see country case insight on Chile, Chapter 3).

■ COO and services

Compared to the copious attention that has been lavished on the effects of COO on physical products, there has been a dearth of similar studies on how COO effects can impact upon services. One review of the COO literature, covering a 20-year period and 24 marketing and general business journals, found only 19 studies in which COO was specifically applied to services; the rapid growth in service economies argues for far more research in this area [16]. Given the predominance of the service sector over the manufacturing sector in most developed economies, such a paucity of research into how COO affects services is extraordinary. One of the rare studies on COO and services measured the country-level images of ski resorts in Switzerland, France and Austria by asking 269 skiers attending a ski show in New York to rate each country on a five-point scale for ten attributes; the images of the three countries were found to be relatively homogeneous, with the American skiers unable to differentiate between the countries [17]. Another of the rare COO and services studies examined the relative effects of national stereotype and advertising information on the selection of a service provider

Table 4.2 Service brand acronyms – visual shorthand or country-of-origin dissimulator?

Acronym	Full name	Service sector
HSBC	Hong Kong and Shanghai Banking Corporation	Finance
RBS	Royal Bank of Scotland	Finance
UBS	Union Bank of Switzerland	Finance
KFC	Kentucky Fried Chicken	Restaurants
BP	British Petroleum	Energy

in the ophthalmology sector – the results from this study indicated that there existed a same-nationality bias in service provider selection, although different-nationality service providers could overcome this bias to some extent by providing consumers with more information in their advertising [18].

Many international service brands have adopted acronyms as their brand names, perhaps in an attempt to minimize any possible negative COO biases against their place of origin. Table 4.2 illustrates some such cases from a range of international service sectors.

It is perhaps not surprising that international financial service brands seek to position themselves as global rather than parochial. HSBC's positioning as 'the world's local bank' effectively combines the prestige and credibility of globalness with the reassuring impression that the brand is conscious of the specific needs of local communities. Consumers may well make the assumption that because a financial service brand is global, it must be successful, well run, reliable, and so on. On the other hand, the bland, not-from-anywhere-in-particular positioning of the major financial services brands may leave a niche open for other brands to occupy with a more explicit COO positioning (see country case insight on Nevis, Chapter 4).

Being too closely associated with one specific COO may leave such brands vulnerable to political or military events beyond their control. This potential vulnerability has been acknowledged by American Express, who conducted research when the 2003 war in Iraq started because they were very concerned about a possible backlash against their brand, given its US-centric name; the company found, however, that in most places in the world people associated the brand with being a global business rather than being American [19].

The international airline sector is an interesting industry with regard to the use of brand management in general and the COO effect in particular. On the one hand, international airlines are investing more and more in branding; on the other hand, leading branding consultancy Interbrand excludes international airlines from its annual Best Global Brands survey on the basis that 'they are still operating in situations where the brand plays only a marginal role. In most cases, the customer decides based on price, route, schedule, corporate policy or frequent flyer points' [20]. The use of COO in the international airline sector is, because of the heritage of national carriers, often explicit. Singapore Airlines, for instance, highlights its COO without compromising its positioning as a widely admired global service brand. British Airways, however, experienced severe turbulence when it attempted to downplay its COO by repositioning itself as BA in an attempt to distance itself from the negative connotations of Britain's imperialistic past. This was perceived to be unpatriotic and caused a political storm in which the then Prime Minister Margaret Thatcher publicly berated the company for its apparent slight against 'Britishness'. One of the key benefits to be derived from a coordinated nation-branding campaign, founded on a healthy public–private sector collaboration, is the avoidance of such unedifying spectacles.

An example of how a coordinated, strategic campaign can overcome resistance to IT services from a country that is not traditionally associated with that service sector can be seen in the country case insight on Brazil (Chapter 6). The Brazil IT campaign is a good illustration of the power of clearly articulated strategy to change attitudes towards a country as a credible and attractive services provider.

■ COO and the product life cycle

The product life cycle (PLC) is a familiar concept in marketing. The thrust of the concept is that products, like other living organisms, undergo a series of life stages. For products, these stages have been characterized as introduction, growth, maturity and decline. In the first two stages, products experience growth; in the third phase (maturity), they reach a plateau in terms of sales, market share, etc.; and in the final phase, the product approaches the end of its commercially viable life, perhaps left behind by changing consumer needs or the arrival of new technology that renders the product obsolete. The usefulness of the PLC concept lies in its ability to let marketers assess the current status of the product and to tailor appropriate marketing strategies according to which stage of the life cycle the product finds itself in. For instance, a new product at the introduction stage of the PLC will require a launch strategy whose marketing communications will be radically different from a well-established product that has reached its maturity phase. However, the PLC concept's inherent flaw is the assumption that products do indeed resemble living organisms and thus follow a similar birth–growth–maturity–death trajectory. The model not only lacks a measurable temporal dimension that would allow marketers to accurately assess the product's stage on the life cycle, it also carries the implication that decline, sooner or later, is inevitable. This defeatist assumption would be challenged by many managers who would see their job as being to ensure that their product remains at the top of its life cycle indefinitely.

There have been some attempts to adapt the PLC concept to the context of COO. One study examined COO marketing over the PLC and found that the use of COO references varied over the PLC, with COO references used more in the introduction stage of the PLC than in the growth and maturity stages [21]. The explanation advanced for this finding was that when a product is launched into a foreign market there will be little or no awareness of the specific product brand, but there may be reasonably high levels of awareness of the country from which the product originates – in such cases, it makes sense to capitalize on the existing country image perceptions in order to establish the product in its new foreign market. The same study found that as the PLC progresses, the tendency is for firms to lessen their use of COO and simultaneously increase their use of brand name marketing. Other studies appear to support the view that COO is used prominently in the product's introduction phase, in order to benefit from the COO halo effect [22], and that the use of COO is highly contextual and evolves over time [23]. When developing export promotion campaigns as one component of overall nation-brand strategy, governments, trade councils and export promotion agencies therefore need to carefully evaluate which of their country's brands will most significantly benefit from initiatives highlighting the product's COO. With tight constraints on export promotion budgets, resources should be targeted at those products for which COO is most relevant.

■ COO and demographics

A product's COO may matter to some consumers and be irrelevant to others. Demographic segmentation can be used to categorize those consumer groups for whom COO is a relevant product cue. Several COO studies have examined the effect that the major demographic variables can have upon product or service perceptions. An early study in the COO field found significant differences towards products of foreign origin amongst different demographic groups – consumers with a high level of education were found to be more favourable towards foreign products than consumers with a lower level of education; female consumers evaluated foreign products more highly than male consumer; and younger consumers evaluated foreign products more highly than older consumers [24].

However, there is little consensus on the impact of COO on different demographic groups. Other studies have supported the contention that the higher the level of a person's education, the more favourable they are to foreign products but have not found evidence of any difference in perception of foreign products between males and females [25]. Whilst such studies rightly examine an important issue in COO, clearly brand managers need to conduct their own, contextualized and brand-specific research in order to ascertain which demographic segments of their targeted markets are influenced by the brand's COO.

■ COO and ethnocentrism

Ethnocentrism has been defined as 'the home-country bias portion of the COO effect' [26]. It refers to consumers' predisposition to favour products from their own country over products from foreign countries. Scales have been devised to measure consumer ethnocentrism, the most widely known of which is the consumer ethnocentric tendency scale (CETSCALE), comprising 17 items based on a 7-point scale, which allow an individual's ethnocentrism to be measured [26]. Consumer demographics such as education, income and social class are believed to affect an individual's ethnocentrism [27]. Brands of foreign origin need to know about prevailing levels of consumer ethnocentrism within specific markets, so that appropriate marketing strategies can be developed and strategic mistakes avoided. It has been found, for example, that the use of a foreign celebrity and an English brand name can be a liability in a country (Austria) with a different cultural heritage and language [28].

When governments are considering developing a 'Buy Domestic' campaign, the overall level of the population's ethnocentrism will need to be researched in order to ascertain the likelihood of such a campaign succeeding. If high levels of ethnocentrism are present, then a 'Buy Domestic' campaign may strike a chord and generate increased demand levels for domestic products; Indonesia is one country in which the overall level of consumer ethnocentrism has been found to be relatively high [29]. However, if ethnocentrism levels are low, then the campaign may prove ineffective and resources may be better directed elsewhere, for example, into enhancing the quality of domestic brands through greater investment in research and development, executive development, design training and so on.

Practitioner Insight

Inverting the COO effect: How Portuguese firm Ecoterra leverages 'country-of-sell' effect

João R. Freire
Brand Consultant for MMG Worldwide; Founder of Ecoterra

The relevance of place marketing is not limited to the attraction of investment, labour or tourism. Positive place image influences and helps sell products manufactured in a specific location. This indicates that the purpose of place-marketing strategy should also take into account the improvement of image in order to sell products in international markets. The relation between place and product is called COO effect. Certain feelings and emotional values that emerge from a brand are a direct result of the COO of the brand, which implies that a country's name is part of the brand name and consumers use places as intrinsic cues to help evaluate products and to make appropriate purchasing decisions.

In a COO context, a product's image may be formed from the perception of the country's ability to produce and market such a product. Country image can either benefit or harm a product depending on whether there is a match or mismatch between the country image and the brand's desired features. Kao, a Japanese company, and one of the largest cosmetic companies in the world, is a good practical example of the COO problem. Although enjoying huge success in Japan and in Asia, this company had a difficult time entering the European and American markets. The reason for this difficulty was only identified when an image study was conducted. Apparently, part of the problem was of a COO nature. European and North American consumers viewed Japanese-made brands as technologically superior and extremely reliable products, but 'short on soul' and for that reason country image was negatively influencing Kao's brand image.

The inverse process also occurs, that is the country, region or city where the product is sold has an impact on brand image, which means that there is a country-of-sell (COS) effect. The strategy developed by Ecoterra, a small Portuguese company dedicated to the branding of foodstuffs, is a good example of the use of the COS effect to enhance brand image. Before entering its domestic market, Ecoterra entered the UK market, specifically in London. The company's objective was to incorporate some of London's values into its brand. It was believed that London would have an impact on the brand at two distinct levels: perceived quality and brand personality. Consumers have the perception that products sold in extremely competitive markets, and in the best shops in the world, will have the highest quality. Therefore, in the domestic market, Portuguese consumers routinely use the factor 'selling in London' as a cue to evaluate product quality. In addition, some of London's traits were successfully associated with the company's brand. Values that are linked to London such as being modern, cosmopolitan and exciting were transferred to Ecoterra's brand personality. With the use of these features, it was possible to differentiate Ecoterra in the domestic market and position it as a high-quality, modern, cosmopolitan and exciting Portuguese brand.

The effect of selling in London was also relevant to create a buzz in the home market. The strategy was set to work in two stages. First, an extensive public relations (PR) exercise was undertaken informing the Portuguese press about a small domestic company that was selling in London's most renowned shops, which included Harrods, Selfridges and Partridges. This PR activity created brand awareness and facilitated the implementation of the second stage – contacting the buyers.

The use of the COS effect can be considered a success because buyers from the best Portuguese gourmet shops were easily persuaded to stock Ecoterra products.

Places trigger feelings and influence brand image. Consequently, place image management is vital to facilitate exports and attract companies that follow a COS strategy. The attraction of resources therefore is not confined to investment, labour and tourism but also to companies that are willing to sacrifice margins and sell in highly competitive markets. The local people are ultimately the beneficiaries of an efficient place image management as they will have access to more products at competitive prices.

*****

■ COO and social identity

One of the more interesting studies in the COO field examined the link between social identity and brand preference in South Africa [30]. One of the interesting aspects of this study was its focus on South Africa rather than the usual Western nations; another interesting aspect was its consideration of the concept of national identity, and more specifically 'within-country diversity', a previously neglected issue in COO research. The study drew attention to the need to be wary of using nationality as a segmentation variable in contexts where other ethnic or religious affiliations may be more powerful than nationality. This idea was amplified in a later study that placed an emphasis on identifying the various subcultures that exist within any society in order to avoid making unsubstantiated generalized claims regarding consumers from a certain country when in reality the subcultural groupings within one country will often display greatly differing characteristics [31]. It has been argued that most cross-cultural studies on COO or PCI effects have implicitly assumed that national markets are composed of homogeneous consumers and such studies are in reality cross-national rather than cross-cultural [32]. The cross-cultural segmentation techniques used by companies in their global branding are thus probably far more sophisticated and well developed in evaluating social identity influences on brand preference than much of the academic research to date.

■ COO and semiotic theory

Semiotics is fundamentally concerned with the study of signs. In semiotics, the concept of the sign is more wide-ranging than it is in normal daily usage. From a semiotic perspective, a sign is 'an all-inclusive notion that comprises words, visualizations, tactile objects, olfactory sensations, and anything else that is perceivable by the senses and has the potential to communicate meaning to the receiver, or interpreter' [33]. A sign has also been defined as 'something physical and perceivable that signifies something (the *referent*) to somebody (the *interpreter*) in some *context* [34]. One of the benefits of adopting a semiotic perspective into the brand management process is that it emphasizes the primacy of context. Signs used in a brand's communications may be interpreted in vastly different ways according to the identity characteristics of the consumer (or interpreter, to use the semiotic vocabulary). In terms of the COO effect, there is enormous scope for brands of all types – whether simple tangible physical products brand at one end of the spectrum or complex multifaceted nation-brands at the other – to make creative use of signs. In his practitioner insight, Jack Yan notes that it is in human nature to want to use semiotics to signal certain brands in our collective minds (see practitioner insight, Chapter 7).

A semiotic approach to the study of COO and PCI effects has been advocated by Askegaard and Ger [35] who argue that a rich set of connotations needs to be used in the analysis of images attached to a product and its place of origin. Taking a semiotic approach, Askegaard and Ger propose a conceptual model of contextualized product-place images (CPPI) containing four dimensions: place, product, market context and usage context. This approach may be considered to be a form of applied semiotics, the utilization of knowledge about signs for the accomplishment of various goals [36]. The acknowledgement of context is central to semiotic theory, which posits that meaning is derived from 'signs and symbols ensconced in their cultural space and time' [37]. This has important implications for branding. Within Arab culture, for example, calligraphy, colour, pattern and symbols represent visual elements that provide coded references to cultural, national and religious identity and as such need to be taken into consideration when constructing the visual manifestation of brands [38].

■ COO perceptions in flux over time

Several studies have indicated that COO perceptions are not necessarily static over time [39–43]. Positive COO perceptions can degrade over time because of numerous factors, including political–military events beyond the control of any company, as appears to have occurred with the US in recent years. On the other hand, COO perceptions can also improve over time as Japan, South Korea and Taiwan can all happily testify to [44]. Taiwan has run a concerted nation-branding campaign for a number of years and appears to have reaped benefits from it in terms of enhanced COO perceptions.

The global country image advertising campaign conducted by Taiwan's Ministry of Economic Affairs over the period 1990–2004 comprised a sequence of advertisements placed in The Economist and Business Week, with key themes introduced in each new campaign [45]. The development of the campaign is summarized in Table 4.3.

Table 4.3 Taiwan's government-sponsored country image advertising campaign 1990–2004

Year	Slogan	Key theme
1990	Not cited	Build basic knowledge about Taiwan's relative advantage of geographic location in the heart of Asia
1992	'It's very well made in Taiwan'	Strengthen perceptions of products associated with Taiwan
1993	'Taiwan: Your source for innovalue'	Present two new attributes about Taiwanese manufacturing (innovation and value), inviting the reader to consider more than just the price-based competitive advantage of the past
1994	'Excellence, made in Taiwan'	Message of excellence linked directly to specific company names and product classes, e.g., Kunnan (golf clubs), Feeler (computer-controlled machinery for heavy industry) and Startek (security systems)
1996	'Today's Taiwan: More and more an important part of our world'	Link Taiwan to a global perspective and position it as an active member of the world business community
1997	'Taiwan: Your source for innovalue'	Previously used slogan now applied to specific Taiwanese brands. Objectives and themes of past ad executions reinforced as salient beliefs
2001	'Taiwan: Your partner for innovalue'	Promote preference, in line with theoretical hierarchy of advertising effects leading from awareness, to interest, knowledge, liking and then preference
2003	'Taiwan: Helping leading companies reach targets'	Strengthen positive linkages already made to the word 'Taiwan', reinforcing salient beliefs in established knowledge networks
Late 2003	'Taiwan stands tall: Reaching out to the world, soaring toward the future'	The use of new and striking attributes of Taiwan, linked to modern architecture and traditional culture. Convey sense of pride and achievement that Taiwan has enjoyed as an 'Asian tiger' over the last 40 years. Advanced technology promoted together with the spectacular natural beauty of Taiwan
2004	'Today's Taiwan'	Position Taiwan as an attractive tourist destination. An emotive appeal quite different from the low-key, objective reasoning of ads from 10 years earlier

Adapted from Amine and Chao (2005) [46].

There are a number of observations to be drawn from Taiwan's country image-advertising campaign. First, it has a coherent long-term structure; second, it displays consistent commitment by the government; third, it shows close collaboration between public and private sectors; fourth, it evolves from basic awareness-building into more specific brand-related claims; and fifth, after firmly establishing product technology quality attributes, it adds another dimension to the country image by promoting its spectacular natural beauty. Fundamentally, it is an illustration of the capacity of a country to seek to manage its image rather than merely remaining as a passive victim of existing external perceptions.

Simon Anholt has observed that it is possible to 'gradually drive the country from the image it has inherited towards the one it needs and deserves' (see practitioner insight, Chapter 1), although the use of the word 'gradually' gives warning that such image enhancement is rarely a speedy process. This view is echoed in the context of Russia and its image-building activities, in which context Lebedenko notes that 'no one has ever managed to change the image of a country in a short time; systemic, long-term efforts are needed' (see country case insight on Russia, Chapter 5). For other nations, there may be a fleeting window of opportunity to establish a positive COO effect where previously there were almost zero levels of awareness of the nation (see country case insight on Estonia, Chapter 9).

■ Combating a negative COO bias

A negative COO bias could cause numerous problems for a nation's PSC brands. Consumers may not wish to be associated with brands that emanate from nations whose COO effects are damaged by poor quality perceptions, animosity towards that nation's political regime, unflattering portrayals in the media, or a multitude of other social, cultural, economic or historical issues. In order to improve a country's image, creating new positive associations may be easier than refuting old negative associations [46]. Kazakhstan might, for example, have more chance of improving its *Borat*-battered image by promoting positive yet hitherto unknown aspects of its nation rather than attempting to refute the unflattering depiction it received in the 2006 film.

All kinds of brands – whether product, service or corporate – may suffer from a negative COO bias. According to the Edelman Trust Barometer, which surveys the opinions of 3100 people in 18 countries, Europeans place most trust in companies from Sweden, Canada and Germany, whereas they place least trust in companies from the emerging BRIC countries and Mexico [47]. The poll's sample has the following demographic characteristics – college-educated, between 36 and 64 years old, reporting a household income in the upper quartile for their country and showing a significant interest in and engagement with the media and current affairs. In other words, a demographic profile that would suggest high receptiveness to brands of foreign origin and a low level of consumer ethnocentrism. Even with such a presumably relatively cosmopolitan demographic segment, the BRIC nations clearly still have work to do in order to combat a negative COO bias amongst European consumers who could hinder future attempts by BRIC nation companies to enter European markets. As Prof. Pasquier points out in his country case insight on Switzerland, nations need to conduct rigorous research to form the basis of promotional activities 'to correct image deficits that could eventually tarnish the image of a country' (see country case insight, Chapter 4).

Country Case Insight – Nevis

Brand Nevis – The role of the financial service sector

Elsa Wilkin-Armbrister
Graduate Teaching Assistant, University of Strathclyde

Is nation branding a feasible option for Nevis? Does a tiny nation such as Nevis have the essential features that would enable it to enter into competition with other nations, who are already ahead of Nevis in this game called 'Nation Branding'? Nevis does, of course, possess the necessary attributes to be branded as a nation, but the challenge it faces is which sector would be the most appropriate tool to utilize in the branding process.

■ 1. Background

Although small, Nevis has had a disproportionate impact on world affairs as far back as when it was rediscovered in 1494 by Christopher Columbus. One of the framers of the US constitution and the architect of the US economy and economic model and the US treasury, Alexander Hamilton, was contributed to the world by Nevis. The island has a rich history, which, combined with its natural beauty, makes it a sought after and exotic destination to those who know it exists. Panache magazine, for instance, a few years ago described Nevis as 36 square miles of sheer natural beauty.

Nevis is the smaller island of the twin island federation of St. Kitts and Nevis. It is located within the archipelago of Caribbean islands, bordered by the Caribbean Sea and the Atlantic Ocean on either side.

Once a former colony of Great Britain, Nevis became the envy of the rest of the Caribbean because it generated wealth and power (which did not compare to its physical size) and established a state of economic prowess for which, coupled with its natural beauty, it was dubbed the Queen of the Caribees. Nevis has a unique constitutional arrangement with its sister island St. Kitts, very similar to that of England and Scotland; therefore, it is politically appropriate for Nevis to be branded independently of St. Kitts.

The two main sources of revenue for the economy of Nevis are tourism and international financial services, and currently tourism takes the lead. The island has a relatively stable economy and minimal unemployment. It also enjoys one of the highest growth rates in gross national product and per capita income in the Caribbean. It has also experienced a balanced budget, a manageable inflationary pace and a current account surplus. In the last 14 years, the Nevis Island Administration was able to accomplish

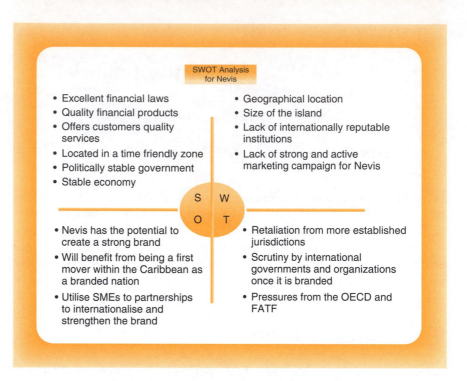

Figure 4.1
SWOT analysis for
Nevis

a balance budget nine times despite being hit by natural disasters such as hurricanes. In this respect, it has shown great resilience.

Today, the island is known as a secluded tourism hideaway for famous movie stars, TV personalities and talk show hosts. The implication of the lack of more generalized international awareness is twofold. It is good for those celebrities who want a quiet place to get away from the rest of the world. However, the island needs greater exposure to allow its international financial service sector to flourish. As a basis for understanding potential nation-brand development for Nevis, an illustration of Nevis' strengths, weaknesses, opportunities and threats is given in Figure 4.1.

■ 2. Why Brand Nevis

Nation-branding expert Simon Anholt (2005) has described how globalization presages that countries compete with each other for the attention, respect and trust of investors, tourists, consumers, donors, immigrants, the media and the governments of other nations: so, a powerful and positive nation brand provides a crucial competitive advantage. It is essential for countries to understand how they are perceived by publics around the world: how their achievements and failures, their assets and their liabilities, their people and their products are reflected in their brand image. According to de Chernatony and McDonald (2003), a successful brand is an identifiable product, service, person or place, augmented in such a way that the buyer or user perceives relevant, unique, sustainable added values that match their needs most closely. The brand and branding process must have a vision of the main objective. It is important for all nations anticipating branding themselves to know the vision and constantly visualize it.

Currently, Nevis lacks a brand image. In the field of international financial services, Nevis is just another island offering such services. However, in order for the island to differentiate itself from its competitors, it needs to become a brand. According to Kapferer (1997), brands perform economic functions in the mind of consumers; the value of that brand comes from its ability to gain an exclusive, positive and prominent meaning in the mind of a large number of consumers. The latter should be the main objective of Nevis. This would be the first step towards becoming known worldwide. In any competitive market, products and services differentiate themselves by becoming a brand. Countries, on the other hand, follow the nation-branding route to attract and acquire economical prosperity and global awareness. Both processes yield competitive advantage, increased profits and economic prosperity.

The financial services provided by Nevis are in the main the preserve of the wealthy. For more than two decades, Nevis has been offering products that assist wealthy individuals and businesses in preserving and protecting their wealth. These individuals view Nevis as a safe haven from frivolous lawsuits, free from draconian laws and legislation that impede free flow of monies. The financial services industry is, like most, very competitive. However, Nevis is off to a good start because it has some excellent products in Asset Protection Trust and Limited Liability Companies (LLCs). Despite having excellent financial service products and laws, Nevis lacks the marketing facilities, internationally recognized financial institutions, international presence and influence to enable it to project a better image required to gain customer confidence. Hence, the need for the island to utilize 'nation branding' as a means of acquiring global recognition and achieving global competitiveness. International financial service brands sometimes seem to downplay their COO: through the use of acronyms Hong Kong and Shanghai Banking Corporation (HSBC) and Royal Bank of Scotland (RBS), for example, appear to deflect rather than attract attention with regard to their COO. For an international financial service brand from Nevis, it could prove beneficial to highlight its COO more explicitly than other international financial services companies do.

■ 3. Potential benefits of branding Nevis

Nation branding can enhance a country's image and global awareness and also give it the impetus to gain competitive advantage over its competitors.

Nevis' physical size and geographical location are sometimes viewed as major barriers to attracting the relatively high level of international attention and foreign direct investment enjoyed by other small islands such as Barbados and Bermuda. One can say that this might be the case because those islands still have residual links to the United Kingdom. Alternatively, Nevis can use its size as an asset instead of a liability. Being particularly hard to find makes Nevis more attractive to some movie stars and investors as they want a niche market to enjoy their privacy, personally and financially.

Some key figures within Nevis have articulated their views regarding the branding of Nevis. The Honourable Mark Brantley (Senator in the Nevis Island Assembly), for example, believes that 'Nevis can and should be branded. This needs to be done because at the moment Nevis lacks a strong presence in the international arena'. This sentiment has been echoed by entrepreneur and former politician Mr Arthur Evelyn and by Mr Laurie Lawrence, Permanent Secretary, Ministry of Finance. As regards the choice of sector to be prioritized by Nevis, opinions differ. Some favour prioritizing financial services whereas others would prefer to see tourism playing the dominant role. Mr Brantley feels that 'although tourism is currently generating more revenue for the island, it has a ceiling effect in terms of the potential it can yield for the economy of Nevis; international financial services, on the other hand, have vastly greater potential and the initial capital outlay is not as exhaustive and large as it is for tourism'. Mr Lawrence also favours support for the promotion of Nevis' financial services, arguing that 'whereas tourism is susceptible to natural disasters, international financial services are not. A hurricane can cause devastating consequences to the tourism industry but with the appropriate telecommunications and legislation, international financial services can be effectively provided'.

However, other figures within Nevis take a different view on these questions. Mr Evelyn is opposed to the idea of branding Nevis by the international financial service sector. He explains his view thus: 'There is greater potential in tourism. There is a greater chance of tourism generating much more wealth for the economy of Nevis than international financial services. Also, the revenue generated by the tourism sector will be dispersed more evenly throughout the economy because tourism employs much more locals than the financial services sector. Moreover, Nevis does and will have more control over the tourism sector but doesn't have that luxury with international financial services as there are international bodies whose influence can greatly affect the growth of the economy. Nevis should be branded, but with the tourism sector as the main focus.'

Nevis' twin sectors of tourism and financial services are also assessed by Mr Cartwright Farrell, Planning Manager for NEVLEC (The Nevis Electricity Company), who makes the following observation: 'Nevis is already seen as a high end tourism destination and this works well since Nevis does not have the space to accommodate a huge influx of tourists at one particular time and nor should it have to. This might spoil its charm and unspoilt natural beauty. As for international financial services, not much is known about that to the ordinary individual in Nevis for it to be used to brand the country. Perhaps we should start with the education of our people at home since they will have a part to play in the branding of the island by whatever means.'

As can be seen, decision-makers in Nevis are well aware of nation branding and its potential applications to Nevis. However, the people of Nevis need to be educated and actively involved in the branding campaign. Nevis can also use its diaspora to assist in the marketing of its brand. Spirited integration, national pride, loyalty and nation branding can greatly assist a country in achieving its most valuable asset – a brand.

■ References

Anholt, S. (2005) *Brand New Justice: The Upside of Global Branding*, Revised Edition. Butterworth-Heinemann, Oxford.

De Chernatony, L. and McDonald, M. (2003) *Creating Powerful Brands*, Third Edition. Elsevier/Butterworth-Heinemann, Oxford.

Kapferer, J.N. (1997) *Strategic Brand Management: creating and sustaining brand equity long term*, Second Edition. Kogan Page Limited, London.

* * * * *

■ Summary

This chapter has reviewed the main themes in the field of COO and related these to the context of nation branding. The COO effect can influence attitude and behaviour towards brands, whether products, services or whole nations. The country case insight on Switzerland that appears in this chapter has shown the importance of monitoring COO perceptions amongst a nation's target audiences so that effective action can be taken where negative perceptions arise, or in cases where a significant gap between perceptions and reality has occurred. COO perceptions can change over time, and it is the responsibility of nation-branding strategists to ensure that such changes evolve in a favourable direction.

■ References

1. Peterson, R.A. and Jolibert, A.J.P. (1995) A meta-analysis of country-of-origin effects. *Journal of International Business Studies*, **26**, 4, 883–900.
2. Al-Sulaiti, K.I. and Baker, M.J. (1998) Country-of-origin effects: A literature review. *Marketing Intelligence and Planning*, **16**, 3, 150–99.
3. Dinnie, K. (2004) Country-of-origin 1965–2004: A literature review. *Journal of Customer Behaviour*, **3**, 2, 165–213.

4. Verlegh, P.W.J. and Steenkamp, J.-B.E.M. (1999) A review and meta-analysis of country-of-origin research. *Journal of Economic Psychology*, **20**, 521–46.

5. Usunier, J.-C. (2006) Relevance in business research: The case of country-of-origin research in marketing. *European Management Review*, **3**, 60–73.

6. Lyons, W. (2005) Clear winner. *Scotland on Sunday*, Food & Drink, October 30, 22.

7. Papadopoulos, N. and Heslop, L. (eds.) (1993) *Product and Country Images: Research and Strategy*. The Haworth Press, New York, NY.

8. Kim, C.K. and Chung, J.Y. (1997) Brand popularity, country image and market share: An empirical study. *Journal of International Business Studies*, **28**, 2, 361–86.

9. Schaefer, A. (1997) Do demographics have an effect on country-of-origin effects? *Journal of Marketing Management*, **13**, 8, 813–34.

10. Zafar, U.A., Johnson, J.P., Yang, X., *et al.* (2004) Does country of origin matter for low-involvement products? *International Marketing Review*, **21**, 1, 102–20.

11. Verlegh, P.W.J., Steenkamp, J.-B.E.M., and Meulenberg, M.T.G. (2005) Country-of-origin effects in consumer processing of advertising claims. *International Journal of Research in Marketing*, **22**, 127–39.

12. Roth, M.S. and Romeo, S.B. (1992) Matching product category and country image perceptions: A framework for managing country-of-origin effects. *Journal of International Business Studies*, **23**, 477–97.

13. Thakor, M.V. and Kohli, C.S. (1996) Brand origin: conceptualization and review. *Journal of Consumer Marketing*, **13**, 3, 27–42.

14. Kwok, S., Uncles, M., and Huang, Y. (2006) Brand preferences and brand choices among urban Chinese consumers: An investigation into country-of-origin effects. *Asia Pacific Journal of Marketing and Logistics*, **18**, 3, 163–72.

15. Roll, M. (2006) *Asian Brand Strategy: How Asia Builds Strong Brands*. Palgrave Macmillan, USA.

16. Javalgi, R.G., Cutler, B.D., and Winans, W.A. (2001) At your service! Does country of origin research apply to services? *The Journal of Services Marketing*, **15**, 6/7, 565–82.

17. Ofir, C. and Lehmann, D. (1986) Measuring images of foreign products. *Columbia Journal of World Business*, Summer, 105–8.

18. Harrison-Walker, L.J. (1995) The relative effects of national stereotype and advertising information on the selection of a service provider: an empirical study. *Journal of Services Marketing*, **9**, 1, 47–59.

19. Mortimer, R. (2007) Card of conscience. *Brand Strategy*, February, 20–3.

20. Interbrand Best Global Brands 2006 FAQ, http://www.interbrand.com/best_brands_2006_FAQ.asp

21. Niss, H. (1996) Country-of-origin marketing over the product life cycle: a Danish case study. *European Journal of Marketing*, **30**, 3, 6–22.

22. Lampert, S.I and Jaffe, E.D. (1998) A dynamic approach to country-of-origin effect. *European Journal of Marketing*, **32**, 1/2, 61–78.

23. Beverland, M. and Lindgreen, A. (2002) Using country of origin in strategy: The importance of context and strategic action. *Journal of Brand Management*, **10**, 2, 147–67.

24. Schooler, R.D. (1971) Bias phenomena attendant to the marketing of foreign goods in the US. *Journal of International Business Studies*, **2**, 1, 71–81.

25. Dornoff, R., Tankersley, C., and White, G. (1974) Consumers' perceptions of imports. *Akron Business and Economic Review*, **5**, Summer, 26–9.

26. Shimp, T.A. and Sharma, S. (1987) Consumer ethnocentrism: construction and validation of the CETSCALE. *Journal of Marketing Research*, **24**, August, 280–9.

27. Jaffe, E.D. and Nebenzahl, I.D. (2001) *National Image & Competitive Advantage: The Theory and Practice of Country-of-Origin Effect*. Copenhagen Business School Press.

28. Chao, P., Wuhrer, G. and Werani, T. (2005) Celebrity and foreign brand name as moderators of country-of-origin effects. *International Journal of Advertising*, **24**, 2, 173–92.

29. Hamin, E.G. and Elliott, G. (2006) A less-developed country perspective of consumer ethnocentrism and 'country of origin' effects: Indonesian evidence. *Asia Pacific Journal of Marketing and Logistics*, **18**, 2, 79–92.

30. Burgess, S.M. and Harris, M. (1999) Social identity in an emerging consumer market: how you do the wash may say a lot about who you think you are. *Advances in Consumer Research*, **26**, 170–5.

31. Lenartowicz, T. and Roth, K. (2001) Does subculture within a country matter? A cross-cultural study of motivational domains and business performance in Brazil. *Journal of International Business Studies*, **32**, 2, 305–25.

32. Laroche, M., Papadopoulos, N., Heslop, L., *et al.* (2003) Effects of subcultural differences on country and product evaluations. *Journal of Consumer Behaviour*, **2**, 3, 232–47.

33. Shimp, T.A. (2003) *Advertising, Promotion, & Supplemental Aspects of Integrated Marketing Communications*, Sixth Edition. Thomson South-Western, USA.

34. Fiske, J. (1990) *Introduction to Communication Studies*. Routledge, New York, USA.

35. Askegaard, S. and Ger, G. (1998) Product-country images: towards a contextualized approach. *European Advances in Consumer Research*, **3**, 50–8.

36. Morris, C.W. (1946) *Signs, Language, and Behaviour*. Prentice Hall, New York, USA.

37. Mick, D.G. (1986) Consumer research and semiotics: exploring the morphology of signs, symbols, and significance. *Journal of Consumer Research*, **13**, 2, 196–213.

38. Acton, M. (2007) Fuel for thought. *Brand Strategy*, April, 54–5.

39. Nagashima, A. (1970) A comparison of Japanese and US attitudes towards foreign products. *Journal of Marketing*, **34**, 1, 68–74.

40. Nagashima, A. (1977) A comparative 'made in' product image survey among Japanese businessmen. *Journal of Marketing*, **41**, 3, 95–100.

41. Papadopoulos, N., Heslop, L., Graby, F., *et al.* (1987) Does country of origin matter? Some findings from a cross-cultural study of consumer views about foreign products. Report No. 87-104, Marketing Science Institute, Cambridge, MA.

42. Nebenzahl, I.D., Jaffe, E.D., and Lampert, S.I. (1997) Towards a theory of country image effect on product evaluation. *Management International Review*, **37**, 1, 27–49.

43. Darling, J.R. and Puetz, J.E. (2002) Analysis of changes in consumer attitudes towards the products of England, France, Germany and the USA, 1975–2000. *European Business Review*, **14**, 3, 170–93.

44. Usunier, J.-C. (2006) Relevance in business research: the case of country-of-origin research in marketing. *European Management Review*, **3**, 60–73.

45. Amine, L.S. and Chao, M.C.H. (2005) Managing country image to long-term advantage: The case of Taiwan and Acer. *Place Branding*, **1**, 2, 187–204.

46. Kotler, P. and Gertner, D. (2002) Country as brand, product, and beyond: A place marketing and brand management perspective. *Journal of Brand Management*, **9**, 4–5, 249–61.

47. Smith, S. (2007) Building the brands we love. *Brand Strategy*, March, 47–9.

CHAPTER 5

Nation branding and national identity

Country Case Insight – Russia

On national identity and the building of Russia's image

Vladimir Lebedenko
Deputy Director of Department for Relations with the Subjects of the Federation, the Parliament, Public and Political Organizations, Ministry of Foreign Affairs of Russian Federation

Russia belongs to the so-called young democracies (even though the hundredth anniversary of parliamentarianism in Russia has already been celebrated), in which many institutes, including a civil society, are at a stage of formation and finding of maturity. In full measure, it concerns institutes of public diplomacy and mechanisms of formation and promotion of image of the country abroad. Unlike the USSR, which possessed a powerful information and propaganda machine and influential ideology, Russia not only has lost such a machine and ideology, but it appeared to find itself during the 1990s in a deep crisis of self-identification and facing a choice regarding its future development, which has clarified only now. As well as after the October revolution of 1917, after 1991, many things had to be started from nothing in terms of the new state and the transition (or more accurately 'return') to another social and political system. If the USSR was mainly object – Russia became during the 1990s the subject of information-ideological influence from the outside, above all from the West.

After the collapse of the USSR, most of the new independent states felt a need for self-identification and the establishment of their image in the world arena. Russia also faced this task, and the approaches to its solution in the last 16 years have undergone a noticeable evolution.

First about self-identification. On the one hand, it was easier for Russia with this than for many new states – after all Russia had behind it a 1,000-year experience of state history and the status of successor to a superpower, the USSR. In addition, even in the Soviet 70-year period many people in the West, for example Charles de Gaulle, had only called the USSR 'Russia'. That is there remained a continuity of the state and nation. On the other hand, there were difficulties as well: the breakup of the USSR had triggered off strong centrifugal tendencies, which had spilled over to Russia too, in particular in the form of manifestations of separatism (examples – Chechnya, Tatarstan). The conflicts that had flared up on ethnic grounds in the post-Soviet area and the virus of nationalism were a most dangerous factor for the stability of our multinational state. Finally, the 'democratic revolution' dealt a powerful blow not only to the Communist party, but to the entire state, with which the party had been in a state of symbiosis. Superimposed on all this was the acute internal political struggle, which developed in October 1993 into a shooting of the parliament building by tanks. Add to this the 'shock therapy', which had cast a whole generation of people of older age below the poverty line, the wild privatization 'for our own men', the 20–25 million Russians who had found themselves overnight and against their will outside Russia, the new boundaries that had narrowed the territory of the country to a state of 500 years ago, and the dubious legitimacy of the Belaya Vezha agreements to dissolve the USSR in the eyes of many people – and you will get the picture of a profound crisis of identity, of a crisis of the nation, its spirit and self-consciousness. So, it was not without reason that the task put forward by the former President Yeltsin of searching for a national idea remained but a declarative slogan. And because few people in the conditions of a permanent power struggle then, in the already distant 1990s, concerned themselves with state interests, so much the less was it the case with the image of the country. Left to its own devices, this image just 'drifted' – by virtue of the tradition of the personification of state authority peculiar to Russia – along with the contradictory image of Boris Yeltsin.

The state had actually withdrawn from the sphere of ideology and given up the implementation of information policy, turning everything over to market forces. And because a vacuum never occurs in this domain, it was quickly filled by product advertising, soap operas, crime films and catastrophe stories. The media themselves quickly fell under the control of oligarchic clans and began to be used by them for political and competitive purposes and for the propaganda of values alien to our society.

By the logic of our narrative it should further be said – 'but now Putin came, and everything has changed'. Unfortunately, so far not everything – well, you cannot all at once clean the 'Augean stables' and repair the image. Yet, the signs of recovery did nevertheless appear, and they are quite a few. And, most important, an understanding has come of the need for serious, systemic work on improving the reputation of Russia. What is this due to?

Above all, it is due to a recognition by all of the considerable harm that is today being inflicted upon Russia by its image, which in many respects has become a hindrance to development and modernization. Russia's reputation in the world is significantly worse than the country really is.

Why did it happen so? Partly because up until recent years in our country no one has seriously concerned themselves with the country's image, and if some did, then it was not ourselves, but other information centers and in the way that suited them and not Russia. Partly our own media are to blame for this, having staked on mass instincts and low taste and having been carried away by negativism and the hyperbolizing of drawbacks. All this has damaged, rather than helped, the provision of objective and full information about developments in Russia. And image is the result of the information that passes.

It is therefore necessary to take up the job of upgrading Russia's image by starting with our own media and first and foremost, television.

And, finally, the real co-authors of the inadequate image of Russia are western media and information centers.

It is intriguing that opinion polls show the ordinary population in the western countries to be far better (more than 50%) disposed towards Russia than their elites, especially the media. According to the think-tank SVOP report, only 17% of the total number of publications of the western media on Russia's transition to market economy can be regarded as positive and realistic. This, by all indications, fits in with the purposive line on discrediting Russia in the western media to weaken its political position and economic competitiveness. Such are the harsh laws of the world competitive struggle. In the Russian analysts' opinion, the situation is unlikely to change radically in the coming years, because the strengthening of Russia on the international scene and the opening by it of new markets do not meet the interests of many foreign partners who regard it as a potential rival.

Because of an inadequate image, Russia's national product is understated by several times, a number of authoritative estimates have shown. This creates serious obstacles to the activities of Russian corporations, lowers their capitalization, narrows the scale of and acts as a brake on investment programs, and is a hindrance to the entry of Russian business into the world market.

The overall unsatisfactory situation with the image of Russia abroad is such that it requires the combining of efforts by all – by authority, at the level of leading decision makers, by the business community, by the media and by the institutions of civil society. In accomplishing the image making of the country, unquestionably, there should, as in the USA, be enlisted professionals too – PR agencies and companies. And what is required is not a utilitarian or sectoral approach towards the promotion of a positive image of the country (a striking example of this approach in recent years was the media promotion of Turkey and its tourism), but crisis management with the participation of the Russian leadership. Classical examples of using the crisis method are Germany and Japan, which were able in a fairly short time after the war to radically change their image as aggressive military states. Evidently, after the Cold War, Russia also has to travel the same road.

Russia has already covered a part of this journey, especially after the assumption of presidential office by Vladimir Putin. The index of his quotability in western media is on the level of leading western politicians. Our President is being seen as an influential partner, he is being listened to, he is being reckoned with on all world problems. The President is the face of the state, and accordingly, the image of the country in foreigners' minds is largely associated with his personality. Russia gains by Putin's personal prestige.

Internal reforms – tax, land – have also begun to bear fruit; they have been highly assessed taking into account our historical experience (the land question was always tackled with difficulty in our country).

Europe's lowest income tax rate of 13% has been established in Russia. The Government has given up further borrowing of money abroad and is on a timely basis – and sometimes also ahead of time – honouring its debt obligations. The country has a surplus budget. Its economy has been developing along an ascending line over the last 3 years, demonstrating pretty high growth rates. The USSR, in its last 30 years, imported grain from America; Russia has become its exporter. All this has been noted and favourably evaluated in the West, including – what is important – by credit-rating agencies.

From being a chronic debtor, the country has turned into the state in fifth place in the world on stocks of currency reserves. Leading brands in the car industry come to the country as well as conservative investors.

The problem of Chechnya has been quite painful for Russia and its image over all recent years. But, in this respect too shifts are in evidence, stemming from the efforts of the Federal Center for political settlement (a referendum on the adoption of a Chechen constitution was held, an election for president of the Chechen Republic took place, restoration of the Republic moves ahead).

On the whole, in recent years, the attention of Russian authorities and society to the necessity of systemic work on improvement of the country's image has noticeably increased. The mechanism of its formation and promotion in the world is not yet well formulated in this regard. Also, as regards the creation of a modern toolkit of soft power, only the first steps have been taken. Nevertheless, a lot of serious projects in various directions have started:

- For the mass media in 2004 'the Valdai club' was created, within the framework of which take place annual meetings of the country leaders with leading foreign political scientists and experts; the president annually addresses mega-press conferences and so forth;
- From the beginning of 2005, there is a weekly journal in English *Russia Profile* (for the USA and other foreign countries);
- From December 2005 began the transmission of an English-speaking TV channel 'Russia Today', designed to show a Russian perspective on Russia and the world (with an annual budget of $30 million);
- Cultural, scientific and educational projects (an action plan within the program 'Years of culture of Russia' in the leading countries, escalating of activity and modernization of the cultural centers of Russia abroad and so forth);
- Sports projects (including participation of Moscow and now Sochi in competitions to host Olympiads);
- Projects such as 'Church diplomacy' and celebrations of memorable historical dates (largest of which are the 300th anniversary of St. Petersburg and the sixtieth anniversary of the Victory in the Second World War);
- Social projects (including the contribution to the struggle against AIDS and rendering assistance to victims of acts of nature).

For the image of Russia, its presidency of the Group of Eight in 2006 (it was promoted also by cooperation with one large western PR company) had a favourable effect.

More active participation in work on improvement of the country's image has been achieved by increased involvement of representatives of a wide range of Russian society, cooperation with the 30 million inhabitants Russian-speaking diasporas abroad, graduates of the Russian (Soviet) high schools, etc.

All these are the signs of the 'recovery' of Russia. Alongside this, Russia's image is also getting better.

At the same time, there are also a number of complexities: weak coordination of all work (today it is coordinated by different divisions of the Administration of the President), lack of general strategy and dispersal of allocated means, underestimation by authorities (except for the President) of the need to work with public opinion both at home and abroad. Often, there is an inability to explain the sense of accepted decisions, a weak position in the world information space, and – most importantly – the state still does not have a distinct ideology and national idea.

A number of these reasons explain the image damage that Russia had in recent years in connection with the 'Yukos' trial, the project 'Sakhalin', and the so-called Russian–Ukrainian gas crisis.

Summarizing, first, the image of the country is a common matter for authority, society and all Russians, including those going abroad as tourists.

Second, Russia has in earnest and for the long term taken up the improvement of its image as a means for strengthening its position in the world and as a factor of economic and social development. There is considerable potential here.

However, no one has ever managed to change the image of a country in a short time; systemic, long-term efforts are needed.

On the whole, the theme of making the country's world image is of particular relevance in the era of globalization and information. Especially, in view of that, the competitive struggle more and more extends into the sphere of country image.

*****

■ Introduction

National identity plays a key role in nation branding. An awareness and understanding of the core features of national identity is a prerequisite for developing nation-branding campaigns, as the essence of any nation-brand derives not only from the country's companies and brands but also from its culture in the widest sense – language, literature, music, sport, architecture and so on all embody the soul of a nation. This is one reason why nation branding is too large an undertaking to be left solely to marketing, branding or advertising people. A deep and authentic nation-brand must include the many elements and expressions of a nation's culture; if it fails to do so, it will rightly be perceived as shallow and superficial and not truly representative of the nation. Branding a nation does not resemble some fast-moving consumer goods (FMCG) branding, where competing products with no real differences are hyped up and promoted on the basis of some spurious differentiation. On the other hand, nation-brands are rooted in the reality of the nation's culture, which is perhaps the truest, most authentic differentiator that any brand could wish to have.

The imperfect knowledge – or often complete ignorance – that people all over the world have with regard to nations other than their own gives rise to what can become a damaging identity–image gap, where a nation's true identity fails to be appreciated by external observers because of either indifference or overwhelming negative stereotypes. The identity–image gap can be exacerbated by something as apparently trivial as an unflattering portrayal in film. Kazakhstan has been the most high-profile victim of this through the 2006 film *Borat*, whilst to a lesser extent Slovakia received a gruesome and sinister depiction through the 2005 horror film *Hostel*. In such cases, a PR damage limitation exercise may bring some short-term benefits but in the longer term a more strategic promotion of the country's culture and identity will be necessary in order to close, or at least reduce, existing identity–image gaps.

This chapter, therefore, provides an overview of the key features of national identity that are relevant to the concept and practice of nation branding. Implications of national identity for nation branding are drawn and areas of particular relevance to nation-brand development are discussed. It has been observed that at least nine academic disciplines have developed theories of nationalism and nation-states and that it is therefore not surprising that authors in one discipline are unfamiliar with theory in another, or that there is overlap and duplication [1]. These disciplines include political geography, international relations, political science, cultural anthropology, social psychology, political philosophy, international law, sociology and history. What follows is an attempt to extract from some of these many disciplines the salient national identity issues for application in culturally informed nation-brand development.

■ Fundamental features of national identity

The fundamental features of national identity include the following: an historic territory, or homeland; common myths and historical memories; a common, mass public culture; common legal rights and duties for all members; and a common economy with territorial mobility for all members [2]. Increasing levels of supranational legislation emanating from regional entities such as the European Union render the last two features less distinctively national than in the past; however, the notions of a historic homeland, common myths, historical memories and a common, mass public culture still prevail as key features of national identity. It is undeniable that the falling of international trade barriers and the border-transcending nature of the Internet have made the world a more interconnected place; yet, national identity retains its deep emotional and spiritual power as a source of identity for many people. The intense pride and emotion in national identity exhibited at international sporting events, for instance, demonstrates that even in our era of globalization, national identity remains a relevant and powerful concept. There are deep wells of culture, attachment and passion for nation-brands to draw from. (Table 5.1)

The visual manifestations of national identity are familiar to all – flags, for example are probably the most potent visual expression of national identity. Their recognition levels result in designs of a country's flag being used as a visual shorthand by products that wish to highlight their

Table 5.1 Dimensions of National Identity

Author	Dimensions of national identity
Smith [2]	A historic territory, or homeland; common myths and historical memories; a common, mass public culture; common legal rights and duties for all members; a common economy with territorial mobility for members
Anderson [3]	The nation as an imagined community, a deep horizontal comradeship
Kearney [4]	To speak of a single 'national past' or a single 'national image' would be to distort the complexity of the history of multinational states such as the UK
Tolz [5]	The main problem of nation-building is how to reconcile civic identities based on inclusive citizenship and exclusive ethnic identities based on such common characteristics as culture, religion and language
Parekh [6]	Identity is neither fixed and unalterable nor wholly fluid and amenable to unlimited reconstruction. It can be altered, but only within the constraints imposed by inherited constitution and necessarily inadequate self-knowledge
Thompson [7]	Contrary to nationalist discourses and commonly held assumptions, the nation is not a unitary entity in which all members think, feel and act as one. Instead, each individual engages in many different ways in making sense of nations and national identities in the course of interactions with others
Kiely *et al.* [8]	'Markers' of national identity can include: place of birth, ancestry, place of residence, length of residence, upbringing and education, name, accent, physical appearance, dress, commitment to place
Bond *et al.* [9]	Attempt to move beyond assumptions that nationalism is essentially cultural and/or narrowly political, primarily past-oriented and defensive. Examine evidence relating to the creative (re)construction of the nation from a contemporary economic perspective

Source: adapted from Dinnie, K. [10].

country of origin (COO). One problem that can arise from this is that any brand from a given country is free to use a design of the flag in its packaging or other forms of marketing communications, and this makes it difficult if not impossible for nations to ensure that only high-quality products and brands use the flag in their branding. Countries can of course establish organizations to promote their country's products and services and create a logo or trademark that can only be used by member companies, and this is one means of protecting quality perceptions of a nation's brands. Other visual manifestations of national identity include uniforms of the armed forces and other institutions, traditional dress and architectural styles. There also exist sonic manifestations of national identity, the most obvious of which is a country's national anthem, but which can also encompass language, regional accents and dialects, and specific voices of well-known individuals who are closely associated with a particular country such as Nelson Mandela in the case of South Africa, Sean Connery in the case of Scotland and so on. Iconic individuals such as these constitute an element of the common, mass public culture identified above as a fundamental feature of national identity.

Landscape represents another powerful visual manifestation of national identity. For example, Mount Fuji, spectacular fjords and Ayers Rock dramatically symbolize Japan, Norway and Australia, respectively. These types of unique, potent iconic landscapes have been used for several decades by national tourism organizations, and consequently, one of the key challenges in nation branding lies in how to position a country so that it is not perceived solely as a tourist destination but also as a credible location for inward investment, a source of high-technology products and so on. For emerging nations yet to fully exploit their tourism potential, the concept of 'cultivating poetic spaces' – the identification of a sacred territory that belonged historically to a particular community [2] – may be adopted as part of a sustainable development agenda centred on the fast-growing ecotourism sector.

One of the most critical issues in national identity is the tension that is frequently observable in many nations between cultural diversity and national unity [11]. It has been suggested that in the context of Russia, for example the main problem in nation-building is how to reconcile inclusive civic identities on the one hand with exclusive ethnic identities on the other [5]. When cultural fault lines intersect within a nation, the social and political consequences can be devastating; alternatively, cultural diversity within a nation can be embraced, celebrated and treated as an asset rather than as a liability. This is a contentious political issue and clearly far beyond the control of any individual or organization engaged in nation-brand campaigns. But, nation-brand teams must be sensitive to the political ramifications of including or excluding certain cultural groups or perspectives from nation-branding campaigns. Derided from the political left for alleged cultural commodification and equally derided from the political right for alleged indifference to and disrespect for the nation's heritage and history, the short-lived 'Cool Britannia' campaign may still make some politicians jittery about committing to a nation-branding strategy. An inclusive, stakeholder approach represents the best means to overcome objections from either end of the political spectrum and to integrate a nation's cultural diversity into its nation branding. Campaigns crudely imposed from above, without prior consultation with the nation's diverse cultural groups, have little chance of resonating with the nation's citizens.

One attempt to tackle the tension between inclusive citizenship and exclusive ethnic identities could be seen in the 'One Scotland' campaign developed by the Scottish Executive in order to tackle and eliminate racism within Scotland [12]. The campaign sought to celebrate the contribution to Scottish life by ethnic communities and can thus be regarded as a form of internal nation branding, based on an inclusive approach. This is in line with the view that the classical distinction between civic and ethnic forms of national identity may be losing its validity in the light of the dynamic nature of social and political processes [13].

To facilitate comparative analysis and to contribute to effective decision-making, efforts have been made to construct scales that objectively measure national identity. One such scale is based on the view that national identity comprises the 'set of meanings' owned by a given culture that sets it apart from other cultures, and this scale identifies four major components of national identity – cultural homogeneity, belief structure, national heritage and ethnocentrism [14]. The scale was designed to allow national identity similarities and differences to be placed in a context that would allow enhanced international marketing decision-making. An alternative scale has been proposed by other researchers, who propose five subscales of national identity – membership (a person's worth for or contribution to the ingroup, in this case the nation); private (a person's view of the ingroup's value); public (other persons' view of this group); identity (contribution of ingroup membership to the self-concept of the person) and comparison (how the ingroup rates in comparison to relevant outgroups, i.e. other nations) [15]. This scale draws upon the principles of social psychology theory and would therefore require adaptation if it were to be used in a branding context.

Although national identity scales can provide a certain degree of useful insight with regard to nation-brand development and communication, it should be noted that national identity is only one form of identity on which overall personal identity may be constructed. Individual self-categorization can also be based on social, supra-national and personal sources of identity, and the salience of each of these identity sources can vary according to the social context [16]. The concept of contingent self-categorization may be extended from the individual and applied also at the level of the nation, whereby nations will highlight appropriate self-categorized aspects of their identity according to context. Northern Ireland, for example, has adopted such a strategy by marketing itself as 'Irish' in Irish-friendly markets and as 'British' in British-friendly markets [17].

Drawing upon a range of potential sources of identification and self-definition, people may be able to 'customize' their social identities [16].

Similarly, a country seeking to brand itself effectively in such a way that its nation-brand covers a sufficiently wide range of product/service sectors must 'customize' its identity according to the geographical and social environment in which it is competing. This view of identity sees identity not as static and fixed but as *produced* and fluid; although, there are clearly limits to this fluidity given that the identity of a person or a nation is not a blank slate [18,19].

Placing the concept of national identity as a fluid phenomenon in an economic context, Bond *et al.* [9] note that the national past continues to have a strong influence upon the means by which economic agents mobilize national identity for contemporary economic ends. They suggest that the need to recognize the continuing importance of the historical influence of national identity, while constructing a contemporary identity, is achieved through four general processes: 'reiteration', which involves the mobilization of a historically positive element of national identity; 'recapture', in which there is an ambition to revisit past success in an area of contemporary problems; 'reinterpretation', in which historically negative factors are presented as contemporary advantages or as largely neutral; and 'repudiation', where negative features that are not suitable for reinterpretation are omitted from contemporary constructions of identity. This concept, which proposes that identity is constructed rather than given, underpins the nation-branding paradigm. Whilst not granting governments *carte blanche* to manipulate national identity for narrow party-political ends, the concept of identity as being both given and constantly reconstituted [6] implies that governments can attempt to harness and highlight certain aspects of national identity in order to shape national image perceptions.

■ The nation as an imagined community

A further key concept in terms of the intangible aspects of national identity is Anderson's [3] consideration of the nation as 'an imagined community'. According to this concept, the nation is 'imagined' as a community because although the members of even the smallest nation will never know most of their fellow members, the nation is conceived of as a deep, horizontal comradeship. The abstract nature of national identity is also examined by Cameron [20], who focuses upon the role of myth in national identity. Cameron observes that myth is inextricably linked with the concept of national identity and many of the symbols that people seize upon to denote their national allegiance are shared with the people of other nations who do not attribute to them the same significance, and although the value of such myths and symbols is in the mind more than in reality, the mind and our deep psychological reactions can govern our attitudes and therefore national myths and symbols have a real potency.

Pittock [21], however, offers a dissenting view on Anderson's concept of 'imagined community', maintaining that although the concept of 'imagining' the nation may be useful to some extent, adopting this concept without interrogation places too much power in the hands of creative writers and created narratives and too little on the lived experience and shared traditions of national communities. Again, in the context of developing a nation-branding campaign, such a perspective would argue in favour of an inclusive approach rather than a fabricated narrative handed down from on high. The issue of national identity-building narratives underpins debates on the teaching of history in a nation's schools and leads to a consideration of one of the most intriguing themes in the national identity literature – the apparently paradoxical concept of 'invented tradition'.

■ Invented tradition

A landmark text in the national identity literature is *The Invention of Tradition* [22], a collection of case studies written by various historians and anthropologists who argue that traditions that appear or claim to be ancient can be quite recent in origin and were sometimes literally invented in a single event or over a short time period. The book argues that there is probably no time or place that has not seen the 'invention' of tradition, although invented traditions occur more frequently at times of rapid social transformation when 'old' traditions are disappearing. A key aim of invented tradition is to establish or symbolize social cohesion and collective identities, and a key characteristic of invented tradition is that the continuity with a referenced historical past is largely fictitious [22]. The fictitious nature of much invented tradition inevitably invites criticism on the grounds that such traditions lack authenticity or legitimacy, and are created in order to benefit the established social order. The invention of a Highland, tartan-clad tradition in Scotland has, for example been vigorously contested:

> 'Tartanry, Highlandism and the rural representation of Scotland . . . were all indicative of the manufacture of a Scottish identity which had little to do with the reality of a rapidly urbanising and industrialising society, but everything to do with the appropriation of symbolic representations of Scotland which were located in a mythical past . . . Because the bourgeoisie and aristocracy peddled such symbols as authentic, it follows that their historical perception would have to be hazy and haphazard for such symbolism to acquire credibility. A rigorous and scientific historical tradition would have exposed this newly fashioned identity as bogus.' [23]

Smith [2] elaborates on the theme of invented tradition by stating that all those monuments to the fallen ceremonies of remembrance, statues to heroes and celebrations of anniversaries however newly created in their present form, take their meaning and their emotional power from a presumed and felt-collective past. The risk of superficiality does however exist to some extent, and it has been claimed that national image can be a complete media creation when the media are the sole source of information [24]. This observation is echoed by Pittock [21], who criticizes the concept of inventing the nation, with its concomitant idea that a mass of people can accept a fraud perpetrated by a publicist or a creative artist as part of their own identity. These well-founded concerns regarding manipulation of national identity need to be acknowledged in the development of nation-branding campaigns. In any country with a free press, the media would not allow any government-sponsored invention of tradition to pass uncontested; hence, the importance of including the full range of public and private sector stakeholders in the development of any nation-brand strategy, particularly where the invention of tradition is being contemplated.

■ Cultural elements of national identity

Culture has been described as 'the most intangible yet the most distinguishing element of any population and country' [25]. As such, a nation's culture may be regarded as constituting the true essence of the nation-brand. Culture's distinguishing role will form the basis for at least some of the nation's brand values, and the integration of culture into the nation-brand will also help elevate nation-branding campaigns above being merely trite, superficial PR/advertising campaigns. It has been argued that international business and especially marketing are a cultural as well as an economic phenomenon [26], and that a perspective on what is important within national cultures is useful to international marketers in building marketing mixes, which will appeal to customers belonging to a national culture [27]. This section therefore provides an overview of some key cultural elements of national identity. It is beyond the scope of this section to conduct an exhaustive, in-depth examination of these cultural elements; rather, it is the relevance of these elements to the nation-branding construct that is of prime interest for our purposes. A number of cultural perspectives on national identity are presented in Table 5.2.

High-context and low-context cultures

A useful and well-known way of analysing cultures is Hall's distinction between high-context and low-context cultures [28]. Using Hall's terminology, in high-context cultures (such as Japanese, Arabic or Chinese cultures), indirect styles of communication and the ability to interpret non-verbal signals and indirect illusions are prized, whereas in low-context cultures (such as the UK and the USA), non-verbal behaviour is often ignored and therefore communicators have to provide more explicit information. Other differences between high-context and low-context cultures can also have an influence on cross-cultural communication and

Table 5.2 Cultural Perspectives on National Identity

Author	Cultural Elements
Anderson [3]	The cultural products of nationalism: poetry, prose fiction, music, plastic arts
McCreadie [29]	The role of language in the formation of national identity
Haydn [30]	The role of history teaching in schools in the formation of national identity
Hall [28]	The contrast between 'high-context' and 'low-context' cultures
King [31]	Through European club football, the outlines can be detected of a new Europe of competing cities and regions, which are being disembedded from their national contexts into new transnational matrices
Shulman [32]	The main cultural components of national identity comprise language, religion and traditions
Tuck [33]	The media evoke particularly strong invented traditions and well-established symbols of national identity in describing the exploits of the English national rugby team.

relationships – for example in high-context cultures, relationships tend to be relatively long-lasting; agreements tend to be spoken rather than written; insiders and outsiders are clearly distinguished; and cultural patterns are ingrained and slow to change. In low-context cultures, the opposite characteristics prevail [34].

Individualism/Collectivism

The link between elements of national identity and consumer behaviour was explored by Aaker and Williams [35] in their study of the influence of emotional appeals across cultures. Cross-cultural persuasion effects are discussed by comparing the effects of emotional appeals across collectivist and individualist cultures. The authors found that appeals relying on other-focused emotions (e.g. empathy, peacefulness) versus ego-focused emotions (e.g. pride, happiness) led to more favourable attitudes for members of the individualist culture (USA), whereas appeals relying on ego-focused emotions, as opposed to other-focused emotions, led to more favourable attitudes for members of the collectivist culture (China). This perhaps surprising finding is explained by the authors as stemming from the notion that the novel types of thoughts generated by the persuasion appeals mediated attitudes, thereby driving the attitudinal and cognitive responses results. Aaker and Williams state, however, that further research is needed in order to understand the specific role of emotions in appeals across cultures.

The issue of individualism/collectivism is central to cross-cultural studies of decision-making and forms a major component of national identity; although, opinion is divided whether the individualism/collectivism construct plays a dominant or merely contributory role in consumer decision-making [36]. Takano and Osaka report that proponents of the individualism/collectivism construct have arrayed a number of country difference findings, but others studying similar kinds of decisions have observed no country differences, and recent meta-analyses find no overall pattern of support for this construct's predictions. Similarly, the validity of highly abstract, general measures of cultural knowledge has been questioned on both methodological and conceptual grounds [37]. Briley *et al.* [38] share this view, declaring that their stance begins with the assumption that cultural knowledge comprises a number of highly specific structures rather than a few monolithic structures, such as an individualist versus collectivist orientation. In terms of developing nation-brand strategy, it is thus clear that appeals to target markets displaying differing levels of individualism/collectivism will need to be framed accordingly. A monolithic nation-brand will lack resonance if it is not adapted to fit its varying markets.

Ethnocentrism

According to Usunier and Lee [39], the concept of ethnocentrism was first introduced in the early twentieth century by Sumner [40] in order to distinguish between 'ingroups' (those groups with which an individual identifies) and 'outgroups' (those regarded as antithetical to the group). Keillor and Hult [14] describe an ethnocentric tendency as one in which individuals, or societies, make cultural evaluations and attributions using their own cultural perspectives as the baseline criteria. Ethnocentrism is included in Keillor and Hult's national identity framework as a means of accounting for the importance placed on maintaining culturally centred values and behaviours. The relevance of ethnocentrism in economic terms is evident, in view of the globalization of the world economy and the increasing competition that now exists in the provision of most products and services. Ethnocentrism may be treated as a potentially useful means of segmenting markets. For example, appeals to highly ethnocentric consumers will highlight the COO of domestic products in order to attempt to achieve favourable attitudes and behaviours towards those products as opposed to imported goods. An understanding of the baseline criteria cultural perspectives of ethnocentric consumers referred to above by Keillor and Hult may therefore be considered as a useful input to the design of nation-branding strategies.

Language

It is important for those involved to develop a heightened awareness of the importance of language when framing nation-branding communications. The role and impact of language as a signifier of a PSC brand's

COO may be considerable. Furthermore, within any one language, there exists a range of linguistic tones or registers that are used every day in social situations. This represents a rich and diverse range of communicative resources, which marketing strategy in general and nation branding in particular could draw upon.

The flexibility and adaptability of language is examined by Macdonald [18] from the theoretical standpoint of sociolinguistics. Sociolinguistic theorizing is said by this author to attempt to retain the idea that we cannot understand the meaning of any one term or inflection in isolation, and that analysis typically focuses upon linguistic practice, variation and change, for example changes in accents, 'registers' and 'codes'. These practices, according to Macdonald, generate a range of possibilities, of different idioms, with different degrees of overlap and spread, which may be variously drawn upon and realized. The author concludes that who the speakers and hearers are, their social positioning, and the manner of utterance and context become crucial. Macdonald's observations on the crucial nature of who the speakers and hearers are, their social positioning, and the manner of utterance and context, are of direct relevance to marketing strategy. Although 'segmentation' is not a term used in the sociological approach taken by Macdonald, from a marketing perspective it could be argued that that is the phenomenon she is referring to, in that appropriate discourses must be utilized in addressing different audiences and stakeholders.

Another important linguistic issue concerns the nature of the relationship between language and reality. The linguist Edward Sapir contends that

'No two languages are ever sufficiently similar as to be considered as representing the same social reality. The worlds in which different societies live are distinct worlds, not merely the same world with different labels attached.' [41]

An implication of this linguistic view that 'no two languages ... represent the same social reality' is that nation-branding communications related to cultural issues may need to be written and designed from scratch by professionals who are members of the target market, rather than merely translated.

Literature

Literature may be viewed as a determinant and also a manifestation of national identity. Novels, poetry, plays and other forms of literature can contribute to a sense of national identity and also occasionally act as state-of-the-nation pronouncements. The relevance of this to nation branding lies in the power of literature to establish in an unplanned way a certain image of the nation, which may or may not chime with the desired image of official bodies such as national tourist boards. The magical realism of Colombian writer Gabriel Garcia Marquez, the novels of Peruvian author Mario Vargas Llosa, the hypnotically compelling stories of Japanese writer Haruki Murakami – all of this literary output represents a deeper and richer route into a country's culture and psyche than could be obtained through any branding campaign, no matter how creative. The implications for nation branding are twofold: first, literature needs to be supported as part of the nation's cultural strategy, and second, a coordinating body needs to be established in order to ensure that when the nation's literary figures make an impact on the world stage, other sectors of the nation benefit from this through coordinated events to boost tourism, branded exports and so on. Without the existence of such a coordinating body, opportunities for synergy will be lost (see Chapter 8).

Music

It could be argued that music as a core element of national identity has been hugely underutilized in country's nation-branding campaigns. Some countries have been receptive to the potential power of music to communicate the nation's identity in a positive, celebratory way. Scottish folk music, for instance, is distinctive and has undergone fusion with more modern musical styles over the past decade, and this represents a potentially powerful influence in the branding of Scotland. This has begun to be recognized by some of the relevant organizations who may be regarded as stakeholders in the branding of Scottish products and services. For example, a recent trade mission by Scottish companies to the Far East was accompanied by the folk–fusion Scottish band Shooglenifty, whose music combines traditional Scottishness with an openness to innovation and world influences in a way that might serve as a source of inspiration for other Scottish sectors on the global stage. Devine [42] observes that rock bands such as Deacon Blue, the Proclaimers and Runrig are emphatically Scottish in style but nevertheless able to convey their music to a much wider overseas audience. Runrig have celebrated Gaelic culture in particular and Scottishness in general to a younger generation of Scots increasingly confident in their own national identity. It would be to squander an opportunity not to incorporate the dynamic fusion of tradition and modernity evident in much current Scottish music into a strategic nation-branding strategy. Whether this would fall under the remit of a government-funded agency, or a private sector body, or some other entity, is a key issue. Musicians, like other creative people, are generally loathe to be dragooned into any kind of formal structure so the rationale for a sonic branding strategy would need to be clearly articulated (in non-brandspeak) and a light-touch policy used.

Food and drink

Few components of national identity could be more expressive of the nation than its food and drink. This is reflected in the proliferation of food and drink-related national promotions that have occurred over recent years. These promotions may be at a national or a regional level. The country case insight in Chapter 3 shows how Chile has coordinated a promotional campaign for that country's wines. Regional campaigns are also natural vehicles for food and drink promotions. The Brittany region of France, for example positions itself with a hint of hyperbole as 'an Olympus for the gods of food and drink' [43].

Sport

Sport engenders high levels of passion and may be considered to be a central contributing factor to a sense of national identity. For example, Bradley [44] cites Spain as a country in which, although there are other important conduits of regional and ethnic identity, football remains symptomatic of the major diversities that exist within society. More than ever before, clubs such as Barcelona, Athletico Bilbao and Real Madrid are the symbols and the focus, as well as the open vehicles for the expression of ethnic, cultural and nationalistic identities and differences within Spanish society.

Whereas, in some countries, the dominant sport contributing to a sense of national identity is football, in other countries different sports fulfil the same function. In New Zealand, for instance, the All Blacks rugby team is a symbol of national pride. With the advent of professional rugby in the mid-1990s, the New Zealand Rugby Union (NZRU) employed Saatchi and Saatchi in order to identify a constellation of 'brand values' for the All Blacks, the national rugby team. Collectively, as a team, the All Blacks were deemed by Saatchi and Saatchi to represent the values of New Zealand, including values such as excellence, humility, teamwork and tradition [45]. A similar study investigating the relationship between rugby union and national identity, in the context of England, was conducted by Tuck [33]. This study found that the English media employed numerous images to describe the exploits of the English national rugby team, evoking particularly strong invented traditions and well-established symbols of traditional Englishness such as bulldog spirit and Anglo-Saxon temperament. Another example of sport's role in identity-building comes from the Caribbean, where during the late 1950s and early 1960s cricket became a powerful expression of Caribbean progress and nationhood with links identified between cricket, black nationalism, Caribbean identity and anti-colonial struggle [46].

The hosting of international sports events such as the Olympic Games or the FIFA World Cup have been effectively used to favourably publicize and re-image a place on a global scale [47]. It has been suggested that incorporating sports into the nation-branding mix is a relatively underused positioning tool [48]. Two countries that now have a tremendous opportunity to enhance their nation-brands on a European, if not global, stage are Poland and Ukraine, who have just won the bidding to host the 2012 European Football Championships. This high-profile sporting event will be watched by around 150 million people and will also attract a vast amount of media attention in the run-up to the event. The way in which Poland and Ukraine manage their nation-branding strategy in the coming 5 years will determine the extent of the benefits that the countries can gain from this historic opportunity to take centre stage in the minds of tens, if not hundreds of millions of Europeans.

Architecture

The use of architecture in the creation of national identity is described by Hess [49], who describes how the architecture and spatial organization of Accra, Ghana, reflects an identification between architecture and a consciously managed national ideal. The post-colonialist Ghanaian administration's reconfiguration of colonial architectural objectives is claimed to have advanced – in its embrace of architectural modernity and reconceptualization of the urban environment – a distinctive notion of the 'nation'. This use of architecture in pursuit of a consciously managed national ideal is examined by Hess in the context of post-colonial identity formation; some may see the creation of the new Scottish Parliament building in a similar light, with Scotland emerging from the shadows of the dominant power, England.

Practitioner Insight

Sonic branding – Capturing the essence of a nation's identity

Daniel M. Jackson
Author of Sonic Branding – An Introduction

Sonic branding is the creation and consistent use of music, voice or sound design as a part of an identity or enhancement of an experience.

How does this discipline relate to the branding of nations? Would it be overstating the case to say it is fundamental, of the essence, essential?

Need some proof? Let's go back about 4,000 years to Joshua, who united the Hebrew nation behind the deeply resonant sound of the ram's horn. On second thoughts, let's skip forward a few thousand years to the 1745 when God Save the Queen was first performed as an expression of British patriotism. While we are on the subject of the UK, we can consider Jerusalem, Land of My Fathers and Scotland The Brave as sonic branding for England, Wales and Scotland respectively.

Need more evidence? For England's attempts to sing about its brand attributes, think of Rule Britannia (popular freedom), Land of Hope and Glory (pride), There'll Always be an England (fighting spirit), Swing Low Sweet Chariot (rugby prowess) and Barmy Army (cricketing underachievement).

Each of these songs or chants fulfils the essential roles of sonic branding.

Firstly, they have been created as expressions of the emotions – both of the essence and of associated values – of nations. Secondly, they have been used consistently over time and across many different 'applications'. Thirdly, they are memorable and fourthly they are distinct (in the main) and thereby only associated with brand England.

Music, which is elemental to all great sonic branding, is so powerful a tool for identifying and uniting a nation that since God Save the Queen, every modern nation on our planet (with the exception of Afghanistan when under the Taliban) has chosen a national anthem for its subjects to sing lustily or solemnly, depending upon the desired mood.

Newly independent nations seeking a musical expression of their national identity may look for inspiration from the five musical genres below that encompass the world's anthems. Such nations should consider one that matches the values they wish to convey and come up with a tune that has major key tonality and is preferably played by a full orchestra!

1. A Hymn
    Slow and melodic, best served solemn and traditional.
2. A March
    Tempo can be slow or fast but all will sound traditional, spirited and thrusting.
3. March 'plus'
    Add some extra sections to the march, include a complex melody and an Italian tenor to do it justice. Your nation will sound strong and traditional but with a bit of extra flair.
4. World Music
    Put together a band of local musicians and have them play in an authentic traditional style. Your nation will be branded proud and individual.
5. A Fanfare
    If you do not want lyrics, find some trumpets and military drums. The world will know you are proud and happy to shout about the greatness of your nation (even if it is only 60 years old).

Of course, the market for new national anthems has not been very active in the recent past (except for some ex-Soviet nations) but what have become more popular in the more recent past are international anthems such as the Internationale (left wing revolutionaries), Beethoven's Ode to Joy (the European Union) and even the UN has an unofficial hymn created by Pablo Casals and W.H. Auden.

The purpose of these supra-national anthems, however, is exactly the same as those of the smallest nations on earth. They are key components in the nation's identity: as important as the flag. They convey the emotions of the nation, some with startling accuracy and others with 'me too' monotony but usually with a decent tune and a stirring lyric.

* * * * *

■ Attitudes and national stereotypes

It is in the area of stereotyping that there is a clear conceptual overlap between the national identity literature on the one hand and the COO literature on the other. Nations are frequently stereotyped in a negative way. A major objective of developing a nation-brand is to counter such potentially damaging national stereotypes.

When used in sociology, the word stereotype means a biased (usually prejudicial) view of a group or class of people, a view that is resistant to change or correction from countervailing evidence [24]. Nations too have stereotypes, which can be positive, negative or neutral, although the stereotypic attributes associated with a nation need have no carryover effect on a specific product [50].

Cultural artefacts can be important determinants of national stereotype perceptions. In an examination of national stereotypes, Higson [19] states that a nation's stereotype can be built up, planned or unplanned, in many ways. Cultural artefacts such as films can have a strong effect on how a nation is perceived. Higson explains how, because the domestic market for British films is not large enough to cover costs, films have to be made with the international market in mind and this inevitably has an impact on the ways in which national identities are represented in them. Such films will often resort to stereotyping as a means of readily establishing character and identity. Whether such glib stereotyping has an effect on consumer behaviour or on perceptions of national image is an area of obvious relevance to nation-brand development. Has Uganda, for instance, undertaken any initiatives to measure the impact of 'The Last King of Scotland' on its own national image? No doubt, a PhD student will do so for a thesis at some point. But from a nation-branding perspective this is clearly not enough. The heightened public awareness of Uganda caused by this film represents a window of opportunity that will slam shut once the film's cinema runs and its DVD life cycle is over.

The role of museums as a vehicle for the expression of national identity has been studied by McLean and Cooke [51], who propose that museums, as sites of representation, are important discursive spaces where images of the nation are produced and consumed. Within a museum setting, suggest the authors, the narratives of nation are constructed through the relationship between the collection, interpretation and display of material culture and the interaction of visitors with the spaces of the museum. Anderson [3] emphasizes that the construction of such narratives of nation is not neutral activity and that museums, and what he terms the museumizing imagination, are both profoundly political. The important role played by museums in the projection of national identity therefore requires to be acknowledged in the development of nation-branding campaigns.

In a marketing context, the relationship between consumer attitudes and national stereotypes is a complex one. Papadopoulos *et al.* [52] found that, on the one hand, stereotypes about the people of a nation can arise from the association with their products (e.g. Hungarians viewed Japanese as trustworthy and likeable on the basis of their products) or, on the other hand, stereotypes may arise from an image of a people applied to their products (e.g. Hungarians rated Swedish products almost as highly as American products, even though few Swedish products at the time were sold in Hungary). This complexity is acknowledged by O'Shaughnessy and Jackson [24], who observe that there is an inherent difficulty in having a coherent image of a nation as people edit out or rearrange certain attributes (we do not really connect Swiss chocolate with Swiss banking to be arranged into some coherent overall image of the nation). Nation-branding strategy must include a significant investment in ongoing research in order to track which attributes people are editing out or rearranging when forming their country image perceptions. The country case insight in Chapter 4 illustrates how Switzerland is addressing this issue.

■ Summary

This chapter has reviewed the fundamental features of national identity, showing the relevance of national identity concepts to the emerging field of nation branding. Key issues in national identity include viewing the nation as an 'imagined community', and the notion of 'invented tradition'. The cultural elements of national identity are wide-ranging, encompassing language, literature, food and drink, sport, architecture, and many other dimensions that nation-branding strategists need to be aware of so that nation-brand development is firmly rooted in the reality and essence of the nation, rather than being merely a creation of advertising, marketing and branding agencies. The country case insight on Russia that appears in this chapter illustrates how nation branding may provide a means to clarify a nation's identity both for internal and also for external audiences.

■ References

1. Treanor, P. (1997) Structures of nationalism. *Sociological Research Online*, **2**, http:www.socresonline.org.uk/socresonline/2/1/8.html (accessed 21/05/01).
2. Smith, A.D. (1991) *National Identity*, Penguin Books, London.
3. Anderson, B. (1991) *Imagined Communities*, Verso.
4. Kearney, H. (1991) Four nations or one? *National Identities: The Constitution of the United Kingdom* (B. Crick, ed.) Blackwell, Oxford.
5. Tolz, V. (1998) Forging the nation: National identity and nation building in post-communist Russia. *Europe-Asia Studies*, September.

6. Parekh, B. (2000) Defining British national identity. *The Political Quarterly*, **71**, 4–14.
7. Thompson, A. (2001) Nations, national identities and human agency: putting people back into nations. *The Sociological Review*, **49**, 18–32.
8. Kiely, R., Bechhofer, F., Stewart, R., and McCrone, D. (2001) The markers and rules of Scottish national identity. *The Sociological Review*, **49**, 33–55.
9. Bond, R., McCrone, D., and Brown, A. (2003) National identity and economic development: reiteration, recapture, reinterpretation and repudiation. *Nations and Nationalism*, **9**, 371–391.
10. Dinnie, K. (2002) Implications of national identity for marketing strategy. *The Marketing Review*, **2**, 285–300.
11. Burgess, S.M. and Harris, M. (1999) Social identity in an emerging consumer market: How you do the wash may say a lot about who you think you are. *Advances in Consumer Research*, **26**, 170–175.
12. The Scottish Executive, http://www.onescotland.com
13. Zimmer, O. (2003) Boundary mechanisms and symbolic resources: Towards a process-oriented approach to national identity. *Nations and Nationalism*, **9**, 173–193.
14. Keillor, B.D. and Hult, G.T.M. (1999) A five-country study of national identity: Implications for international marketing research and practice. *International Marketing Review*, **16**, 65–82.
15. Lilli, W. and Diehl, M. (1999) Measuring national identity, Working Paper, Nr 10, *Mannheimer Zentrum für Europäische Sozialforschung*.
16. Burgoyne, C.B. and Routh, D.A. (1999) National identity, European identity and the euro, in *National Identity* (K. Cameron, ed.), Intellect Books, England.
17. Gould, M. and Skinner, H. (2007) Branding on ambiguity? Place branding without a national identity: Marketing Northern Ireland as a post-conflict society in the USA. *Place Branding and Public Diplomacy*, **3**, 100–113.
18. Macdonald, S. (1997) *Reimagining Culture: Histories, Identities and the Gaelic Renaissance*, Berg, Oxford.
19. Higson, A. (1998) Nationality: National identity and the media, in *The Media: An Introduction* (A. Briggs and P. Golbey, eds.) Longman.
20. Cameron, K. (ed.) (1999) *National Identity*, Intellect Books, Exeter, United Kingdom.
21. Pittock, M.G.H. (1999) *Celtic Identity and the British Image*, Manchester University Press, Manchester.
22. Hobsbawm, E. and Ranger, T. (eds.) (1983) *The Invention of Tradition*, Cambridge University Press.
23. Finlay, R.J. (1994) Controlling the past: Scottish historiography and Scottish identity in the 19th and 20th centuries. *Scottish Affairs*, **9**, Autumn, 127–142.
24. O'Shaughnessy, J. and Jackson, N. (2000) Treating the nation as a brand: Some neglected issues. *Journal of Macromarketing*, **20**, 56–64
25. Pant, D.R. (2005) A place brand strategy for the Republic of Armenia: 'Quality of context' and 'sustainability' as competitive advantage. *Place Branding*, **1**, 273–282.
26. Bradley, F. (2005) *International Marketing Strategy*, Fifth Edition, FT Prentice Hall, UK.
27. Muhlbacher, H., Dahringer, L., and Leihs, H. (1999) *International Marketing: A Global Perspective*, Second Edition, Thomson, UK.
28. Hall, E.T. (1976) *Beyond Culture*, Anchor Press/Doubleday, USA.
29. McCreadie, R. (1991) Scottish Identity and the Constitution. *National Identities: The Constitution of the United Kingdom* (B. Crick, ed.) Blackwell, Oxford.

30. Haydn, T., Arthur, J., Davies, I., *et al.* (2001) *Citizenship through Secondary History*, RoutledgeFalmer, London.
31. King, A. (2000) Football fandom and post-national identity in the New Europe. *British Journal of Sociology*, **51**, 419–442.
32. Shulman, S. (2002) Challenging the civic/ethnic and west/east dichotomies in the study of nationalism. *Comparative Political Studies*, **35**, 554–585.
33. Tuck, J. (2003) The men in white. *International Review for the Sociology of Sport*, **38**, 177–199.
34. Mead, R. (2005) *International Management: Cross-Cultural Dimensions*, Third Edition, Blackwell Publishing, USA.
35. Aaker, J.L. and Williams, P. (1998) Empathy versus pride: The influence of emotional appeals across cultures. *Journal of Consumer Research*, **25**, 241–273.
36. Takano, Y. and Osaka, E. (1999) An unsupported common view: Comparing Japan and the US on individualism/collectivism. *Asian Journal of Social Psychology*, **2**, 311–341.
37. Peng, K., Nisbett, R.E., and Wong, N.Y.C. (1997) Validity problems comparing values across cultures and possible solutions. *Psychological Methods*, **2**, 329–344.
38. Briley, D.A., Morris, M.W., and Simonson, I. (2000) Reasons as carriers of culture: Dynamic versus dispositional models of cultural influence on decision making. *Journal of Consumer Research*, **27**, 157–192.
39. Usunier, J.-C. and Lee, J.A. (2005) *Marketing Across Cultures*, Fourth Edition, FT Prentice Hall, UK.
40. Sumner, G.A. (1906) *Folk Ways*, Ginn Custom Publishing, New York, USA.
41. Sapir, E. (1929) The status of linguistics as a science. *Language*, **5**, 207–214.
42. Devine, T.M. (1999) *The Scottish Nation 1700–2000*, Penguin Books, London, UK.
43. Advertisement in The Guardian Weekend magazine, *The Guardian*, April 21 2007, p. 111
44. Bradley, J.M. (1995) *Ethnic and Religious Identity. in Modern Scotland: Culture, Politics and Football*, Avebury, England.
45. Motion, J., Leitch, S., and Brodie, R.J. (2003) Equity in corporate co-branding: The case of adidas and the All Blacks. *European Journal of Marketing*, **37**, 1080–1094.
46. James, C.L.R. (1963) *Beyond A Boundary*, Stanley Paul, London.
47. Jun, J.W. and Lee, H.M. (2007) Enhancing global-scale visibility and familiarity: The impact of World Baseball Classic on participating countries. *Place Branding and Public Diplomacy*, **3**, 42–52.
48. Rein, I. and Shields, B. (2007) Place branding sports: Strategies for differentiating emerging, transitional, negatively viewed and newly industrialised nations. *Place Branding and Public Diplomacy*, **3**, 73–85.
49. Hess, J.B. (2000) Imagining architecture: The structure of nationalism in Accra, Ghana. *Africa Today*, **47**, 34–58.
50. Elliott, G.R. and Cameron, R.S. (1994) Consumer perceptions of product quality and the country-of-origin effect. *Journal of International Marketing*, **2**, 49–62.
51. McLean, F. and Cooke, S. (2000) From Oor Wullie to the Queen Mother's Tartan Sash: Representation and identity in the Museum of Scotland. *Image into Identity Conference*, University of Hull, United Kingdom.
52. Papadopoulos, N., Heslop, L.A., and Beracs, I. (1990) National stereotypes and product evaluations in a socialist country. *International Marketing Review*, **7**, 32–47.

CHAPTER 6

From country-of-origin and national identity to nation branding

Country Case Insight – Brazil

Brazil IT: Taking Brazil's successful domestic IT industry abroad

Renata Sanches[1] and Flavia Sekles[2]
[1]*Projects Unit Coordinator, APEX Brasil and* [2]*Executive Director, Brazil Information Center*

In late March of 2007, A.T. Kearney's Global Services Location Index showed Brazil advancing five spots from its position in 2005 in the general ranking of countries offering offshore outsourcing, reaching the fifth position after India, China, Malaysia and Thailand.

The study, as well as many other similar items that have started to appear with increasing frequency in newly published research from other IT-consulting firms such as Gartner and Forrester showing the growth of Brazil as one of the most competitive outsourcing destinations, is welcome news to Brazilian IT companies and Brazilian export promotion organizations. Since early 2004, several interested sectors in the Brazilian economy have worked in tandem to put the Brazilian IT industry on the global map. Even though Brazil is one of the 10 largest IT markets in the world, worth approximately $15 billion a year, it exports a relatively small percentage, especially when compared with India, which exports nearly 75% of its IT production. The effort to boost the Brazilian IT sector as an exporter has received ample encouragement from the Brazilian government, through Brazil's export promotion agency, APEX Brasil.

It is widely recognized by all players in the Brazilian IT sector that to achieve significant export growth, the Brazilian IT industry would have to gain recognition as a capable producer of IT services and products outside of Brazil, specifically in the USA, the world's largest consumer of IT products. Before 2004, Brazil was hardly ever identified in industry research and analyst reports as an up and coming outsourcing destination. In fact, countries with much less-developed IT industries than Brazil's, such as Ukraine, Costa Rica and Vietnam, were frequently mentioned as the emerging IT outsourcing destinations by well-known industry analysts, whereas Brazil was largely ignored. This reflected a clear image problem.

To begin to change this perspective, APEX Brasil launched in 2004 what initially was a 3-year effort focused on the dissemination of Brazil IT services and products and of Brazilian IT companies as better suited partners for US companies seeking differentiated service closer to home.

Having identified the Gartner Group as a key opinion-making institution, both for its industry analysts as well as for their myriad IT trade shows, APEX decided to participate in the Gartner ITxpo in October 2004, in Orlando. APEX also chose to work with several Brazilian companies that were already established in the US market to develop an action plan that could, in the longer term, be applied to other Brazilian companies not yet selling their services to the USA. A key point of interest: Brazilian IT companies that worked in the USA at that time were also hurt by the lack of knowledge about the country's IT industry abroad, and about the lack of knowledge about Brazil in more general terms. As one executive said, at each sales meeting, the company had to expend a significant amount of time explaining that Brazil did indeed have an IT industry, cutting down on the time he had for selling his product. The initiative would also work as a uniform tool for companies developing business in the USA, creating a common strategy, using each other's efforts to leverage overall sales, transforming individual guerilla sales pitches into a coordinated market-conquering war.

Working with several IT Clusters throughout Brazil, individual IT companies and the Brazil Information Center, a non-profit trade organization based in the USA that promotes Brazil to American opinion makers and consumers, APEX Brasil, started brand development – using the term Brazil IT both as a noun and as a verb, as in 'Brazil it!', and consistently disseminating the competitiveness and areas of excellence of Brazil's IT industry, as well as the competitive advantages Brazil holds over other leading outsourcing destinations.

A new logo for Brazil IT was created, and the brand trademarked in the USA. The tools used for dissemination were video, Internet – www.brazil-it.com, traditional print media and consistent trade show participation. The message was focused on a few key points such as Brazil's strong domestic IT market, cultural and business environment similarities to the USA, geographical proximity and time zone compatibility, geopolitical stability and the creative power differential of Brazilian IT engineers when compared with IT engineers in other parts of the world. Areas of excellence such as Brazil's banking system, healthcare and e-gov were chosen as focus points to show a degree of world class quality and adaptability. Rather than selling itself as another potential India – where companies have thrived in wholesale outsourcing services, Brazil IT meant to differentiate Brazilian IT service and software developers as 'value aggregators' in a different league, providing services with business expertise capable of developing and implementing creative, 'out of the box' solutions.

Brazil IT's inaugural participation at a large trade show in the USA happened at the Gartner ITxpo in 2004, bringing nearly 30 Brazilian IT companies to the First Timer pavilion. The participation was so successful from the companies' point of view – measured by new contacts made and interest from Gartner Symposium participants – that the group returned in 2005 with a much larger presence, as Market Place Sponsors, bringing to the event an institutional space to promote knowledge about Brazil IT as well as five individual booths occupied by individual Brazilian IT companies – some with an established presence in the USA and others still considering whether the time was right to enter the American market.

In 2006, Brazil IT's strategy evolved yet again to participation in several Gartner events, many of these focused on specific industry segments. Investment in marketing activities grew alongside with investment in more events and included a re-launch of the Brazil-IT website in 2005, a new video, and – in 2006 – the launch of Brazil IT News, a newsletter about Brazil IT which is distributed at trade shows and sent to the growing list of IT executives who have made contact with Brazil IT during participation at Gartner events over the last 3 years. The industry-focused Gartner events allow the presentation of Brazil IT success cases to small but captive audiences of key IT executives. In June 2006, Brazil IT was awarded 'Best Enterprise Vendor Presentation' at IT ChannelVision. At the 2006 Gartner ITxpo, Brazil IT jumped onto the renewable energy bandwagon and presented a case study on how IT (software) has been successfully used in Brazil to allow the low cost production of flex-fuel cars. It is a case with global ramifications that is not well known abroad, where many still believe that the flex-fuel versus optimal engine equation must be resolved through hardware.

Parallel to the work of Brazil IT coordinated by APEX Brasil, other industry associations in Brazil stepped up their work. Of note, Actminds, a group of about 10 small Brazilian IT companies based in Campinas, in the outskirts of Sao Paulo, opened its first US representation, joining larger companies such as Stefanini, Politec and CPM, some of which already have multiple locations in the USA serving dozens of clients. Other IT clusters, such as in the northeastern state of Paraíba and Pernambuco, experienced sustained IT exports growth in the range of 30–50% per year, according to APEX Brazil, and were able to bring an increasing number of smaller companies that had never considered going abroad to participate in trade shows. The Brazilian Association of Software & Service Export Companies, Brasscom, created in 2004 by Brazil's six largest IT service providers CPM, Datasul, DBA, Itautec, Politec and Stefanini, with the objective of fomenting IT exports, has now grown to include Accenture, HSBC, Promon, Braxis, BRQ, CenPRA, Sun and TIVIT, and hired A.T. Kearney to study the best alternatives and opportunities in the international market, as well as the roadmap to Brazil's insertion in it.

More and more Brazilian companies are achieving the coveted capability maturity model (CMM) rating, increasing industry credibility. Individually, companies such as Stefanini, CPM and Politec, which are among most active in the US market, are earning independent recognition: in 2006, Stefanini IT Solutions was ranked among the top ten end-to-end global outsourcing vendors in a survey by the Brown & Wilson Group, and CPM and Politec were included in the Global Services GS100, a prestigious annual list of the world's 100 most innovative service providers, as selected by Global Services magazine.

As a whole, these initiatives and successes reflect the positive results of a joint, if not always coordinated, will to grow Brazil's IT industry abroad, in order to reach the $2 billion export target set by the Brazilian government in 2004. To keep the momentum going, APEX Brasil is continuing its support of the Brazil IT program for the years of 2007 and 2008, stepping up once again trade show participation and publicity efforts, while demanding increasing investment from Brazil's private sector in promotion activities.

*****

Introduction

Country-of-origin and national identity are two related fields that underpin the concept of nation branding; yet, rarely have the two fields been integrated. In this chapter, we identify the areas of commonality between country-of-origin and national identity and relate them to the differentiating power of branding that forms the basis of nation-brand development. A conceptual framework for nation branding is presented in the form of the category flow model, drawing upon key issues identified in the twin fields of country-of-origin and national identity. The country case insight on Brazil shows how a nation can promote an economic sector that does not necessarily coincide with existing stereotypes of the nation, whilst the practitioner insight focuses on the paradox of a product and a national icon.

National identity and country-of-origin: Areas of commonality

The national identity literature has rarely been drawn upon by country-of-origin researchers. This is surprising, in that many of the determinants of country-of-origin image perceptions are grounded in the cultural, social and political contexts that constitute national identity. Existing country-of-origin research has largely focused upon the effects of 'Made In' labels on consumer decision-making, without seeking to examine the cultural dimensions of national identity that contribute to country image. Papadopoulos and Heslop [1] point out that the vast majority of product-country image studies have asked respondents to assess the *products* of various *countries*, equating the results with the countries' images – which, of course, they do not. It is a weakness of much country-of-origin research that the construct of country image has been approached in such a narrow way, making simplistic equations between product image and country image. Country image is determined by a far broader mix of factors than a country's products and services alone.

By taking into consideration determinants of national identity such as the invention of tradition, the role of education and sport, it is possible to provide a richer and more culturally informed basis from which to construct marketing strategies related to the branding of nations. The implications of national identity for marketing strategy have rarely been addressed in the country-of-origin literature; yet, the trend towards country branding will make such integration-of-identity issues into marketing strategy imperative. In an increasingly globalized economy, nations that fail to plan the strategic management of their nation-brand may struggle to compete with nations that take a more pro-active approach to this issue. Some of the common constructs to be found in the areas of national identity and country-of-origin are shown in Figure 6.1. These constructs play an important role in nation branding, influencing country image formation processes and providing the context within which nation-brand strategy is developed.

The intersection of the common constructs between national identity and country-of-origin (Figure 6.1) can be located in the general domain of culture. 'Culture' is a term with different meanings for different people. It will be helpful to consider how culture has been defined, in order to clarify how we may consider expressions of culture as a determinant of country image perceptions and as a significant component of a nation-brand. Danesi and Perron [2] define culture as 'a way of life based on a signifying order' passed along from generation to generation. The term *signifying order* referred to by Danesi and Perron is the aggregate of the *signs* (words, gestures, visual symbols, etc.), *codes* (language, art, etc.) and *texts* (conversations, compositions, etc.) that a social group creates and uses in order to carry out its daily life routines and to plan its

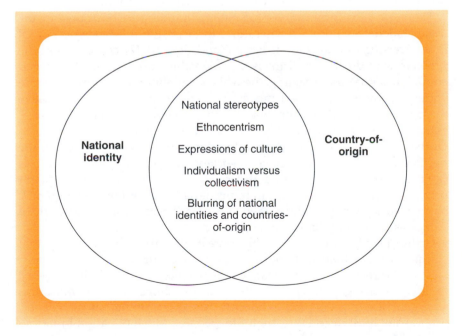

Figure 6.1
Common constructs in national identity and country-of-origin

activities for the future. Other definitions of culture that have relevance to national identity and country-of-origin are provided by Goodenough [3], who states that culture is a set of beliefs or standards, shared by a group of people, which help the individual decide what is, what can be, how to feel, what to do and how to go about doing it. A similar definition of culture is given by Child and Kieser [4], whose definition is given in anthropological vocabulary but which could also be viewed in terms of marketing segmentation. Child and Kieser define culture as patterns of thought and manners that are widely shared; however, they also emphasize that the boundaries of the social collectivity within which this sharing takes place are problematic, and therefore, it may make as much sense to refer to a class or regional culture as to a national culture. From the above definitions of culture, it can be seen that many hitherto under-examined aspects of culture have direct relevance to the creation of nation-branding campaigns, in that a country's image is formed largely by its culture and not solely by consumer perceptions of a country's products or services. This view is largely echoed by Kotler and Gertner [5] who contend that a country's image results from its geography, history, proclamations, art and music, famous citizens and other features.

In the context of organizations, Handy [6] states that a culture cannot be precisely defined, for it is something that is perceived, something felt. According to Handy, factors that influence culture and structure for an organization include history and ownership; size; technology; goals and objectives; the environment and the people. It can therefore be seen that a nation-branding strategy must take into consideration issues pertaining to organizational culture as well as the more obvious manifestations of popular culture that tend to receive more media attention.

There are also implications for nation branding to be found in the organizational identity (OI) literature. In an insightful discussion of OI in a diversified organization, Barney and Stewart [7] contend that the problem with diversified firms is that the value-based OI must be broad enough to signal convergent goals while clear enough to support a wide variety of knowledge-based means (i.e., core competencies) to achieve those goals. The authors' conclusion is that in order to generate the necessary breadth of values, highly diversified firms may have to create an OI that is defined in terms of moral philosophy – a statement about the right and wrong ways to behave in society and in a company. Managers can then take these moral imperatives and apply them in managing their particular subsidiary business. In terms of nation branding, a nation may be viewed as a highly diversified organization requiring a breadth of values as defined by Barney and Stewart.

Griffin [8] places culture in the context of tourism by affirming that culture is more than just the heritage of a destination and that heritage is the remains of the past, whereas culture is the living essence of it, comprising heritage (streetscapes, buildings, events); museums and galleries (ancient and modern); arts (performing, music, dance, drama) and lifestyle (daylife, nightlife, people). Much of nation-branding strategy constitutes an effort to embrace both the past heritage and the present living culture alluded to by Griffin, so that outdated images do not obscure consumer perceptions from what may be vibrant modern societies.

■ Branding's differentiating power

At this point, it is useful to reiterate the nature and impact of branding techniques alluded to in Chapters 1–3. We focus here on some of the salient characteristics of branding that may usefully be applied in a nation-branding context. Governments around the world are turning to branding techniques to differentiate their nations on the global stage and also to give themselves a competitive edge over rival countries with which they must compete in both international and domestic markets [9–16]. Many scholars and practitioners have defined the nature and impact of branding. Keller [17], for example states that a brand is a product but one that adds other dimensions that differentiate it in some way from other products designed to satisfy the same need; these differences may be rational and tangible and related to product performance of the brand, or symbolic, emotional and intangible and related to what the brand represents. Aaker and Joachimsthaler [18] also acknowledge the differentiating impact of branding and assert that the key to most strong brands is brilliant execution that bursts out of the competitive clutter, provides a boost to the brand and creates a cumulative impact over time.

Kapferer [19] echoes the notion of branding's cumulative impact over time by positing that along with R&D, a consumer orientation, an efficiency culture, employee involvement, and the capacity to change and react quickly, brands are one of the very few strategic assets available to a company that can provide a sustainable competitive advantage. Riezebos [20] shares this view and states that within marketing circles there is now a greater awareness that brands represent not only a financial but also a strategic value for the company. In an interesting study based on the premise that there has been a dearth of research into how branding principles may apply in the services sector as compared with the product sector, De Chernatony and Dall Olmo [21] contend that branding principles are common between products and services at the conceptual level and that in either sector, brands must be developed as the link mirroring the set of functional and emotional values created by the company and the way these are perceived by consumers. The CBBE perspective argues that a brand is something that resides in the minds of consumers [22], and governments around the world are taking an increasingly active approach to managing their nation-brands, so that what resides in the minds of consumers is a more favourable set of perceptions than would be the case if governments left national reputation to stereotype and cliché.

Practitioner Insight

Greek olive oil – The paradox of a product and a national icon

Anthony Gortzis
Chairman of One Team Consultancy; Vice-President of the Hellenic Management Association

In Greece, olive oil is a sacred product. The olive tree is the symbol of the Greek landscape. At the same time, it is strongly linked to Greek antiquity when the branches of the olive trees were used to crown the winners of the Olympic games. Even the Greek Orthodox religion gave a central role to olive oil that is used in many religious practices, as for example in the baptism service. In all its preciousness, olive oil in Greece is paradoxically a commodity.

Greece is the third country in the world in terms of the quantity of olive oil produced. Greek production not only covers the needs of the country but a large quantity is also exported. Greek olive oil is very recognizable because of its deep green colour and its balanced taste. Greeks are very negative towards consuming olive oils from other countries. Within Greece, the majority of olive oil that is consumed is bought in bulk, straight from the producer. The branded olive oil market makes up approximately 30% of the quantities sold and consumed in Greece. Greeks have the highest per capita consumption of olive oil – approximately 13 kg annually. Consumer benefits that have an appeal beyond the domestic Greek market and that are also relevant to international markets are as follows:

Health: The Mediterranean diet, famous for its health benefits, is very strongly linked to olive oil. Therefore, the perception is that olive oil contributes to longevity. For individual olive oil brands, the problem with this concept is the fact that it is linked to olive oil as a category rather than a specific brand.

Origin: In Greece, there are various olive oil-producing areas. The climate and conditions in each area can lead to olive oil of different tastes. The importance of origin for olive oil has been acknowledged by the European Union through its 'protected designation of origin' (PDO) symbol, which guarantees that the olive oil is extracted from a specific variety of olives, cultivated in a specific geographical area. The rationale behind establishing the PDO symbol is twofold – first, to ensure that farmers and producers are fairly rewarded for producing high-quality products, and second, to provide a guarantee to consumers that they have purchased an authentic, high-quality product.

Taste: This is a step further than the origin concept because it focuses directly on the issue of different taste profiles. Furthermore, it is something that a brand can ensure rather than a generic characteristic of the olive oil category. For example, one olive oil brand variant was launched as an extra virgin olive oil of strong, ripe taste from the Peloponnese. With this product, the brand catered to consumers who appreciate strong-tasting olive oil. At the same time, the Peloponnese is an important point of reference as it is an area that is famous for its olive oil.

As can be seen, Greek olive oil is much more than just a commodity – the paradox is that this product which appears to be just a commodity is, in reality, a symbol of national identity for Greece as well. Greek olive oil has been recognized both by consumers and also by the European Union (through its PDO symbol) for its outstanding high quality. In the coming years, Greek olive oil will be highlighting its country-of-origin much more than it has done in the past. The importance of olive oil to the Greek economy was acknowledged in April 2005 by the country's Economy Minister, George Alogoskoufis, who announced a plan to improve the branding of Greece's olive oil supported by a budget of €5 million. The Minister declared that 'the aim is that olive oil will be one of the vehicles for the promotion of Greece, tourism and Greek products in general' (Hatzidakis, 2006). Olive oil as a symbol of Greece's national identity should therefore be well positioned to capitalize on the high profile that the nation-brand of Greece obtained during not only the Athens 2004 Olympics, but also during the Greek football team's amazing triumph in the European Football Championship in the same year. Greek olive oil – the fusion of a national icon, positive country-of-origin effect and a great product.

■ Reference

Hatzidakis, G. (2006) 'Greece Targets Olive Oil Branding to Help Boost Demand, Economy', http://www.bloomberg.com, updated April 17, 2006.

*****

■ Nation branding conceptual framework

Based on some of the key issues in branding, COO, and national identity discussed in Chapters 1–5 and integrating these with the original country case insights, academic perspectives and practitioner insights that appear throughout the chapters of this book, the conceptual framework embodied in the category flow model shown in Figure 6.1 proposes a network of relationships amongst nation-branding antecedents, properties and consequences. As can be seen from Figure 6.2, the numerous possible antecedents of the nation-branding construct have been grouped

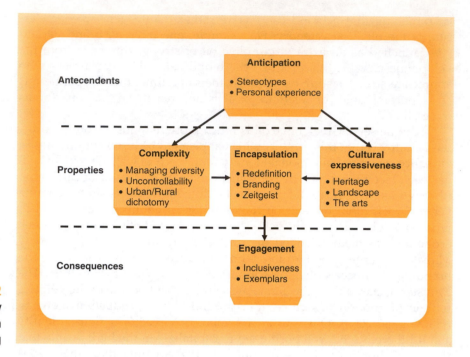

Figure 6.2
The category flow
model of nation
branding

into the category of 'anticipation'; the properties of the nation-branding construct include the categories of 'complexity', 'encapsulation' and 'cultural expressiveness'; whilst the consequences of the construct are presented in the category of 'engagement'.

The category flow model suggests a sequential flow from an initial category of anticipation to two further categories, complexity and cultural expressiveness. Complexity and cultural expressiveness comprise those elements of the nation-brand construct that require encapsulation through the development of a nation-brand strategy in order to achieve engagement, the ultimate stage in this conceptual framework for nation branding.

The category of anticipation represents the initial category in the model. This category derives from the existing consumer perceptions of the nation, before any attempts to consciously create a nation-brand. These perceptions must be analysed and understood as an initial step in the nation-branding process in order to gain an awareness of the stereotypes and personal experience that individuals draw on in forming their perceptions of the nation. The antecedents of anticipation may be based on superficial stereotyping, misinformation or isolated personal experience, none of which may truly reflect the essence of the nation-brand. Therefore, two further categories have been conceptualized in order to reflect the multi-faceted nature of nation branding, lifting the construct above the facile stereotypes that can blight perceptions of a country's image.

The category of complexity acknowledges the uncontrollability of many of the factors that impact upon the nation-brand, such as political events, war, natural disasters, the behaviour of prominent citizens, the performance of national sports teams and so on. This category also contains the related concepts of managing diversity and the urban/rural dichotomy that exists in most countries.

The category of cultural expressiveness encompasses cultural elements such as the arts, language and history as well as landscape, which can play a significant role in the formation of national identity. A nation-brand that did not acknowledge and incorporate these cultural elements would be a shallow, overtly commercially driven artifice, unlikely to secure engagement from its stakeholders.

The categories of complexity and cultural expressiveness thus recognize and encompass the rich, complex and multi-faceted nature of the nation-brand. These two categories flow into, and are assimilated by, the category of encapsulation. It is within the category of encapsulation that explicit branding techniques emerge. By acknowledging the complexity of the processes involved in the nation-brand construct, and by integrating into the nation-brand, a high degree of cultural expressiveness, marketers can then seek to encapsulate the essence of the nation in a multi-faceted yet coherent nation-brand. Such encapsulation entails redefinition of the nation-brand values in harmony with the prevailing zeitgeist. This demands a managerial skill set and a level of cultural awareness far exceeding that required when branding a PSC brand. Once encapsulation has been achieved, from this should flow the final category, engagement. Without engagement from a wide range of stakeholders, little success can be expected for the nation-brand. The relationship between encapsulation and engagement suggests a linkage between the effectiveness with which the nation-brand redefines and brands itself in the context of the prevailing zeitgeist, and the subsequent level of engagement that may be achieved in support of the nation-brand. Manifestations of such engagement may be perceived in terms of the degree of stakeholder inclusiveness achieved by the nation-brand, the existence of motivating exemplars, and a reasonable level of transparency in the development and management of the nation-brand.

The categories of the model and their constituent elements are discussed below.

Anticipation: Stereotypes and personal experience

In terms of antecedents of the nation-branding construct, the category of anticipation focuses on the expectations that consumers have of a certain nation, what is hoped for from the nation and what consumers are prepared for. Disconfirming such expectations is a risky strategy. However, if the existing stereotypes of a nation are negative, then the nation-brand must be managed in such a way that these stereotypes can evolve in

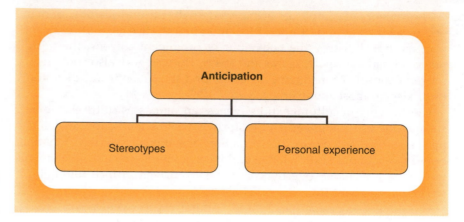

Figure 6.3
'Anticipation'
category

a more positive direction. Therefore, an understanding of the concepts underpinning the category of anticipation is required (Figure 6.3).

The concepts of 'stereotypes' and 'personal experience' constitute the elements of the category of 'anticipation'. The issue of stereotypes is one of the common constructs identified in both the country-of-origin and the national identity literatures [23–25], whilst personal experience has recently attracted attention in the country-of-origin literature as one of the potential determinants of country image [26]. Stereotypical perceptions tend usually to be of a negative nature, and this can present a problem to nations attempting to enhance their reputations amongst external audiences. Effective nation-brand management seeks to counter the potentially damaging caricatures that national stereotypes can embody. In his academic perspective (see Chapter 10), Prof. Stephen Brown observes that 'nation branding strategies are moving beyond hackneyed stereotypes'. Hackneyed stereotypes are insulting to those on the receiving end, tedious to more well-informed observers and possibly detrimental to the nation's economic welfare, and therefore, it is not surprising that governments are increasingly using branding techniques to overcome such stereotypes. Bolivia, for example has long suffered from an image of misery and poverty that has obscured the richness of the country's culture and nature, and a coordinated nation-branding campaign represents a potential means to replace the old negative image with a more positive one (see country case insight on Bolivia, Chapter 7).

It is important, however, to recognize that stereotyping is not always negative. The anticipated imagery associated with a nation can very often be positive. In terms of developing the nation-brand, the conceptual issue centres upon how to harness the positive anticipated imagery without allowing the nation-brand to become pigeonholed by a too narrow range of associations. Nation branding requires an acknowledgment, but then surpassing, of anticipated imagery.

The second concept within the category of anticipation, 'personal experience', represents an important aspect of the nation-branding construct. Personal experience can range from visits by an individual to a particular country to personal interactions with citizens of other nations. Personal experience can also derive from the consumption of products or services from a particular country, which underlines the importance for export promotion agencies to support the international marketing activities of the country's exporters. Switzerland has taken an innovative approach in this regard. In response to research demonstrating that external audiences perceived Switzerland to be weak in terms of one particular attribute – 'Strong influence of citizens on political decisions' – the Swiss Confederation decided to finance Research Chairs on federalism in foreign universities to explain and promote the Swiss federal system (see case county insight on Switzerland, Chapter 4). In this way, foreign students and academics may revise existing negative perceptions of one aspect of Switzerland's governance through the personal experience of interacting on a regular basis with academics explaining and promoting the Swiss federal system.

Complexity: Uncontrollability, the urban–rural dichotomy and managing diversity

The intricacy and convoluted nature of nation branding presents a major challenge to marketers wishing to develop a successful nation-brand. The complexity of a nation-brand is far greater than that of a PSC brand because of the multi-faceted character of the nation-brand and also the multitude of stakeholders whose concerns and interests must be taken into consideration (Figure 6.4).

Managing diversity is a critical component of the nation-brand construct. With increasing global integration, there are now higher levels of migration across national boundaries, leading to far greater heterogeneity in many nations' populations than existed previously. Cultural and social diversity poses an important challenge to the application of branding techniques in developing a consistent message about the nation. Moreover, the diversity of organizations involved in nation-branding activities represents a considerable managerial challenge in terms of achieving effective coordination and avoiding wasteful duplication of effort. Finally, the wide range of different audiences for the nation-brand poses yet further challenges in managing diversity.

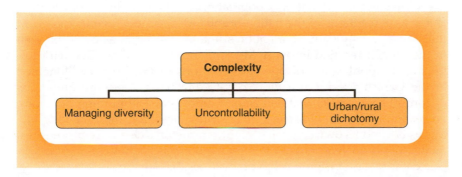

Figure 6.4
'Complexity' category

All nations have to contend with a diversity of internal stakeholders as well as a diversity of external audiences. De Chernatony has noted that there are 'numerous, powerful stakeholders seeking to influence the nature of the nation-brand which has to appeal to diverse stakeholders' (see academic perspective, Chapter 1). Switzerland is one country that has recognized that the diversity of issues relating to the promotion of the country leads to a proliferation of agencies and organizations focusing on different aspects of the country's promotion, and that a coordinating organ needed to be created to optimize the overall promotion of the nation (see country case insight on Switzerland, Chapter 4). In large, ethnically diverse nations, the challenge of managing diversity assumes even greater proportions. In India, for instance, it has been stated that 'despite a mixture of creeds that have longer standing rivalries than some in the Middle East, India has managed to present a united front; its president has gone as far as to discuss nation branding to its domestic audience' (Jack Yan, practitioner insight, Chapter 7).

The strategies adopted by individual nations in order to manage diversity vary according to the specific needs of each country. Estonia, for example has developed a nation-brand model that takes this diversity into account and that uses a series of coordinated and reinforcing messages that can be used by Estonia's different public and private sector organizations when addressing specific audiences (see case country insight on Estonia, Chapter 9). As a general principle that holds for all nations regardless of size, the application of CRM technology and techniques is essential if nations are to successfully manage their diverse stakeholders and audiences. CRM expert Francis Buttle states that 'any functionality that marketing, sales and service personnel want to enable them to understand, service and satisfy a nation's many customers effectively and efficiently is available in today's CRM systems' (see academic perspective, Chapter 3).

The concept of uncontrollability is related to that of managing diversity. The greater the diversity of the nation, the less controllable are its constituent elements and the more challenging it will be to develop a consistent, widely accepted nation-brand. Brands in any sector of the economy are subject to the impacts of unexpected environmental factors. However, nations are subject to a far wider range of impacting factors than individual PSC brands, given that the behaviour and actions of every member of the nation's population are potentially a contributing factor to perceptions of the nation-brand. Also, sudden events can erupt that can seriously damage a nation's image overnight, as could be seen in the violent reaction in many Moslem countries against Denmark following the publication of offensive cartoons of the Prophet Mohamed in the Danish press. On a more day-to-day basis, there are numerous uncontrollable factors that can impact upon nation-branding activities. For example, Egypt's Business Image Unit identified the following factors as beyond its own control: corruption, customs clearance procedures, quality of products, sclerosis of politics and infrastructure amongst others (see country case insight on Egypt, Chapter 2).

The urban/rural dichotomy refers to the gulf that can exist between urban and rural manifestations of the nation. Managing this dichotomy in such a way that the urban and rural appeal and imagery of the nation complement rather than contradict each other is clearly a complex task. The presence of a nation-branding coordinating body, for example would help prevent the nation's image being dominated by traditional rural imagery as is often promoted by national tourism organizations, to the detriment of also positioning the nation as a desirable place for companies to invest (for which more suitable imagery would focus on modern infrastructure, cutting edge technology and so on rather than bucolic rural imagery).

A solution to the dilemmas posed above in terms of managing diversity and uncontrollability may be found in the development of a nation-brand strategy that adopts and implements the basic marketing technique of segmentation. A crude, monolithic approach to branding the nation would fail because it would lack sensitivity to the specific needs and wants of clearly identified sectors. The bases for market segmentation that may be employed by the nation-brand are diverse and limited only by the imagination of the marketers involved in managing the nation-brand. Possible segmentation variables that have been identified in the country-of-origin literature include consumer ethnocentrism [27], gender [28] and segmentation along cultural rather than geopolitical lines [29]. Whichever segmentation variables are selected, it is important that the nation-brand frames an appropriate appeal to the selected market. Ignoring this important consideration can lead to ineffective use of resources.

Cultural expressiveness: Heritage, landscape and the arts

Heritage, landscape and the arts are the constituent concepts of the category of cultural expressiveness. Anholt [30] has argued that successful nation branding requires the integration of a country's cultural and artistic expression in order to achieve unique and sustainable differentiation. The category of cultural expressiveness reflects this proposition in terms of the three concepts in this category, namely heritage, landscape and the arts (Figure 6.5).

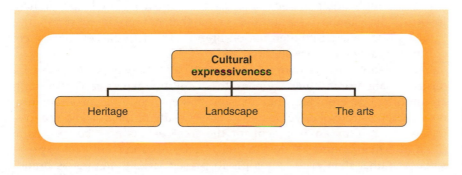

Figure 6.5
Cultural expressiveness category

'Heritage' as a concept encompasses issues such as a country's history, traditions and architecture. The challenge in this respect is to develop a modern nation-brand, with resonance for contemporary audiences, without throwing away the heritage that has given rise to the current nation. Leading international consultancy firm Interbrand took this into consideration when developing a nation-brand for Estonia, by seeking to bring Brand Estonia to life in a way that reflected the country's heritage, unique qualities and what the country has to offer the world (see country case insight on Estonia, Chapter 9).

'Landscape' is treated in the present analysis as a concept rather than merely a physical presence because of the extremely powerful emotional and symbolic value that is placed upon landscape by many people. This supports Gray's contention [31] that landscape and geology play a defining role in the formation of national identity. Nepal and Bolivia are two countries for whom their unique, beautiful landscapes constitute key elements of their respective nation-brands (see academic perspective, Chapter 2; country case insight, Chapter 7). However, there is a need to ensure that an exaggerated focus upon traditional rural imagery does not obscure the fact that a country can have tourist-attracting scenery as well as a vibrant modern economy that is also an attractive destination for inward investment and so on.

The third and final concept in the category of cultural expressiveness is 'the arts'. Several elements of the arts that play an important role in the creation of national identity, for example literature, music and other cultural artefacts. Literature and music are important elements of cultural expressiveness. However, the individualistic, creative temperament normally associated with those active in the creative arts does not sit easily with structured marketing campaigns. Considerable hostility from writers and musicians can be predicted if they were seen to be being dragooned into acting as cultural representatives of the nation. Therefore, a challenge exists for those involved in developing the nation-brand strategy with respect to how to integrate expressions of culture such as literature and music without doing so in a crude and manipulative manner. Japan's nation-branding efforts provide an illustration of how a country's cultural assets – in this case, primarily music, movies and food culture – can be leveraged as part of an overall strategy to improve the country's image and reputation (country case insight, Chapter 9).

It is through organizations such as the British Council, the French Institute, the Goethe Institute and so on that nations incorporate cultural expressiveness into their nation-brands. The activities of some such cultural organizations are summarized in Table 6.1.

Every nation has its own idiosyncratic cultural expressions, and in terms of nation-brand management, these cultural expressions represent an important differentiator that decision-makers need to incorporate into nation-brand strategy development. State subsidy of the arts and the fostering of a healthy environment for the creative arts may be seen as a more effective manner of developing a nation-brand's cultural expressiveness rather than crude attempts to present artistic figures as brand

Table 6.1 Vehicles of cultural expressiveness		
Nation	**Arts Organization**	**Activities**
France	French Institute	French language classes; programmes of French films; multi-media libraries; personal appearances by French cultural figures
Germany	Goethe Institute	Promotes the study of German abroad and encourages international cultural exchange; fosters knowledge about Germany by providing information on its culture, society and politics
United Kingdom	British Council	Connects people with learning opportunities and creative ideas from the UK to build lasting relationships around the world; emphasis on English language teaching and studying in the UK

ambassadors for the nation. Organizations such as the French Institute, Goethe Institute and the British Council play a crucial role in promoting their respective nation's culture.

Encapsulation: Redefinition, branding and zeitgeist

Encapsulation may be viewed as a crucial element in the nation-brand construct. Given the diversity and multifaceted nature of nations, it is necessary to encapsulate an appropriate set of brand characteristics that can be communicated in a clear and consistent way to the target audience. Without a conscious process of encapsulation, there is the danger that an incoherent babble of contradictory messages could be sent out by the nation-brand.

Redefinition of the nation, branding and integration and awareness of zeitgeist are the constituent concepts of the category of 'encapsulation'. The category of encapsulation focuses on the requirement for a nation-brand to compress and capture a diverse range of brand values, and at the same time to tap into the prevailing zeitgeist, which is one of the concepts underpinning this category. We have defined a nation-brand as *the unique, multi-dimensional blend of elements that provide the nation with culturally grounded differentiation and relevance for all of its target audiences.*

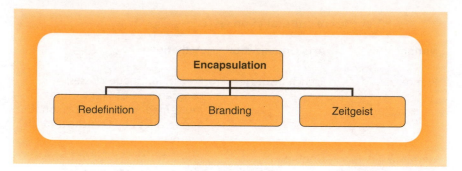

Figure 6.6
'Encapsulation'
category

This definition acknowledges the multi-faceted nature of the nation-brand and the consequent challenge that exists for marketers seeking to encapsulate this in a consistent, clearly differentiated way (Figure 6.6).

Redefinition, one of the concepts underpinning the category of encapsulation, refers to the efforts that can be made to actively redefine the ways in which the nation wishes to present itself to internal and external audiences. It focuses on the need for nations to consciously redefine their values and decide on which values they wish to project, both internally and externally. This is a central tenet of nation branding, the contention that if a nation does not actively define itself, then others will define the nation through stereotyping and myths that very often are negative and derogatory [32]. Russia is one country that found itself in need of redefinition during the 1990s, a period in which the country suffered a crisis of self-identification and an associated lack of direction regarding its future development (see country case insight on Russia, Chapter 5). Russia has subsequently engaged in a concerted effort to establish a positive reputation on the global stage. Other nations that have experienced the need for redefinition include Bolivia, which has in the past been positioned mainly as an Andean country neighbouring Peru, but which now needs to assert its identity on its own terms rather than as just a next-door neighbour to Peru (see country case on Bolivia, Chapter 7), and the much larger Brazil, which needed to redefine itself as a credible and attractive nation in the global IT services sector (see country case on Brazil, Chapter 6).

The process of redefinition needs to be made manifest through branding, the second of the concepts underpinning the category of encapsulation. One could argue that the task of branding always concerns encapsulation of values, but when applied to such a rich and diverse entity as a nation, this represents a particularly difficult challenge. According to De Chernatony, the concept of brand can be applied to nations in that the brand concept represents 'a cluster of values that enables a nation to make a promise about a unique and welcomed experience' (see academic perspective, Chapter 1). For some nations, there is the added complication posed by a degree of ambiguity regarding the country's status as a nation – Northern Ireland, for example has a debatable nation-status, as well as unfortunate associations with a number of undesirable attributes (see academic perspective, Chapter 10). The identification of a set of positive attributes upon which to build a strong brand can be seen in the case of the ongoing Brazil IT campaign mainly targeting the US market, a campaign in which the following key attributes have been utilized: Brazil's strong domestic IT market, cultural and business environment similarities to the USA, geographical proximity and time zone compatibility, geopolitical stability, and the creative power differential of Brazilian IT engineers (see country case on Brazil, Chapter 6).

As was identified in Chapter 4, country images are dynamic rather than static, and this may be regarded as a motivating factor for marketers attempting to improve their country image perceptions through a nation-branding strategy. Given that country images are not fixed, there is no excuse for a fatalistic attitude towards managing country image through the use of appropriate branding techniques.

The third concept in the category of encapsulation is 'zeitgeist', which is closely related to the first concept of 'redefinition' in that the development of the nation-brand is an ongoing process that must, as is the case with many PSC brands, adapt to global economic and political developments, evolving social trends and changing market conditions. The concept of zeitgeist is the third of the concepts constituting the category of encapsulation. Zeitgeist has been defined [33] as 'the defining spirit or mood of a particular period of history'. Although zeitgeist is a difficult concept to identify exactly, it represents an essential concept in the nation-brand construct because nation branding does not operate in a vacuum. The social trends and phenomena contributing to zeitgeist require to be monitored and taken into consideration if the nation-brand is to have resonance and relevance within society at large.

Certain countries may be better positioned than others to exploit the prevailing zeitgeist. For example, the consumer trend towards natural and organic food and drink chimes happily with the country-of-origin connotations possessed by nations that have a competitive advantage in those sectors. In this case, the implication for the development of a nation-brand would be to incorporate the brand value of 'naturalness' into the overall nation-brand. This would allow the nation-brand to leverage the maximum potential from the prevailing zeitgeist in respect of the trend towards natural, pure products. Mounting concern about global warming has raised interest in renewable energy, and the Brazil IT campaign has acted upon this current interest by making a presentation at an international conference on how IT software has been used in Brazil to enable the production of low-cost flex-fuel cars (see country case insight on Brazil, Chapter 6).

A further aspect of zeitgeist that informs the nation-brand construct lies in the prevailing attitude of particular societies towards marketing and branding as desirable or undesirable activities. Although there is a significant backlash against marketing and branding in the developed world, embodied by Naomi Klein's influential anti-branding book *No Logo* [34], this is counter-balanced by the emergence of many countries onto the global stage, which are using branding techniques to differentiate themselves in order to compete in the increasingly globalized economy. It is an ongoing social debate whether branding *per se* is an exploitative process as claimed by Klein, or whether branding in itself is neither good nor bad, it depends upon the use to which the techniques of branding are put. Smaller, less wealthy, and emerging nations are applying branding techniques to their nations in order to establish themselves on the global stage, and if such techniques can help reduce poverty and contribute to sustainable development for these nations, then it would be hard to argue that this application of branding is exploitative.

The nation-brand construct cannot therefore be viewed outwith the context of the prevailing zeitgeist. Should there be considerable resistance to the application of branding techniques to the nation, then the nation-brand strategy will need to focus on the less-visible aspects of nation-brand building such as the development of business networks throughout the world, and the exploitation of the nation's diaspora.

Engagement: Inclusiveness and exemplars

The concepts in the category of 'engagement' are inclusiveness, exemplars and transparency. Engagement is as a major foundation of nation branding. Without engagement, no basis exists for nation branding and no resonance for the nation-brand throughout the wider society beyond the limited confines of political decision-makers and those marketing and branding specialists employed to develop the nation-brand (Figure 6.7).

The concept of 'inclusiveness' refers to the need to establish a level of commitment to the nation-brand from its full range of stakeholders. Such a pact will not occur if some stakeholders feel excluded from the nation-brand. There are, however, difficulties in this respect. It is extremely problematic to try and include every stakeholder in the nation-brand, and high levels of hostility can be expected from those who feel that

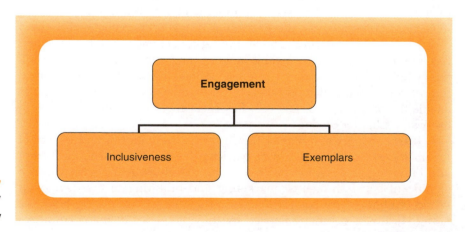

Figure 6.7
'Engagement'
category

the brand does not reflect their own values. The utilization of Delphic brand-visioning technique may be one solution to this dilemma (see academic perspective, Chapter 1). The attempts at taking an inclusive approach to their nation branding by countries such as Egypt, Russia, Iceland and France can be seen in the country case insights in Chapters 2, 5, 8 and 10.

A further aspect of inclusiveness exists with regard to the nation's diaspora. Many nations possess large diasporas. Greece and Italy, for example are two European nations with a large diaspora present in countries as geographically distant as the USA and Australia. Members of diaspora networks are often intensely patriotic, albeit at a distance, and well disposed to helping the homeland in its economic development. There exists, therefore, considerable reputation-building capacity offered by the existence of ready-made diaspora networks that may be harnessed in cultivating the nation-brand. The strategic development of diaspora networks may well represent a more effective manner of building strong nation-brands rather than glossy television-advertising campaigns, for example.

The concept of inclusiveness also needs to be refined in order to distinguish between an ideal state of full inclusiveness, and on the other hand, an actual state of programme-specific inclusiveness. This important distinction is discussed in Chapter 8.

The second concept in the category of engagement is 'exemplars'. Exemplars, in the form of examples of best practice or other types of success stories, are crucial to secure engagement for the nation-brand in the face of apathy, cynicism or hostility. Any nation-branding activity that is funded by public money will find itself under intense scrutiny from the media, and therefore, it is essential to provide some examples of tangible benefits delivered from such branding activity. Also, in order to boost credibility, specific nations will need to provide examples of success and testimonials from relevant sources to bolster the nation-brand's credentials. For example, the New France campaign used testimonials from senior executives in top international corporations such as FedEx, Toyota, Xerox, GE and Sony in order to improve perceptions of France as an attractive proposition for inward investment.

The issue of transparency is closely related to the concept of 'inclusiveness'. Strikingly divergent views may exist regarding the desirability of transparency in the nation-branding process. The issue of transparency therefore represents a key challenge in the development of the nation-brand. If governments or other agents involved in nation-brand development operate in a transparent manner, communicating to the nation the aims and objectives of the nation-brand, will this achieve buy-in to the nation-brand or will it have the opposite effect and unleash a cacophony of competing claims? Lack of transparency could result in few stakeholders buying in to the strategy. On the other hand, a less publicly visible approach to building the nation-brand may be taken in order to avoid a storm of dissenting voices from derailing the nation-brand strategy before the strategy can deliver its first benefits.

Country Case Insight – Germany

Branding Germany – Managing internal and external country reputation

Gianfranco Walsh[1] and Klaus-Peter Wiedmann[2]
[1]*Professor of Marketing and Electronic Retailing, University of Koblenz-Landau and* [2]*Professor of Marketing, Leibniz University of Hanover and Reputation Institute Country Director for Germany*

At this point in time, Germany is faced with the challenge of finding ways of presenting and representing its past economic, social, cultural achievements alongside its modern achievements in ways that appeal to internal and external stakeholders. In the summer of 2006, Germany hosted the football World Cup. The German philosopher Gunter Gebauer mused that the World Cup gave Germans a glimpse of who they want to, and could, be. Previously touted as dour and humourless, during the World Cup Germany came across as fun-loving and friendly. The German Foreign Secretary, Frank-Walter Steinmeier, said that although other nations had expected perfect organization from the Germans, the degree of enthusiasm, openness and tolerance during the 4-week-long football spectacle was a surprise. In this context, the British Prime Minister Tony Blair argued the World Cup 'beat all expectations … the old clichés have been replaced by a new, positive and fairer image of Germany'. Indeed, it appears Germans have pulled off a fundamental re-branding of their country.

According to the Anholt Nation Brand Index (2007), Germany is one of the world's top three countries in terms of nation-brand equity. The Anholt Nation Brand Index suggests the brand 'Germany' is worth almost US $4.6 billion, only surpassed by Japan (US $6.2 billion) and the USA (US $17.9 billion). Furthermore, Germany was among the strongest climbers between 2005 and 2006. This has led to a special mention in one of the latest Anholt Reports: 'As the country that hosted a successful Soccer World Cup, it could have expected to experience a boost in its international image. The increase in Germany's score in this period was a respectable 2.3%, enough to move it from 6th place at the end of 2005 to 2nd place in the last two surveys. Until the last quarter of 2006, its year-on-year increase was even higher, over 3%' (Anholt Nation Brand Index 2007, p. 9).

Figures like these suggest that much is to be gained if a country's brand equity is harnessed and its brand is managed effectively. If we accept the notion that Germany shed its old reputation and successfully re-branded itself in the course of a few weeks, we may also render it possible that a comprehensive national branding programme could lead to a sustainable change in Germany's reputation. But, of course, it is a bit short-sighted to believe that successful event marketing might be sufficient to dramatically increase a nation's brand equity. As important as such a globally highly observed sports event might be in creating an effective communications platform, many more activities are necessary to gain convincing and sustainable branding effects. To manage Germany's reputation, it is necessary to gain an understanding of the dimensions of Germany's, or any other county's, reputation from the perspective of internal and external audiences and stakeholders. As a rule, national branding programmes are directed at foreigners (Fan, 2006), aiming to improve one country's reputation in the eyes of the rest of the world. However, it is equally important to create programmes that aim at that country's own people, because in the long-term a nation is perceived also through its individuals.

Nobody doubts the football World Cup organized in Germany was a success. But, what has led the Germans to come out of the shell and to become the people that have been credited for a wonderful sporting event? And what helped to prevent the disaster of nationalistic acts of violence breaking out? We should not forget the decisive warnings about Germany in the run-up to the World Cup, especially about cities in the eastern part of Germany that tourist guidebooks or other media warned about, for example in the 'Rough Guide', 'Frommer's Germany' and 'Cultureshock', the Australian-British tourist guide 'Lonely Planet', the British 'Time out'. 'Skinheads', 'Glatzen', 'Neo Nazis' were introduced to the international audience as a very concrete risk for foreigners.

In the case of nation branding, there is not only one institution that is planning, implementing and controlling a branding strategy. Many institutions, as well as individuals, get involved in such processes, and in the end a nation brand is not only developed through displaying the national flag on different objects or marking products with a 'Made in Germany' sign. The focal point of nation-branding activities is the whole national brand identity that is influenced by

1. the national reality in the past, present and the potential future consisting of the economic, technological, political, cultural and natural infrastructure, the behaviours of all citizens and institutions, all achievements, offerings and artefacts (products, architecture, works of art, etc.),
2. the perceptions of and the associations with the national reality that form brand images relevant to the different internal as well as external stakeholders,
3. the nation's overall reputation as a result of the interplay between the different brand images in relation to reality as well as reflecting the attitudes, and especially the support potentials and supportive behaviours of all relevant stakeholders.

This description of the different components of a nation's brand identity clearly shows that nation brand management is a complex task. It deals with the idea of influencing national reality as well as the images of this reality aiming for an overall reputation, which is helpful for the future development of a nation and its relations to other nations. Against this background, brand management has to be conceptualized as an activity that involves all processes and arrangements geared towards canalizing and supporting developments within the national reality. Moreover, nation-branding strategies have to pay heed to the perceptions of relevant stakeholders that display supportive behaviours to ensure a desired development of a nation from different perspectives (e.g., economic, political, cultural).

Although not one single institution may try to influence such processes and arrangements, we have to take very different goal systems into account when developing nation-branding strategies because without any coordination we may end up in a disjointed incrementalism that is not very effective and efficient. However, in reality, a nation brand will not only be developed consciously. More often than not, no purposeful brand management activities whatsoever take place; nevertheless, brand images will occur because eventually, all perceptions, associations and impressions will contribute towards shaping the nation's brand.

To give a very brief overview over the institutions possibly getting involved in nation-branding processes, we may differentiate between governmental institutions, economic institutions (e.g. companies, associations, trade unions) and social institutions in the areas of science, culture, religion, media, sports, etc. As evidenced in the recent 'Du bist Deutschland' (You are Germany) campaign (see Table CS6.1), two or more of such institutions can collaborate and make a concerted effort

Table CS6.1 Overview over Major Campaigns

Title	Campaign Summary
'Perspektive Deutschland' (Perspective Germany)	*Main focus and objectives*: causing a societal change through public information and discussion, especially aiming for a change of mood, and activating new initiatives. No specific target groups, but only implemented in Germany
	Core components of concept: a) incorporating huge online surveys each year since 2001 identifying and analyzing public opinions about relevant societal issues, b) developing reform proposals, and c) publications, events, etc. *Initiator and partners*: McKinsey, stern, ZDF and WEB.DE; private corporate sponsors and the former President, Richard von Weizäcker as patron *For more information see*: www.perspektive-deutschland.de. Status: ongoing
'Du bist Deutschland' (You are Germany)	*Main focus and objectives*: causinga change of mood, increasing national pride and joy, activating all citizens and institutional representatives to take responsibility for Germany's future and to get active creatively and innovatively. Target groups: all citizens, all national media, important advertising and PR agencies, enterprises, non-business organizations and initiatives. Period of main activities: 2005 and 2006 flanking the football World Cup, but still ongoing as an initiative on a lower level
	Core components of concept: advertising and PR campaigns spread over a wide range of media and planned along a three-step concept – 1. 'detonation': starting with celebrities convinced to take part for nothing, 2. 'widespread

(Continued)

Table CS6.1 (Continued)

Title	Campaign Summary
	effect': motivating all kind of institutions to join in with their own theme and example supported by agencies at no more than cost, and 3. 'communication of success' through presentations, events, articles, etc., also trying to get more and more institutional representatives and citizens involved. Along all three phases an internet platform providing information as well as options for interaction played – and stills plays – a major role
	Initiator and partners: initiated and organized by Bertelsmann A.G., supported by 25 important media companies, joined by numerous business and non-business institutions as well as private citizens over time *For more information see*: www.du-bist-deutschland.de. Status: ongoing, since 2007 on a lower level
'Deutschland – Land der Ideen' (Germany - Land of ideas)	*Main focus and objectives*: strengthen and maintain Germany's reputation as 'Land of Ideas' both within Germany and abroad, especially focussing on: nation of science and culture – the land of poets and thinkers, innovative products 'made in Germany'. Target groups: all citizens within Germany and abroad, but especially concentrated on decision-maker in all kinds of business and non-business institutions achieve their support and willingness to invest in Germany
	Core components of concept: advertising and PR campaigns spread over a wide range of media as well as events, presentations, lectures, publication of books, which support the claim 'Land of Ideas' with historical and present-day evidence, from Gutenberg right up to the present day. Building a network of people and institutions to support all kinds of innovative initiatives, especially new business ventures, flanked by an internet portal to organize information and exchange
	Initiator and partners: German government and commerce and industry, represented by the German Industry Association (BDI) and leading corporations. German President Horst Köhler as patron. FC Deutschland GmbH was founded for the implementation of 'Germany – Land of Ideas' *For more information see*: www.land-der-ideen.de
'Partner für Innovation' (Partner for innovation)	*Main focus and objectives*: establish a well-functioning cooperation between all relevant institutions in business, politics and science to initiate innovation processes, and especially to help to get as soon as possible from ideas to market maturity. Target groups: experts and decision makers in all kind of institutions, and young people as well as small and medium sized companies who might have potential for future success
	Core components of concept: building networks of people and institutions to support all kind of innovative initiatives, especially new business ventures by consulting and venture capital. Some advertising and PR campaigns, but mainly events, presentations, lectures, publication of books, etc., flanked by an internet portal to organize information and exchange
	Initiator and partners: initiated in 2004 by the former Chancellor, Gerhard Schroeder, supported by the Federal Ministry of Economics and Labour, and over 200 companies, unions and other institutions
	For more information see: www.innovationen-fuer-deutschland.de. Status: ongoing.

to improve Germans' perceptions of themselves. Those 'joint ventures' formed together temporarily to realize common projects will be dissolved after having reached their goals.

For example, the initiative 'Germany – Land of Ideas' focusses on different target groups and stakeholders abroad, and continues to try to convey many examples for Germany as a nation of science and culture – the land of poets and thinkers, innovative products 'made in Germany'. The message stands for a world-renowned quality of Germany: its inventiveness and creative passion. There is plenty of historical and present-day evidence of this wealth of ideas, from Gutenberg right up to the present day. Another initiative 'Partner for Innovation' was established to flank and support this initiative. The main purpose is to build up and maintain an effective network to help in particular young scientists, and small and medium-sized companies to develop and implement their ideas.

In sum, a nation brand should not only be seen as a complex symbol, but rather as a very complex brand identity that is the result of a specific national reality, its perceptions and evaluations by many different internal and external stakeholders (brand images), and is characterized by a specific overall reputation containing the 'good will' as well as the 'bad will' of different audiences. To manage a country's reputation, it is necessary to explore and understand gaps between national reality, and the internal and external reputation of a country. The internal view of the country held and to some extent, shared, by a country's citizens may differ from that held by multiple external groups, such as potential foreign investors and tourists to the country. Arguably, effective nation-branding management hinges on establishing a convincing national reality and reducing the perception gap between reality and its perception as well as between internal and external views.

■ Reference

Fan, Y. (2006) Branding the nation: What is being branded? *Journal of Vacation Marketing*, January 1, **12**, 1, 5–14.

*****

■ Summary

Although they have to a large extent be treated separately in the past, country-of-origin and national identity share many common constructs and these constructs infuse the emerging concept and practice of nation branding. Whereas COO research has focused mainly on the effects of the 'Made In' label, national identity examines the essence of nations, their culture and character – those elements which constitute the reality of the nation and which must therefore form the basis of the nation-brand. The category flow model offers a conceptual framework for understanding nation branding, based on a set of interlocking categories including anticipation, complexity, encapsulation, cultural expressiveness and engagement.

■ References

1. Papadopoulos, N. and Heslop, L. (2002) Country equity and country branding: Problems and prospects. *Journal of Brand Management*, **9**, 294–314.
2. Danesi, M. and Perron, P. (1999) *Analyzing Cultures: An Introduction & Handbook*, Indiana University Press, Indiana.
3. Goodenough, W.H. (1971) *Culture, Language and Society*, Modular Publications, **7**, Addison-Wesley, Reading, MA.
4. Child, J. and Kieser, A. (1977) A contrast in British and West German management practices: Are recipes of success culture bound? Paper presented at the *Conference on Cross-Cultural Studies on Organisational Functioning*, Hawaii.
5. Kotler, P. and Gertner, D. (2002) Country as brand, product, and beyond: A place marketing and brand management perspective. *Journal of Brand Management*, **9**, 249–61.
6. Handy, C. (1999) *Understanding Organizations*, Penguin Books, England.
7. Barney, J.B. and Stewart, A.C. (2000) Organizational identity as moral philosophy: Competitive implications for diversified corporations, in *The Expressive Organization: Linking Identity, Reputation, and the Corporate Brand* (M. Schultz, M.J. Hatch and M.H. Larsen, eds.) Oxford University Press, England.
8. Griffin, J. Making the most of culture and tourism, http://www.locum-destination.com/lf2jg.htm (accessed 09 May 2003).
9. Leonard, M. (1997) *Britain™: Renewing Our Identity*, Demos, London.
10. Olins, W. (1999) *Trading Identities: Why Countries and Companies are Taking Each Others' Roles*, The Foreign Policy Centre, London.
11. Gilmore, F. (2002) A country – Can it be repositioned? Spain – the success story of country branding. *Journal of Brand Management*, **9**, 281–93.
12. Gnoth, J. (2002) Leveraging export brands through a tourism destination brand. *Journal of Brand Management*, **9**, 262–80.
13. Chisik, R. (2003) Export industry policy and reputational comparative advantage. *Journal of International Economics*, **59**, 423–51.
14. Gardner, S. and Standaert, M., Estonia and Belarus: Branding the Old Bloc, http://www.brandchannel.com/features (accessed 23 April 2003).
15. Jaworski, S.P. and Fosher, D. (2003) National brand identity & its effect on corporate brands: The nation brand effect (NBE). *Multinational Business Review*, **11**, 99–113.
16. Quelch, J. (2003) The return of the global brand. *Harvard Business Review*, **81**, 22–6.
17. Keller, K.L. (2003) *Strategic Brand Management: Building, Measuring, and Managing Brand Equity*, Second Edition, Prentice Hall, USA.
18. Aaker, D.A. and Joachimsthaler, E. (2000) *Brand Leadership*, Free Press, USA.
19. Kapferer, J.-N. (2004) *The New Strategic Brand Management: Creating and Sustaining Brand Equity Long Term*, Kogan Page, UK.

20. Riezebos, R. (2003) *Brand Management: A Theoretical and Practical Approach*, FT Prentice Hall, UK.
21. De Chernatony, L. and Dall Olmo, F.R. (1999) The Challenge of Financial Services Branding, www7.open.ac.uk/oubs/research/pdf/WP00_6.pdf
22. Kotler, P. and Keller, K.L. (2006) *Marketing Management*, Twelfth Edition, Pearson Prentice Hall, USA.
23. Harrison-Walker, L.J. (1995) The relative effects of national stereotype and advertising information on the selection of a service provider: an empirical study. *Journal of Services Marketing*, **9**, 1, 47–59.
24. Higson, A. (1998) Nationality: National identity and the media, in *The Media: An Introduction* (A. Briggs and P. Golbey, eds.), Longman.
25. Lotz, S.L. and Hu, M.Y. (2001) Diluting negative country of origin stereotypes: A social stereotype approach. *Journal of Marketing Management*, **17**, 105–20.
26. Jaffe, E.D. and Nebenzahl, I.D. (2001) *National Image & Competitive Advantage: The Theory and Practice of Country-of-Origin Effect*, Copenhagen Business School Press.
27. Lantz, G. and Loeb, S. (1996) Country-of-origin and ethnocentrism: An analysis of Canadian and American preferences using social identity theory. *Advances in Consumer Research*, **23**, 374–8.
28. Heslop, L.A. and Wall, M. (1985) Differences between men and women in the country of origin product images. *Administrative Sciences of Canada Proceedings*, Montreal, Canada, pp. 148–58.
29. Duany, J. (2000) Nation on the move: The construction of cultural identities in Puerto Rico and the diaspora. *American Ethnologist*, **27**, 5–26.
30. Anholt, S. (2002) Foreword, special issue: Nation branding. *Journal of Brand Management*, **9**, 229–39.
31. Gray, A. (1997) *Why Scots Should Rule Scotland 1997*, Canongate Books, Edinburgh.
32. Papadopoulos, N. and Heslop, L. (2002) Country equity and country branding: Problems and prospects. *Journal of Brand Management*, **9**, 294–314.
33. *Concise Oxford Dictionary* (1999) Tenth Edition, Oxford University Press, UK.
34. Klein, N. (2000) *No Logo*, Flamingo, London.

PART 3

Ethical and pragmatic issues in nation branding

CHAPTER 7

Ethical imperatives in nation branding

Country Case Insight – Bolivia

Using nation branding to move beyond 'trickle-down tourism': The case of Bolivia

Ximena Alvarez Aguirre[1] and Ximena Siles Renjel[2]
[1]General Director of Discover the World Marketing in Bolivia, former Vice-Minister of Tourism in Bolivia (2004–2005) and
[2]Risk Analyst and Relationship Manager in different industries and sectors in Bolivia and Ecuador

Bolivia lies at the heart of South America. The country, rich in terms of natural resources and diversity, is a fascinating place to visit. From the Amazon to the Andes, the different regions, varied climatic zones and diversity of people offer visitors a wide range of destinations. This cultural and ecological array makes Bolivia a unique place to visit. In terms of nature, the identity that Bolivia has tried to show to the world is based on its unique attractions, including

- Uyuni Salt Flats: This is the biggest salt flat in the world, surrounded by coloured lagoons, exotic rocky formations, diversity of animals, volcanic craters and fumaroles.
- Lake Titicaca: The highest navigable lake in the world is shared with Peru. This lake is famous because it was the centre of culture and religion of all the high-plateau cultures.
- Chiquitania: Jesuit Mission temples that were founded between 1691 and 1767 and have remained intact after hundreds of years.
- Madidi National Park: Considered the door to the Bolivian Amazons, where unique flora and fauna are found. This protected area has the largest biological diversity in the world.
- Colonial Cities: Like Potosi and Sucre, amazing cities that are an example of ancestral cultures.

Bolivia's identity is based on two characteristics: its culture and nature. In terms of culture, the true identity of Bolivia is in its 'ancestral cultures', cultures that have been maintained without any alteration throughout time and that make Bolivia a unique place in comparison with its neighbouring countries. The main characteristic of the Bolivian culture is the respect to the traditions in terms of folklore, clothing, food and all the ancestral traditions of native origins. In terms of nature, the identity of Bolivia is based on its unique natural features such as Uyuni Salt Flats and Madidi National Park, which make the country a unique place to visit.

For many decades, the country has suffered from not being able to show to the world all the beauty, attributes and resources it has, whereas the image that has been portrayed to the outside world is a negative one of poverty and misery. It is important to recognize that Bolivia is a poor country, but it also has different realities that ought to be shown to the world. Bolivia is a rich country in terms of natural resources and has a lot to offer to visitors. However, all the incredible attributes of the country have remained a 'secret' for the rest of the world. The country has suffered from an absence of promotional strategies to show its treasures to potential visitors. This situation has been aggravated because of the social and political uncertainty of recent years, which has threatened the development of the tourism sector of the country. Through adopting a nation-branding campaign focused on the tourism sector, Bolivia may be able to start countering this negative image and begin to create a more positive, balanced and beneficial image.

Bolivia needs to develop a marketing plan in order to create a new image to show to the world an image that highlights the diversity and attractiveness of the country, which would create and/or develop the interest of people all around the world to think about Bolivia as an attractive tourist destination. Tourism has tremendous potential for contributing to the Bolivian economy, but because of various social, political and economic factors, this potential has not yet been realized. According to experts in the field, Bolivia could live from the tourism sector, based on its incredible natural, cultural and historic attractiveness. However, the industry has not yet been properly developed.

Studies have shown that potential tourists have very low levels of awareness about Bolivia as a country and as a tourist destination. Many people do not even know which continent Bolivia is in. One reason for this is that Bolivia as a country has not had clear and sustained marketing strategies, and there has been little involvement and coordinated work between the different stakeholders. Furthermore, few resources have been committed in order to promote the country.

Kotler and Gertner (2002) mention that the image of a country can be related to many things such as history, art, music, etc., but sometimes country image can also be related to societal ills. Unfortunately, it appears that Bolivia is suffering from the latter type of association. The image of Bolivia that has been shown to the world has always been of poverty, and with the recent political and social conflicts, there has also been a negative perception about the country in terms of stability and safety. This point confirms the strong power that the media has on consumers/tourists and how important it is to manage the communication process and to control and measure the intensity of its impact. The perception that many have about Bolivia is associated with generalized perceptions about South America as a continent. Corruption, drugs and a laidback lifestyle feature among the most commonly held perceptions.

The Bolivian Tourism Institute (IBT), which is an independent entity, has made several efforts in order to promote Bolivia to the world. However, in order to more effectively promote the image of Bolivia, there needs to be a clear strategic vision for the development of targeted markets. To date, Bolivia has been positioned mostly as an Andean country, which is connected to Chile and to the ruins of Machupichu in Peru. There has been a so-called 'trickle-down' tourism effect from Peru to Bolivia whereby some tourists visiting Peru have been tempted to add on a visit to Bolivia. However, Bolivia needs to promote itself to the world based on its own attractiveness, and not merely as a next-door neighbour to Peru. In recent years, there has been a boom in the eco-tourism and adventure tourism areas, and Bolivia is uniquely well endowed to be able to benefit from this trend.

In terms of marketing strategies and communication channels, Bolivia has been utilizing a logo and the tag line 'lo autentico aun existe' – 'the authentic still exists' – which is coherent with the country's identity and conveys the main message that Bolivia wants to send to the world, namely that the country offers an authentic experience in terms of nature and culture.

Source: Tourism Vice-Ministry – Bolivia, 2006.

The former Vice-Ministry Tourism authorities developed a website (www.turismobolivia.bo) that provides important and relevant information for tourists. However, following a change of administration, this website has been left adrift. There is a feeling in the tourism industry that there has been a lack of continuity regarding the communication channels and elements that have been utilized.

It is critical for Bolivia to analyse its current situation and take the necessary steps in order to reposition itself in the mind of potential tourists. According to Cromwell (2006), a self-analysis is the starting point of the nation-branding process. Bolivia needs to identify, analyse and understand the internal and external environmental forces. In an internal context or environment, Bolivia needs to be aware of its strengths in order to exploit them but also needs to identify its weaknesses in order to face them and work to overcome them. When referring to the external environment, it is critical for the country to identify the opportunities in the market and take advantage of them, but it is also important to be aware of the threats so as to be prepared to confront them. Table CS7.1 presents some of the internal and external factors which are identified as part of the self-analysis process.

This self-analysis is critical for the country in order to structure the branding process, and as mentioned by Cromwell (2006), it is important because it will help to develop a truthful and believable brand.

Table CS7.1 Internal and External Analysis – Bolivian Tourism Sector

Strengths	Weaknesses
• Unique natural attractions • Distinctive culture • Ancestral history • Inexpensive place to visit	• Lack of resources for the promotion of the tourism industry • Lack of involvement of the different stake-holders • Negative image shown to the world
Opportunities	**Threats**
• Growing interest in eco-tourism all over the world • Attention attracted to the country because of the recent presidential election • Strategic geographic position in South America in order to attract tourists and conventions/conferences	• Strong competition from neighbouring countries in terms of tourist attractiveness • High cost of travelling to South America and within the continent • Volatile political and social situation of the country

■ Conclusion

The level of awareness about Bolivia as a country and as a tourist destination is very low. This, accompanied by the negative image projected to the outside world and the lack of marketing and branding strategies, is making it difficult to position the country in the mind of potential tourists in an international context. For these reasons, it is fundamental first to develop a strategic vision for tourism in the country and to re-define Bolivia's identity and reposition its image, based on a clear view of the target audience whom the country wants to attract. Bolivia is a rich country in terms of its nature and culture, and can take advantage of the opportunities in the market such as the growing interest in eco-tourism and adventure-tourism and focus its efforts in that niche of the market.

It then becomes important to design the strategies to promote the country to the outside world, conveying a clear and real message, which is by developing adequate programmes in order to send a truthful message to create, change and improve the image of Bolivia in an international context. However, this is only going to be possible by having the commitment of the different stakeholders that are involved in the process, which includes not only the government but also the private sector and the country's citizens. This will take time, but it is imperative for the country to take the first steps for the branding or re-branding of Bolivia, which must be a priority in order to augment the economic and social development of the country.

■ References

Cromwell, T. (2006) Why Nation Branding Is Important For Tourism, EastWest Communications. www.eastwestcoms.com [Online] [Last accessed May 27th, 2006].
http://eastwestcoms.com/Why-Nation-Braning-Is-Important-For-Tourism.htm
Kotler. P. and Gertner, D. (2002) Country as brand, product, and beyond: A place marketing and brand management perspective, *Journal of Brand Management*, **9** (4/5), 249–262.
Vice-Ministry of Tourism – Bolivia (2006) (Vice-Ministerio de Turismo de Bolivia) www.desarrollo.gov.bo [Online] [Last accessed on April 24, 2006].
http://www.desarrollo.gov.bo/turismo/Bolivia-Travel/setframeING.htm
http://www.turismobolivia.bo/loader_en.php?n1=1&n2=1&n3=&n4=

*****

■ Introduction

It is impossible to divorce nation branding from a number of ethical imperatives, given that every citizen of a nation is a stakeholder in the nation-brand and is therefore affected by activities connected to the nation-brand. The fact that public funds will almost certainly be allocated to a country's nation-branding strategy means that there will be a high level of critical scrutiny of the strategy. Ethical issues surrounding nation branding include the overall legitimacy of applying brand management techniques to whole nations rather than to mere product brands; who has the right to identify and select nation-brand values; and, ensuring that nation-brand strategy contributes to the nation's sustainable development.

■ The legitimacy of nation-brand management

If nation branding is to become accepted by both governments and citizens, it needs to establish itself as a socially and politically acceptable activity. A key ethical question that must be answered centres on the following issue: If a nation is to be treated as a brand, who has the right to be the nation-brand manager? Evidently, the only individual who can claim the legitimacy of a democratic mandate to fulfil the role of nation-brand manager is the elected head of state. However, few politicians possess the requisite business and marketing skills to perform a brand management role. On the other hand, professional marketers and brand managers possess (at least to some extent) the required skill set, but they do not possess the democratic mandate. This dilemma in itself may lead some to dismiss nation branding as a conceptual dead-end and an exercise in futility.

Such cursory rejection of nation branding would, nonetheless, be short-sighted. The solution to the dilemma of legitimacy can be found in collaborative public–private sector structures and programmes wherein citizens' interests are represented by elected politicians, and commercial interests are represented by industry associations and individual companies. This collaborative model reflects the reality that no single individual can realistically be considered to be the 'nation-brand manager'; instead, the infinitely wide scope of nation-branding activity can only adequately be conducted through an inclusive stakeholder approach.

A further ethical imperative to be taken into consideration when debating the legitimacy of nation-brand management resides in an issue that affects every citizen, namely why should any nation tolerate the perpetuation of inaccurate, outdated, and offensive stereotyping and caricature? If a nation itself does nothing to counter negative stereotypes, then there is nothing to stop the enduring degrading effect that such stereotypes can have. Nations do not have the choice of being branded or not; on the contrary, nations can merely make a simple choice between allowing others to brand the nation – through ignorant stereotyping – or, alternatively, nations can embrace the challenge of projecting a truer, more accurate and more uplifting image of the nation to the rest of the world.

As can be seen in Jack Yan's practitioner insight in this chapter, another ethical justification for nation branding is that it can benefit smaller, less-developed nations that cannot compete with larger, more powerful countries in the global economy. Smaller, emerging nations do not possess the economic, diplomatic and military power of larger nations, but this disadvantage can be confronted through creative coordination of the country's assets – unique culture, environmentally sustainable policies, diaspora networks and so on. Nation branding thus hugely transcends the inanity of crass advertising campaigns, which are incorrectly thought by some to be what nation branding is all about. Done correctly, nation branding represents a culturally sensitive yet commercially driven set of techniques and strategies to deliver tangible social and economic benefits to those nations most in need of it.

Practitioner Insight

Smaller nations enter the global dialogue through nation branding

Jack Yan
CEO of Jack Yan & Associates, and a Director of the Medinge Group

Nation branding is a very real concept. And why not? The twentieth century has shown us that branding has, by and large, worked. In some cases, it has worked for all the wrong reasons and causes. But you cannot distance the human nature to want to belong to tribes by exhibiting certain brands, or the use of semiotics to signal those brands in our collective minds.

But nation branding, on the other hand, has not caught on quite as rapidly as organizational branding or even personal branding. There is some logic there: personal branding relies on the conduct and publicity of one person in his or her interaction with the audience, so it is reasonably easy to control. Organizational branding has a finite group of people, but it is still possible to communicate, symbolize and differentiate them as an entity. There have been traditional departments that take care of branding, so it is, for better or for worse, fairly easy to pigeonhole it.

Nation branding is another matter. By its definition, it must be governmentally sponsored. However, governments are voted for very short terms, much shorter than what a branding campaign necessitates. In addition, governments have not always been stellar exhibitors of promotion. Which department must helm a nation-branding campaign? Groupthink tends to set in (or worse, corruption), and the resulting nation brand is no different to what the country started out with.

But nation branding's practical weakness with many established, and usually occidental, countries may be its strength with smaller nations wanting to play on the world stage. Simon Anholt has already shown, time and time again, how brands contribute to the bottom lines of their nations of origin, ahead of any wealth that may have come from the state.

Nations such as Sri Lanka are blessed with populations that are quite centralized, with passionate leaders who want to see their country strong and part of the global community. There is an opportunity to have a *carte blanche*, for a government to approach these leaders, who in turn take the question back to their communities. Because of that unified desire to do well in the global economy, there is less dispute about which department must helm the development of a nation brand.

Indeed, India has been doing well with tourism branding (Incredible India) and is beginning to examine how profits from the technology sector might be used in impoverished rural areas. Despite a mixture of creeds that have longer standing rivalries than some in the Middle East, India has managed to present a united front; its president has gone as far as to discuss nation branding to its domestic audience. Again, this has stemmed from a unified desire to do well as a nation, helped in some part by the freedom of movement of its citizens and its capital, particularly when it involves the Indian diaspora in the Middle East and the USA. By the second part of the twenty-first century, India will probably be the source from which the west will learn how to nation brand.

Nation branding may well be the great equalizer, just as branding has worked for the corporate sphere. Some may say the Internet was the democratizer that allowed the self-employed businessman to beat the large corporation, but that hardly explains the rise of Richard Branson or, in New Zealand, Angus Tait, both later knighted. Both men relied to some degree on brands. They managed to play with larger companies. Thus, brands for nations will allow smaller, perhaps even less-developed, countries to participate in the global dialogue and economy, competing successfully with the G7.

As citizens of the twenty-first century, we have become accustomed to reading the signals of branding and interpreting them, in addition to what nature blessed us with. We know, oftentimes, what a bad brand is (one with little corporate citizenship that fails to follow through with its promises) and what a good brand is (the means through which an organization lives its promises and fulfils its *raison d'être* to all audiences). That same training will allow us to judge, fairly, a good nation brand with a bad one – and in 2007, the occident has not picked up the baton anywhere nearly as quickly as the Asian subcontinent.

*****

■ Identification and selection of nation-brand values

Any nation-branding campaign needs to be guided by the identification and selection of a set of appropriate brand values. Who has the right to identify such values and then decide which values will be used as foundations of the nation-brand strategy? In terms of values, nations do not start with a blank slate. Advertising agencies or branding consultants cannot be given a free rein to conjure up a set of values that do not adhere to the cultural norms and expectations that prevail in the nation. The identification of nation-brand values needs to be based on extensive research, both qualitative and quantitative in nature, that takes an inclusive approach to all the nation's stakeholder groups. An example of this type of transparency in action could be seen in Taiwan's brand-building exercise in 2005, when the people of Taiwan were invited by their government to vote on which out of 24 iconic Taiwanese images should be used to represent the Taiwan brand to the rest of the world [1].

Without extensive consultation on the values by which the nation-brand should be driven, there may be little buy-in to the positioning and imagery derived from those values. Many countries already have a motto that encapsulates certain values embodied in the nation. This can provide a useful starting point for nations embarking on an exercise in identifying and selecting nation-brand values. Some examples of nations and their existing mottos are summarized in Table 7.1.

The identification and selection of nation-brand values may be facilitated through inviting key stakeholders to surface their vision for the nation-brand and then through the use of the Delphic brand-visioning technique, attempting to arrive at a consensus vision (see academic perspective, Chapter 1). As an example of the kinds of values that can be used to underpin nation-branding campaigns, the following values were identified as being suitable for underpinning the action plan devised by Egypt's Business Image Unit: integrity, guardianship, inclusion, initiative, teamwork and accountability (see country case on Egypt, Chapter 2).

Table 7.1 Nation mottos	
Nation	**Motto**
Columbia	'Liberty and Order'
France	'Liberty, Equality, Fraternity'
Argentina	'In Union and Freedom'
Botswana	'Rain'
Scotland	'No one provokes me with impunity'
Pakistan	'Unity, Discipline, and Faith'
Tunisia	'Order, Liberty, Justice'
Australia	'Advance Australia Fair'
Cuba	'Homeland or Death'
Greece	'Freedom or Death'
Norway	'All for Norway'
Armenia	'One Nation, One Culture'
Senegal	'One People, One Goal, One Faith'

Compiled from Wikipedia [2].

■ Is 'brand' acceptable?

For some, there is a deep-seated hostility to the very idea of treating a nation as a brand. To some extent, the hostility towards the idea of branding a nation may be rooted in an aversion to the word 'brand', and if alternative terminology was used, for example to talk in terms of building a nation's 'reputation' rather than 'brand', then there would perhaps not be the same degree of scepticism towards the concept of nation branding. In recent years, there has been a trend towards integrating ethical considerations into brand management, with many companies turning to ethical branding to gain differential advantage as consumers become more ethically conscious [3]. Emphasis has also been placed on the power of branding to contribute to progress [4]. Specifically, in the context of nation branding, it has been argued that 'branding does not equate with the commercialisation of local culture, but with the protection and promotion of diversity' [5].

■ Sustainability and nation branding

In recent years, there has grown ever-increasing concern on a global level regarding the dire threat to the environment from pollution, greenhouse gases and other consequences of industrialization. Environmental awareness has spread from the traditional sphere of conservation activism into the economic and political mainstream. In the same way that corporate social responsibility (CSR) has focused public attention onto the ethical behaviour of commercial organizations, the heightened concern for good environmental stewardship represents an opportunity to spotlight the level of responsibility with which nations are managing their environmental resources. Which of the world's nations are behaving in an environmentally responsible way and which are failing in their duty to engage in sustainable development? Through the efforts of various organizations, there now exist various sustainability indexes that allow the ranking of individual countries with regard to the quality of their environmental stewardship. We shall look at one of these indexes in some detail – the Environmental Sustainability Index (ESI) – and briefly compare this index with alternative sustainability indexes. How well or how poorly a country performs in such indexes may impact upon that country's nation-brand image. High-performing countries can expect to benefit from an enhanced nation-brand image whereas poor-performing countries may see their image damaged. If the results of the sustainability indexes are highlighted to the general public and widely disseminated through the media, national government policymakers may be encouraged to improve their sustainable development credentials.

Although perhaps not readily associated with being at the cutting edge of environmental activism, the World Bank has contributed significantly to the sustainable development agenda in recent years, particularly through the publication in 2005 of its report 'Where is the Wealth of Nations' [6]. This report argues that current indicators used to guide development decisions – national accounts figures, such as gross domestic product (GDP) – ignore depletion of resources and damage to the environment. The World Bank goes on to propose other measures of total wealth, including natural resources and the value of human skills and capabilities, which show that many of the poorest countries in the world are not on a sustainable path. Although the report's conclusions show a general lack of sustainability in many nations' development path, the World Bank offers some examples of countries that have successfully embraced sustainable development principles – Mauritania, for instance, is praised for enhancing its sustainable development trajectory through better management of its fishery resources, whilst Botswana also distinguishes itself through specific provision in its budget to ensure that mineral revenues are invested rather than consumed through government expenditures – a policy that can both finance future investments and also buffer the government budget from swings in diamond prices. These achievements should be promoted to the world by Mauritania and Botswana so that their respective nation-brands receive due recognition for their commitment to sustainable development.

In a similar vein to the World Bank, the United Nations Environment Programme has also sought to encourage sustainable development by calling upon nations to make well-directed investments in the environment such as terracing agricultural land to slow erosion, which can have a payback rate of $3 or more for every dollar invested [7]. The economic argument for good environmental stewardship is likely to carry more weight amongst national policymakers than purely ethical appeals. At this juncture in world affairs, nation branding can play a key role in aiding implementation of the sustainable development agenda by allowing individual countries – whether emerging nations, established economic superpowers or anywhere in between – to project and benefit from enhanced positive country image if their national environmental stewardship has been good. There has been much debate in recent years about the decline of Brand America [8,9]. In a recent poll of over 26,000 people in 25 countries, BBC World Service found that the image of the USA was deteriorating, and only 29% of those surveyed felt that the USA currently had a positive influence on world affairs [10]. Whilst numerous factors have contributed to the USA's declining nation-brand and no single, isolated remedial measure can reverse this decline, there can be little doubt that re-connecting with global environmental concerns could bolster the USA's tarnished image. Failing to ratify the Kyoto Protocol was widely regarded in the rest of the world as an abdication by the USA of its global environmental responsibilities, even though there were some legitimate reasons for the USA's stance. But, for a nation that aspires to lead the rest of the world, a more committed approach to participation in international environmental initiatives could represent one potential means to help re-establish some of the USA's recently depleted moral authority.

Environmental Sustainability Index

Perhaps the most high-profile country-ranking list for sustainable development is the ESI, produced by a team of environmental experts at Yale and Columbia Universities [11]. The ESI is an environmental scorecard that was launched at the World Economic Forum (WEF) on January 27, 2005, in Davos, Switzerland. The Executive Summary to the full report explains how the ESI attempts to benchmark the ability of nations to protect the environment over future decades by permitting country-by-country comparison across five fundamental components of sustainability:

- Environmental systems (air quality, biodiversity, land, water quality, water quantity)
- Reducing environmental stresses (reducing air pollution, reducing ecosystem stresses, reducing population growth, reducing waste and consumption pressures, reducing water stress, natural resource management)
- Reducing human vulnerability (environmental health, basic human sustenance, reducing environment-related natural disaster vulnerability)
- Social and institutional capacity (environmental governance, eco-efficiency, private sector responsiveness, science and technology)
- Global stewardship (participation in international collaborative efforts, greenhouse gas emissions, reducing transboundary environmental pressures)

A comparison between the ESI and two other widely used sustainability indexes – the Ecological Footprint Index (EFI) and the Environmental Vulnerability Index (EVI) is summarized in Table 7.2.

Table 7.2 Sustainability indexes

Sustainability index	Source	Scope
Environmental Sustainability Index (ESI)	Yale Center for Environmental Law and Policy, Yale University; Center for International Earth Science Information Network, Columbia University; in collaboration with World Economic Forum, Geneva, Switzerland and Joint Research Centre of the European Commission, Ispra, Italy	The ESI integrates 76 datasets – tracking natural resource endowments, past and present pollution levels, environmental management efforts and a society's capacity to improve its environmental performance – into 21 indicators of environmental sustainability. It aims to enable national governments to take a more data-driven and empirical approach to policymaking.
Ecological Footprint Index (EFI)	Same source as ESI	The EFI converts a country's total resource consumption into the equivalent of hectares of biologically productive land and then divides this by population to obtain a final value of hectares per capita. High levels of resource consumption are not sustainable long-term; however, countries with small footprints are not necessarily sustainable if their footprints are small because of a lack of economic activity and pervasive poverty
Environmental Vulnerability Index (EVI)	South Pacific Applied Geoscience Commission in collaboration with the United Nations Environment Programme and others	The EVI aims to provide a sense of the environmental conditions that predispose a country to internal and external shocks that adversely impact its physical entities (people, buildings, ecosystems), economy and wellbeing. This includes susceptibility to natural hazards, sea-level rise, natural resource depletion, fragile ecosystems and geographical isolation. High environmental vulnerability creates a variety of impediments to sustainable development

Adapted from 2005 Environmental Sustainability Index [11].

From the ESI analysis, several conclusions emerged relating to the benchmarking of nations' environmental stewardship. For instance, the report notes that whilst no country appears to be on a fully sustainable trajectory, at every level of development, some countries are managing their environmental challenges better than others. Also, measures of governance such as the rigour of regulation and the degree of cooperation with international policy efforts correlate highly with overall environmental success. A further key conclusion, with significant political implications for the future of environmental sustainability, is that environmental protection need not come at the cost of competitiveness. Prof. Daniel C. Esty of Yale University, and creator of the ESI, states that

'The ESI provides a valuable policy tool, allowing benchmarking of environmental performance country-by-country and issue-by-issue. By highlighting the leaders and laggards, which governments are wary of doing, the ESI creates pressure for improved results.' [12]

This increased pressure for improved results should help drive the sustainable development agenda at a global level. The 'leaders' referred to by Prof. Esty should maximize the positive halo effect that good environmental stewardship may bestow upon their nation-brand, whereas the 'laggards' should improve their performance in order to avoid degradation of their nation-brand with the associated negative consequences of lower global esteem. In this respect, it is interesting to compare the top 20 countries in the ESI with the top 20 countries in the Anholt-GMI Nation Brands Index (Table 7.3). By making this comparison, the potential for the future integration of environmental sustainability into nation branding may be identified.

There is a striking divergence between the top 20 country rankings of the ESI ranking on the one hand and the NBI ranking on the other. Before drawing any hasty conclusions from a comparison of the two rankings, it is important to note that whereas the ESI covers a total of 146 countries, the NBI covers only 25 countries, which obviously places a severe limitation on any comparative analysis of the two rankings. However, some pertinent observations can still be made based on the respective top 20 lists from both indexes.

From the perspective of smaller, less-developed or emerging nations, it can be seen that a high ranking on the ESI is more achievable than on the NBI. Given that countries such as Bolivia do not currently possess the necessary recognition levels to make an impact on the NBI, such countries may benefit more than most from highlighting their impressive ranking on the ESI. In an era that has seen the rise of the ethical consumer, countries such as Bolivia can hope to use their ESI ranking to enhance country image perceptions which in turn could generate increased tourism from environmentally conscious consumers, as well as increase willingness to buy Bolivian products on the part of ethical consumers. Good performance in environmental sustainability could contribute to a generalized positive halo effect around the overall nation-brand. For less-developed and emerging countries that do not have the financial resources to fund

Table 7.3 Top 20 nations in Environmental Sustainability Index and Nation Brands Index

Top 20 country ranking	Environmental Sustainability Index	Nation Brands Index
1	Finland	Australia
2	Norway	Canada
3	Uruguay	Switzerland
4	Sweden	United Kingdom
5	Iceland	Sweden
6	Canada	Italy
7	Switzerland	Germany
8	Guyana	Netherlands
9	Argentina	France
10	Austria	New Zealand
11	Brazil	United States
12	Gabon	Spain
13	Australia	Ireland
14	New Zealand	Japan
15	Latvia	Brazil
16	Peru	Mexico
17	Paraguay	Egypt
18	Costa Rica	India
19	Croatia	Poland
20	Bolivia	South Korea

Adapted from Environmental Sustainability Index [11] and GMI Poll [13].

expensive image-building advertising campaigns, committing to the sustainable development agenda and communicating this commitment to the rest of the world represents perhaps a unique opportunity to build a strong nation-brand.

Remote countries, in particular, may benefit from committing to environmental sustainability as a means of overcoming their lack of proximity to large markets. Such a policy has been advocated, for example in the case of Armenia whose products may have more chance of succeeding in international markets if they are 'characterized by environmental quality distinction and are marketed vigorously as ecologically qualified and certified products' [14].

■ Summary

This chapter has discussed the key ethical imperatives related to nation branding. The concept of nation branding is far from universally accepted and some people remain sceptical as to whether a nation can, or should, ever be treated as a brand. The legitimacy of nation branding therefore needs to be established if the concept and practice of nation branding is to find wide acceptance and buy-in from a broad range of stakeholders.

■ References

1. Li, L. (2006) Branding Taiwan. *Taiwan Panorama*, April, p. 14.
2. Wikipedia, http://www.wikipedia.com, accessed 5 April 2007.
3. Fan, Y. (2005) Ethical branding and corporate reputation. *Corporate Communications*, **10**, 341–350.
4. Ind, N. (2003) A Brand of Enlightenment, in *Beyond Branding* (N. Ind, C. Macrae, T. Gad and J. Caswell, eds.), Kogan Page, UK.
5. Freire, J.R. (2005) Geo-branding, are we talking nonsense? A theoretical reflection on brands applied to places, *Place Branding*, **1**, 347–362.
6. The World Bank (2005) Where is the wealth of nations? http://www.web.worldbank.org, (accessed 15 September 2005).
7. *The Economist* (2005) Greening the books, September 17, p. 96.
8. Anholt, S. and Hildreth, J. (2004) *Brand America: The Mother of All Brands*, Cyan Books, UK.
9. Martin, D. (2007) *Rebuilding Brand America*, Amacom, USA.
10. Frost, R. (2007) Brand America: Taming Wild Perceptions, http://www.brandchannel.com, 2 April.
11. Environmental Sustainability Index (2005) http://www.yale.edu/esi
12. Esty, D.C. (2005) Finland Tops Environmental Scorecard at World Economic Forum in Davos, *Yale News Release*, http://www.yale.edu/opa/news, January 26.
13. GMI Poll Press Release (2005) Australia Is The World's Favorite Nation Brand, http://www.gmi-mr.com/gmipoll/release, August 1.
14. Pant, D. (2005) A place brand strategy for the Republic of Armenia: 'Quality of context' and 'sustainability' as competitive advantage. *Place Branding*, **1**, 273–282.

CHAPTER 8

Pragmatic challenges to the nation-branding concept

Country Case Insight – Iceland

The case of 'Iceland Naturally' – Establishing an umbrella brand to increase country image impact and coherence

Inga Hlín Pálsdóttir
Project Manager, Trade Council of Iceland

'Iceland was probably the worst marketing case in the world. Leifur Eiriksson named it Iceland and no one wanted to go there. Then, having learned from his mistake, he went to what was truly an ice land, and named it Greenland thinking that if it got a better name, people would go there...'

Ilves, Toomas, 2003.

This statement is not entirely accurate, as in reality it was not Leifur Eiriksson who named the country; it was Hrafna-Flóki around the year 860. But does it have some truth in it? The population of Iceland is around 300 000. This puts the country in a group with the least populated countries in the world; yet, despite its small size, it is a rich country that enjoys high standards of living. The name of Iceland is likely to have affected the country in some way, either positively or negatively. It is a fact that many people associate Iceland with the stereotype of 'ice and cold', which is not a true or balanced picture of contemporary Iceland. The name might, though, work in favour for some industries according to Baldvin Jónsson, an Icelandic marketing specialist working on the US market: 'Iceland is a good name. The name of the country is good, both for tourism and for food production. Cold and fresh,' (Morgunblaðið, 26 June 2005).

Iceland does not generally get much attention from the outside world. However, at the end of 2006, the Icelandic government decided to allow whale-hunting to start again, despite warnings about possible hostile reaction to this in the rest of the world. The negative reactions have been considerable. For example, one of the negative reactions was that the General Manager of the Whole Food Market chain in the USA, Kenneth J. Meyer, sent a declaration to the Icelandic Minister of Fisheries, Einar K. Guðfinnsson, in December 2006, in which he declared that the stores had decided not to put any emphasis on Iceland in their marketing strategy for the Icelandic products sold in their stores. It was thought that the resumption of whale-hunting had had a negative influence and that the goodwill that the customers had for the Whole Food Market stores could be damaged (Fréttablaðið, 8 December 2006). The Chairman of the Iceland Chamber of Commerce, Mr Erlendur Hjaltason, has also concluded that by starting whale-hunting again the nation was upsetting the environment in such a way that it could affect the long-term interests of the nation (Fréttablaðið, 8 February 2007; Morgunblaðið, 7 February 2007).

The Icelandic government and its industries were not ready for this kind of attention. It is safe to say that Iceland's country image was affected in a negative way. In February 2007, Iceland was ranked at number 19 in the Anholt-GMI Nation Brands Index, shockingly for Iceland as that made it the lowest of the OECD countries as well as the lowest of the Nordic countries. Both in relation to this and to other recent developments, the government and private companies have been evaluating how it is possible to protect and affect the image of Iceland in a positive and strategic way. One of the first ways that the Icelandic government has chosen to make the country recognizable in today's global market is the Iceland Naturally programme (IN programme), which was launched in 1999 in North America and is still running. Even though the programme has not been identified by the government and other associations as nation branding, the attempt to build up a unified identity for the country can be recognized.

In 2000, the Icelandic Minister of Foreign Affairs, Mr Halldór Ásgrímsson, concluded in one of his speeches that the IN programme was probably the first step towards developing a clear image of the country. The IN programme is a joint marketing programme between tourism and business interests. It has been developed to increase demand for and to promote the purity of products from Iceland and also to encourage travel to the country. The programme combines efforts of the New York office of the Iceland Tourist Board and the Icelandic Foreign Service Overseas Business Services (OBS), within which the Ministry of Communication and the Ministry of Foreign Affairs represent the government along with eight leading Icelandic companies and associations: Iceland Group plc, Icelandair, Icelandic Agriculture, Iceland Spring Natural Water, Leifur Eiriksson Air Terminal, 66°North, the Blue Lagoon and Glitnir Bank.

Before the launch of the IN campaign, research on perceptions of the country was carried out by the Icelandic government in 1999 in the North American market. The purpose of the research was to find out about the general level of knowledge that the average American had about Iceland. The results were disappointing, as the general awareness about Iceland and its products was low. Another of the results was that there were a lot of inconsistent messages in the market from many companies in the same industry. This resulted in a lack of impact and coherence. The results clearly showed that the public–private sector partnership could benefit from delivering consistent messages. The research also conclusively demonstrated that 'Icelandic companies and the government can benefit by working together to create a strong brand image for Iceland' (Ministry of Communication, 1999).

After these discussions, the government decided to start a promotional campaign using the IN programme. The main idea of the programme is to increase the awareness of Iceland, its products and its services by using various marketing tools including events, advertising in leading travel and lifestyle publications, a website, monthly newsletters, sweepstakes and other promotional techniques.

Companies were offered the chance to join for a 5-year period. The government was prepared to pay two-thirds of the campaign budget, with the remaining one-third to be contributed by participating companies. It was decided that the slogan for IN would try to capture the diversity of the country and also attempt to create a warmer image of Iceland. The IN brand was designed to represent the essence of Iceland in terms of its purity and unspoiled natural environment. It was considered that it would be possible to use the 'IN' logo for promoting almost everything related to Iceland, when promoting flights, business, tourism, food products and so on. Soon the largest Icelandic companies in the North American market were prepared to join the programme. The final version of the IN logo can be seen in Figure CS8.1. When looking at the IN programme as an umbrella brand, it can be seen that it covers many of the leading industries in Iceland and perhaps it can be seen as the first step in creating a brand for Iceland.

The government and the private sectors have set the tone by establishing the IN programme and by trying to control – or at least manage with a light touch – what kind of messages should be sent. However, one dimension that is thought to be missing from the process of the IN programme is the perception of the nation, what the internal view of the country is and what the companies and associations think should be embodied in the brand. The programme is one of the first attempts by the Icelandic government to affect the image of the country in a strategic

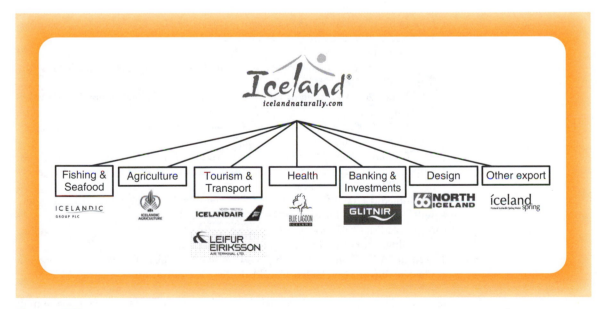

Figure CS8.1
The 'IN' umbrella brand

way. Since the programme started, research to measure awareness of Iceland and Icelandic products among US consumers has also been conducted in 1999, 2000, 2003, 2004 and 2006. The research clearly indicates positive trends in key areas such as associations with Iceland, interest in Iceland as a tourist destination and interest among the younger audience and outdoor types (Iceland Naturally, 2007). The programme expanded over to Europe in 2006 with the same terminology used, even though not all the same companies decided to take part in the programme. Three leading countries were chosen: France, Germany and Great Britain. Now it remains to be seen whether the same approach will work as well in European markets as it has in North America.

From the above strategic initiatives, it can be seen that the Icelandic government recognizes the importance of trying to influence the image and reputation of the country and great steps have been taken. Companies involved in IN have also shown interest and commitment by taking part in the programme. In early 2007, the Prime Minister of Iceland, Mr Geir H. Haarde, announced that the government will put together a group of qualified people to discuss the image and reputation of Iceland and how it is possible to achieve a better performance (Fréttablaðið, 8 February 2007). Key public and private sector stakeholders in Iceland have acknowledged that it is important to have a clear strategy on how the nation wants to be seen and what messages should be sent out to the world in order to attract tourists, investors, entrepreneurs and consumers.

■ References

Frettabladid (2006) *Marketing campaign cancelled because of whaling* [Markaðssókn hætt vegna hvalveiðanna], 8 December, p. 2.

Frettabladid (2007) *The debate showed that actions were needed,* [Umræðan sýndi að aðgerða var þörf], Interview with Mr. Erlendur Hjaltason and Mrs. Halla Tómasdóttir, February 7, p. 13.

Frettabladid (2007) *Whaling ill-judged decision* [Hvalveiðar misráðin ákvörðun], 8 February, p. 2.

Frettabladid (2007) *The country low in image comparisons* [Landið neðarlega í ímyndarsamanburði], 8 February, p. 22.

Ilves, Toomas (2003) *Marketing Estonia: Making Estonia's image mean business,* http://www.balticsworldwide.com/news/features/selling_estonia.htm (accessed 23 May 2005).

Morgunbladid (2005) *Sustainable and Satisfying* [Sjálfbært og Seðjandi], Interview with Mr. Baldvin Jónsson, June 26, pp. 18–21.

Morgunbladid (2007) *Icelanders Whaling Taunt to the Environment* [Hvalveiðar Íslendinga storka umhverfinu], 8 February, p. 4.

The Ministry of Communication (1999) *Fleishman Hillman Company Research.* Sent via e-mail from Ms. Helga Haraldsdóttir, Director at the Ministry of Communication.

Iceland Naturally (2007) *What we have achieved.* Presentation sent via e-mail from Mr. Hlynur Guðjónsson, Trade Commissioner, Consulate General of Iceland.

The Iceland Chamber of Commerce (Viðskiptaráð Íslands) (2007) *Anholt Nation Brands Index, Iceland 2006*, February, Reykjavik, Iceland, p. 1.

The Ministry of Foreign Affairs (2000) *Ræður Halldórs Ásgrímssonar; Ræða Utanríkisráðherra um utanríkismál á Alþingi (13 April)*. Speeches of Mr. Halldór Ásgrímsson: The speech of Minister of Foreign Affairs at Althingi (13 April), http://www3.utanrikisraduneyti.is/frettaefni/raedur-radherra/nr/867 (accessed 18 July 2005).

*****

■ Introduction

From a managerial perspective, there are several pragmatic challenges to the nation-branding concept. The extent of stakeholder participation represents one such key challenge. Further challenges relate to the coordination of nation-brand touchpoints, the need to develop a coherent nation-brand architecture and the highly politicized nature of nation branding.

■ Who needs to be involved?

The wide-ranging nature of nation branding necessitates the involvement of many parties in the formulation and implementation of nation-brand strategy. The principle of inclusiveness holds that all the relevant stakeholders need to be involved in campaign development. However, the inclusiveness concept is moderated by the unique set of circumstances prevailing within individual nations. Therefore, it is useful to distinguish between two forms of inclusiveness. First, the ideal state, or fully inclusive approach. Second, the actual state, or programme-specific inclusiveness.

Ideal state: Fully inclusive approach

The benefits of an inclusive approach to strategy may be considered in terms of motivating employees, generating buy-in and commitment, stimulating creativity, and aligning stakeholders behind the corporate vision. Such issues have been well documented in the internal/employer-branding literature [1,2]. De Chernatony has identified some of the key stakeholders in the nation-brand as including representatives from government, commerce, not-for-profit organizations, tourism and the media (see academic perspective, Chapter 1), whilst Sri Lanka has been cited as an example of a country with passionate leaders who want to see their country strong and part of the global community; this represents an opportunity for government to approach those leaders who then take the question back to their communities (see practitioner insight, Chapter 7). The need for inclusiveness is also highlighted in the case of Bolivia, where the country's nation-branding objectives can only be met 'by having the commitment of the different stakeholders that are involved in the process, which includes not only the government but also the private sector and the country's citizens' (see country case insight on Bolivia, Chapter 7); similarly, in order for Russia to improve its unsatisfactory image abroad, there will need to be a fully inclusive combining of efforts by all stakeholders, including government, the business community, the media, the institutions of civil society, as well as cooperation with the 30 million members of the Russian diaspora (see country case insight on Russia, Chapter 5).

Applying the principle of inclusiveness to the context of nation branding, the fully-inclusive stakeholder (FIST) approach shown in Figure 8.1 provides a framework indicative of the range of potential stakeholders in the nation-brand. The framework is not exhaustive, as every individual nation will have its own specific range of stakeholders; however, the framework offers a basis for analyzing the diversity of stakeholders that will need to be consulted in the development of the nation-brand.

The FIST approach may be considered to represent the ideal state, rather than the actual state, regarding levels of stakeholder inclusiveness in the formation of nation-branding strategy. It is a truism that nations truly come together only as a defensive impulse in response to an external threat such as imminent invasion or attack, and that once such a threat passes, nations return to their old political and social divides. In times of peace and relative prosperity, a nation's actors (institutions, political parties, corporations, individual citizens and so on) perhaps have the luxury of not needing to reach out from their comfort zones to try and establish a consensual vision for the nation-brand. However, many other less developed, transition or emerging nations may be able to act more

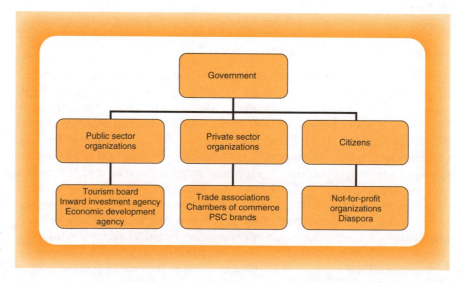

Figure 8.1
The FIST (fully-inclusive stakeholder) approach

decisively in a fully inclusive, consensual way in order to face down the spectres of poverty and under-development. When the need for concerted action is more urgent, the greater the opportunity for governments to unite the nation's stakeholders behind an inclusive programme. Yan illustrates this in the case of Sri Lanka, where 'because of that unified desire to do well in the global economy, there is less dispute about which department must helm the development of a nation brand' (see practitioner insight, Chapter 7).

It can be seen from the FIST framework that the government is the only one of the nation's key actors that can realistically aspire to coordinate nation-brand activities encompassing the full range of stakeholders. The establishment of a coordinating body is essential in order to avoid fragmentation and duplication of activity by the different stakeholders. The coordinating body needs to be set up by government, but the coordinating body also needs to possess a degree of political independence so that nation-brand strategy, which is a long-term undertaking, does not veer off-course every time a new Minister is appointed. As is discussed later in this chapter, nation branding is a highly politicized activity and efforts need to be made to minimize disruption of nation branding activities because of the waxing and waning of individual politicians' careers.

Public sector organizations represent a key component of the FIST approach. Tourism boards, inward investment agencies, economic development agencies and so on all have their own agendas and goals, and there is increasing evidence that many nations are successfully coordinating the activities of such organizations in order to achieve important economic goals (see country case insights on France, Iceland, Brazil). Public sector organizations frequently work closely with private sector organizations – export promotion agencies, for example will inevitably have close links with at least some of the nation's key export companies – yet, there is little evidence of countries within which the representatives of civil society are being included in overall nation-branding activity. Given that much of the funding of nation-branding activities comes from the tax-payer, governments need to give some consideration to the ways in which the nation's citizens can be included in the development of nation-brand strategy.

Actual state: Programme-specific inclusiveness

Whereas the ideal state of full inclusiveness may be attained by nations facing acute economic threat, or by nations that are in the process of emerging onto the international stage for the first time or which need to effect a radical change in their international image, a more realistic aspiration for other nations will be to achieve good levels of programme-specific inclusiveness in their nation-branding activities. This has been achieved by various nations, and therefore, we name programme-specific inclusiveness as an *actual* state rather than an *ideal* state. This does not, of course, imply that all nations have achieved an actual state of programme-specific inclusiveness. On the other hand, many nations may find their nation-branding efforts stymied by political corruption, power struggles or a lack of strategic vision on the part of the country's ruling elites. Even in such unpromising circumstances, it should still be possible for nations to initiate nation-branding activity that embodies a modicum of programme-specific inclusiveness.

In this section, we shall look at three campaigns that illustrate the concept of programme-specific inclusiveness – 'Brazil IT', 'Iceland Naturally' and 'The New France'. The stakeholder participants in each of these three campaigns are summarized in Table 8.1.

Although Brazil, Iceland and France are very different nations and facing different nation-branding challenges, each of the three campaigns summarized in Table 8.1 demonstrates the importance of fostering programme-specific inclusiveness for nations of any size, regardless of their stage of economic development or status in the global economy. In terms of campaign objectives, two of the above campaigns – 'Brazil IT' and 'The New France' – illustrate how it is possible for a clearly defined strategy to remedy a country image deficit. In the case of 'Brazil IT', before the campaign was launched, there was little awareness or recognition of Brazil as a provider of IT services and products. Brazil benefits from tremendously positive associations in other respects, such as football, music and other hedonic appeals; yet, these associations conferred no COO advantage onto Brazilian IT providers. A different type of country image deficit was identified in the case of 'The New France' campaign, whose key objective was to improve foreign investor opinions of France in order to attract new business and increase inward investment. Pre-campaign, the image of France as a nation, was dominated by highly positive perceptions in terms of the country as an attractive tourism destination and a country with fine food and drink; however, perceptions of France as a business destination were much weaker and 'The New France' campaign was launched to remedy this country image deficit. The 'IN' campaign differs notably from the 'Brazil IT' and 'The New France' campaigns in that for Iceland, the challenge was not to overcome pre-existing dominant associations but rather to develop an effective awareness-raising programme that would communicate to targeted markets the closeness of the fit between Icelandic products and the country's overall image of purity and naturalness.

It is notable from the country case insights (see Chapters 6, 8, 10) that all three campaigns fulfil the basic marketing principles of segmentation, targeting and positioning. 'Brazil IT' primarily targeted the US market, 'IN' also targeted the North American market before expanding to include Europe, whilst 'The New France' targeted five key investment countries – the USA, the UK, Germany, Japan and China. The clear strategic focus of each campaign may be viewed as an important condition for establishing the wide-ranging stakeholder participation that each campaign achieved.

Table 8.1 Stakeholder participants in nation-branding campaigns

Campaign	Brazil IT	Iceland Naturally	The New France
Key Objectives	To gain global recognition for the Brazilian IT industry as a capable producer of IT services and products, particularly in the USA, the world's largest consumer of IT products	To increase demand for Icelandic products in the North American market To promote the purity of Icelandic products To encourage travel to the country	To raise France's economic profile among five leading target investment countries: the USA, the UK, Germany, Japan and China To improve foreign investor opinions of France to attract new business and increase inward investment To create solid relationships with foreign investors for long-term dialogue
Stakeholder Participants	Brazilian government through Brazil's export promotion agency, APEX Brasil Several IT clusters throughout Brazil Individual IT companies Brazil Information Center, a non-profit trade organization based in the USA, which promotes Brazil to American opinion-makers and consumers	Icelandic government through the Ministry of Foreign Affairs and Ministry of Communication Icelandic Foreign Service (Overseas Business Services) Iceland Tourist Board Eight leading Icelandic companies and associations: Iceland Group plc, Icelandair, Icelandic Agriculture, Iceland Spring Natural Water, Leifur Eiriksson Air Terminal, 66°North, Blue Lagoon, Glitnir Bank	Campaign developed and run by the Invest in France Agency, a government organization; UBIFrance, international business development agency; Maison de la France, the national tourist office; Information Service Department; Ministry of Foreign Affairs; French Economic Mission; Sopexa, the national agricultural marketing and communication consultant; EDUFrance, the education promotion agency; Treasury Directorate; French State Council; Pierre Dauzier, communications expert and ex-president of advertising company Havas

Source: adapted from country case insights in Chapters 6, 8, 10.

Government involvement in all three campaigns and commitment to achieving the campaign objectives are essential in order to sustain the participation of all the necessary stakeholders, although the degree of government involvement may be contingent upon the nature and stage of each individual campaign. Government involvement could be most active in the initial stages, in order to kick-start the campaign and galvanize stakeholder participation, and then government involvement may become more hands-off as private sector companies engage more actively in the campaign's development. 'Brazil IT', 'IN' and 'The New France' demonstrate the different types of public sector bodies that can be involved in specific campaigns; these campaigns also show that there is no rigid blueprint for nation-branding campaigns, whose diversity defies easy categorization – there is no set checklist of stakeholder participants for nation-branding campaigns, and the appropriate range of participants will vary according to each campaign's specific strategic objectives.

Nations should benefit from a cumulative effect in terms of stakeholder participation in specific campaigns. Participation in any campaign should allow the formation of social networks that can usefully endure beyond the shelf life of the campaign in question and underpin future campaigns. Social network theory in the context of the firm offers some interesting perspectives for those involved in nation-branding campaigns. It has been argued, for example that firms can draw on their unique social networks of relations to make a difference to their strategies rather than accepting strategy as merely a function of the market or of internally driven forces, and moreover, managers need to identify and develop network structures that are 'resourceful, rare and inimitable' [3]. For nation-branding campaigns, such network structures are embodied in the range of stakeholder participants actively engaged in the three campaigns analyzed here. An additional network at the disposal of nations is their diaspora, and governments are beginning to appreciate the potential benefits of engaging with their diaspora networks as key participants in developing a powerful nation-brand (see Chapter 9).

■ Coordinating nation-brand touchpoints

Brand touchpoints exist whenever and wherever the brand is experienced by any of its stakeholders or audiences. Brand touchpoints occur most obviously during consumption of the brand, although touchpoints also exist pre-consumption and post-consumption through multiple channels and occasions. Touchpoints consist of planned, controllable brand-building activities such as advertising, promotion, PR, customer service and so on, as well as unplanned touchpoints beyond the control of brand managers – blogs, discussion boards on the web, the personal behaviour of individuals associated with the brand and so on. For any PSC brand, there exists a multiplicity of brand touchpoints; for complex and multifaceted nation-brands, with their vast range of internal and external stakeholders and audiences, the number of brand touchpoints assumes almost infinite proportions. The reason that brand touchpoints matter is that they can all contribute to, or detract from, brand equity in terms of the positive or negative perceptions that occur in audience's minds because of the assessments they make of how satisfying the brand touchpoint experience was. The totality of brand touchpoints cannot be controlled but they can be managed, based on ongoing research that identifies and evaluates brand touchpoints as and when they occur. Brand expert Ian Ryder has noted that in place branding, 'you need to know where the touchpoints are that will make a difference in the acceptance or management of the brand' [4]. Nation-brand touchpoints can be bewilderingly diverse, from the potentially harmful effects on Iceland's country image because of that nation's resumption of whaling (see country case insight on Iceland, Chapter 8) to the potentially positive reputational effects of improved business formalities on perceptions of Egypt as a business destination (see country case insight on Egypt, Chapter 2). In the context of Brand Estonia, Interbrand consultancy point out that 'as well as the more obvious communication points that a new brand needs to touch, public infrastructure and public services are the most noticeable and memorable national symbols for visitors and those who come to work in a country' (see country case insight on Estonia, Chapter 9).

In many respects, there are similarities between corporate branding and nation branding. Both types of branding involve more complexity than is the case with product brands. The added complexity of corporate and nation branding lies in the wider range of stakeholders that the brand has, the multiplicity of communications channels that need to be used in order to reach those audiences, the difficulty of encapsulating a multifaceted entity into the distilled essence of a brand and the unlimited number of uncontrollable factors that can affect perceptions of the brand.

Hankinson [5] has proposed five guiding principles for the management of destination brands based on an adaptation of corporate-branding theory. Whilst a destination brand could be a single town, city, resort or other relatively limited entity, it could also be a whole nation and many destination-branding campaigns are run at a national level. Hankinson's five guiding principles may therefore be considered as having potential application at a nation-branding level. His five principles are as follows: first, strong, visionary leadership; second, a brand-oriented organizational culture; third, departmental coordination and process alignment; fourth, consistent communications across a wide range of stakeholders; and fifth, strong, compatible partnerships. Further insight into the potential adaptation of corporate-branding theory to the context of nation branding is provided in this chapter's academic perspective by Olutayo B. Otubanjo and Prof. T.C. Melewar. The need for consistent communications across a wide range of stakeholders alluded to by Hankinson is illustrated in the case of South Africa, where there was a realization that the country was suffering from certain perceptions that needed to be changed, but the uncoordinated proliferation of messages emanating from the country was not helping to challenge the problem – '... there were many messages entering the international arena, and these messages were as varied as the sources and did very little to change the perceptions. They added to the confusion', (see country case insight, Chapter 1).

Academic Perspective

Corporate brand differentiation in the financial services industry – Applying the highest central common factor concept to nation branding

Olutayo B. Otubanjo[1] and T.C. Melewar[2]
[1] Former Account Executive, CMC Connect Lagos, Nigeria; and
[2] Professor of Marketing and Strategy at Brunel University, London, UK

Corporate brand differentiation is one of the most challenging business practices in corporate brand management. It provides the platform through which firms distinguish themselves from competitors. Whether in theory or practice, corporate brand differentiation drives firms towards unique positions in the minds of stakeholders. Although corporate brand management has been an aspect of corporate marketing since the 1950s, it did not develop fully as a marketing practice and discipline until the early 1980s. Many firms in Europe and most importantly those operating in the financial services industry in the UK have since the early 1990s embraced corporate branding as a strategic tool for corporate differentiation. The widespread adoption of such branding techniques by nations is a yet more recent development.

For many years, the British financial services industry has been dominated by a strong generic corporate brand. Many financial services firms that emerged successfully from the business and economic turbulence of the 1980s consciously sought ways of differentiating themselves from competition. Plush and exquisite corporate visuals were deployed to break the generic mould that dominated this industry. However, the notion that there is no real difference between these corporate brands grows evermore.

To address this challenge, successful corporate brand differentiation requires self-determination, willpower, creativity and innovation. Distinct corporate brands can evolve in the financial services industry by identifying and communicating the 'highest central common factor' (HCCF), which binds the universal characteristics of diversified business portfolios (i.e. retail, commercial, corporate and investment banking) together (see Figure 8.2). The HCCF may be one thing or a combination of factors that gives members of a firm a sense of belonging. It may be the informal and formal set of rules or a firm's unique history or conditions of employment. The HCCF concept may also apply to nation-brands, whereby the diversified business portfolios of corporate financial service brands (retail, commercial, corporate and investment banking)

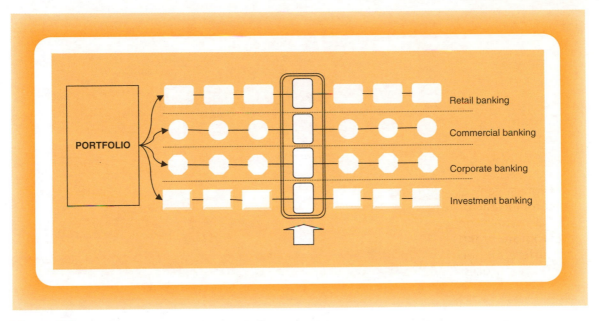

Figure 8.2
Highest central common factor (HCCF)

are mirrored by the diverse agencies engaged in the nation-brand, e.g. inward investment, tourism, export promotion and so on.

The notion behind the HCCF holds that there is a cultural identity common to all business portfolios no matter how diversified a firm and its culture may be. It is these common characteristics that serve as a glue binding the firm together. HCCF is a phenomenon reflective of the largest common character denominator prevailing in sub-business cultures. It is that unique character that prevails and is commonly embedded in the sub-cultural systems. It is the distinct collective corporate character of firms that, when fully conceptualized, cannot be imitated by competitors.

The HCCF is a four-stage corporate brand differentiation process that begins with a rigorous and comprehensive review of the corporate characteristics in the firm's diversified business portfolio followed by an identification of characteristics common to all business portfolios. In the third stage, an internal assimilation of the characteristics takes place. As can be seen in Figure 8.3, the process is completed with the presentation of the characteristics to external stakeholders through various forms of corporate communications.

*****

To adequately address the multiple audiences that a nation-brand possesses, the principles of integrated marketing communications (IMC) need to be applied. The emergence of IMC has been driven both by the proliferation of new media channels in the digital age and by the fragmentation of previously homogeneous audience 'blocks' into smaller

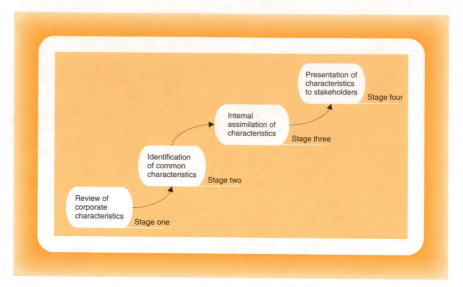

Figure 8.3
Highest central
common factor
(HCCF) four-stage
corporate brand
differentiation
process

and more numerous discrete groups. IMC has been defined as 'the practice of unifying all marketing communication tools – from advertising to packaging – to send target audiences a consistent, persuasive message that promotes company goals' [6]. The marketing communication tools that are available to brands include traditional media advertising such as TV, radio, newspapers and magazines; online advertising; event marketing; publicity; trade journal advertising; conferences and expos, and so on. Nation-brands can utilize such marketing communications tools to pursue their objectives in the same way that PSC brands have used such tools. For example, an illustration of the use of IMC in nation branding is provided by 'The New France' campaign, which used the following communications options: print advertisements in top economic news publications such as the *Financial Times*, *Wall Street Journal*, *Handelsblatt* and *Nikkei*; billboard advertisements in major airports in the USA, UK, Japan, China and France; sector videos; a book available in five languages entitled 'France means business', with 10 000 copies distributed in 60 different countries; a microsite, www.thenewfrance.com, containing testimonials and information on doing business in France; and face-to-face meetings with economic leaders and potential investors at high-profile events such as the World Economic Forum in Davos, the Forbes CEO Conference, the BusinessWeek Leadership Forum and the Fortune Innovation Forum (see country case insight on France, Chapter 10).

Iceland and Brazil have also implemented the principles of IMC in their nation-branding activities, unifying their marketing communication tools in order to send their target audiences a consistent, persuasive message. The 'IN' programme, for example created a logo for the campaign and used a variety of marketing tools including events, advertising in leading travel and lifestyle publications, a website, monthly newsletters, sweepstakes and other promotional techniques (see country case insight on Iceland, Chapter 8). The 'Brazil IT' campaign also created a new logo and trademarked the brand in the USA, and then drew upon a range of communication tools such as video, the www.brazil-it.com website, traditional print media and consistent trade show participation (see country case insight on Brazil, Chapter 6). The visual coordination of nation-brand touchpoints is relatively straightforward compared with the management of the many uncontrollable touchpoints that every nation-brand has. New Zealand, for example has for many years used its silver fern logo to unify the visual aspect of its sport, education, trade and tourism promotions, and it has been observed that 'origin devices like the fern have a deep connection people, culture, tradition, pride and national heritage' [7].

The coordination of nation-brand touchpoints is therefore a complex, challenging and necessary undertaking. A report by the Oxford Said Business School on developing a brand for Latvia, for example states that the coordinating role in the nation-brand should be played by a Brand Steward whose activities should be enabling rather than directive, providing the different groups working for the nation-brand with 'tools that will ensure their efforts are harmonious with those of their counterparts in other arenas to guarantee a joint national vision' [8]. Weak coordination of nation-branding activities in the past has been identified as a problem now being addressed by Russia (see country case on Russia, Chapter 5), whilst a similar lack of coordination has been observed in Switzerland's past nation-branding activities – 'the promotion of Switzerland's image had previously been managed in a fragmented manner by various public and private sector organisations' – in response to which the coordinating body 'Presence Switzerland' was established in order to coordinate the activities of other organizations such as Pro Helvetia, Swiss Info, Location Switzerland, OSEC Business Network Switzerland and Swiss Tourism (see country case insight on Switzerland, Chapter 4).

■ Nation-brand architecture

A further pragmatic challenge in nation branding is the question of deciding upon a suitable nation-brand architecture (NBAR). Brand architecture is a key concept in brand theory. It has been defined as 'an organizing structure of the brand portfolio that specifies the brand roles and the relationships among brands and different product-market brand contexts' [9]. Temporal believes that 'brand architecture is possibly the most difficult area of brand management, in that there are simply no rules, and endless opportunities to try out many variations. Some variations work, while similar ones don't' [10]. Yvonne Johnston, CEO of the International Marketing Council of South Africa, has described how that country has developed a brand architecture that has defined the relationship between the mother-brand and the various sub-brands that comprise Brand South Africa.

One of the clearest and most useful descriptions of brand architecture is given by Olins [11] who distinguishes between three basic brand portfolio structures: monolithic, endorsed and branded. In the monolithic structure, there is a single dominant corporate umbrella brand. In the endorsed structure, individual brands have their own brand names and identity but are clearly endorsed by the parent brand. Finally, in the branded structure, each individual brand stands alone with its own identity and the parent brand is not visible. Examples of a monolithic brand structure can be seen with companies such as Canon (where the umbrella brand covers printers, fax machines, cameras, etc.) or Mitsubishi (financial services, cars, domestic appliances); an endorsed brand structure is used by General Motors (Chevrolet, Buick and so on); finally, a branded structure is used by Johnnie Walker Red Label, where the parent brand (Diageo) is not visible to the consumer and the individual brand stands alone. Within these three basic structures, there can be endless permutations and variations; yet, Olins' monolithic-endorsed-branded perspective remains a robust framework for brand architecture analysis and development.

Why do companies use different brand architectures and how can they decide upon the most appropriate brand architecture for their own unique brand portfolios and markets? The rationale for a monolithic brand structure derives from the ability of a monolithic brand to create a unified, powerful and consistent image across different markets. Corporate brands such as Yamaha are so strong that they can enter sectors as disparate as motorbikes and guitars, and many other product categories in between. A risk with the monolithic structure, however, is that if one sub-brand receives bad publicity or performs poorly, this may taint the other brands in the portfolio. The rationale for an endorsed structure is that an endorsed brand can enjoy the best of both worlds – it benefits from the power of the parent or umbrella brand, whilst simultaneously establishing its own individual brand identity. A drawback of the endorsed structure is that the sub-brand's freedom to position itself in its target markets is restrained by the need to conform to the parent brand's positioning. The rationale for a branded structure is that it allows maximum potential to develop a clearly differentiated brand that can stand alone and prosper without being associated with the parent brand. The branded structure is commonly used in the spirits drinks sector, where quirky, heritage-focused, or in other ways highly individualistic brands would gain no benefit – and in fact would almost certainly lose brand equity – if they were associated with the faceless multinational corporations that own them. However, a weakness of the branded structure is that there may be a failure to benefit from the positive associations of a powerful parent brand.

Douglas *et al.* [12] contend that establishing a coherent international brand architecture is an important element of a firm's international marketing strategy because it provides a structure that enables the firm to leverage strong brands into other markets, and to integrate strategy across markets. Transposing the concept of brand architecture to the specific case of South Africa's nation branding, Dooley and Bowie [13] show how South Africa has developed a 'nation umbrella brand' whose purpose, like that of a corporate umbrella brand, is to link together individual sub-brands; the 'sub-brands' referring to regions, cities and their industry sectors such as tourism, exports and FDI.

There are no universal guidelines for firms that are trying to select the correct brand architecture for their own brand portfolios. For lazy managers, who need the crutch of off-the-shelf solutions to their problems, this is perhaps unfortunate, but for motivated nation-branding teams who are energized by the pride they take in the honour of working to develop their nation-brand, the lack of rigid formulae is a positive thing in that it represents an exciting opportunity to do original, creative and effective work to promote the nation's economic and social well-being.

Although there exists no brand architecture panacea, on a general level managers must analyse the existing corporate and sub-brand equities of their portfolios in the light of the markets they operate within and those markets they are contemplating entering. These equities must be evaluated in terms of what value the umbrella brand and the sub-brands are currently contributing, and the potential value that they could deliver in the future. In nation-branding terms, the corporate or umbrella brand is evidently the nation as a whole. The nation's 'sub-brands' include its cities, regions and landmarks; PSC brands from all sectors; tourism, FDI and export promotion agencies; sporting teams, at both national and club level; cultural and political figures, and so on. The purpose of the brand architecture concept is to instil some order and structure on this otherwise sprawling and disjointed list of sub-brands, in order to achieve synergistic benefits and to advance the overarching nation-brand. The NBAR model in Figure 8.4 shows one possible NBAR that could enable the nation to introduce some strategic coordination and direction to its host of sub-brands. In the NBAR model, the nation-brand represents the 'umbrella brand'; at the next level down can be found 'endorsed brands' such as the nation's tourism, exports, inward investment, talent attraction and sports; whilst the third level comprises a mix of 'endorsed' and 'standalone' brands.

Mentally stimulating though it may be, the development of effective and coherent NBAR is not an intellectual game. The strategic purpose of NBAR is to fully leverage the overarching, umbrella nation-brand and all the 'sub-brands' of the nation in order to achieve maximum synergy on a long-term basis. It requires a creative and concerted effort to overcome the silo mentality that afflicts many large corporations. Whereas corporations need to foster cross-functional collaboration between marketing, R&D, operations, finance and so on, nations on the other hand must address a similar challenge in facilitating fertile collaboration between distinct bodies such as tourism boards, inward investment agencies, tertiary education providers, export promotion agencies and others.

The NBAR model proposes a brand architecture that encompasses the umbrella, endorsed and branded structures. The model is intended to stimulate the creative development of synergistic linkages between

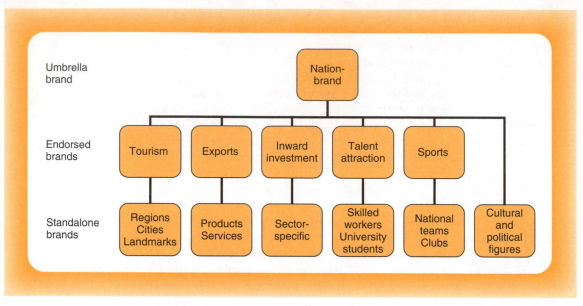

Figure 8.4
The NBAR (nation-brand architecture) model

different sub-brands, for example between tourism and talent attraction, or between exports and sports. It is also designed to prevent the proliferation of uncoordinated visual branding systems that could cause confusion in target audiences and reduce potential synergies. Under the umbrella nation-brand, an endorsed structure is suggested for the main agencies, sections and dimensions of the nation-brand such as tourism, exports, inward investment, talent attraction, sports, and cultural and political figures. However, this endorsed structure comes with one important caveat – the visual expression of endorsement by the umbrella brand should be merely the name of the nation-brand, accompanied by a logo, for example the New Zealand fern. It is probably futile to try and boil down the essence of a nation to a single-phrase slogan, as such a slogan would have to be so broad and all-encompassing that it would actually be vacuous and pointless. It is at the endorsed, sub-brand level that each sub-brand should produce a slogan appropriate to its own specific target markets.

■ A highly politicized activity

There is no getting away from the fact that nation branding is a highly politicized activity. Governments are assumed to represent the people of a nation, and therefore, governments must play a key role in nation-branding strategy. Private sector organizations do not, on their own, possess the legitimacy to lead the direction of nation-brand strategy. The country case insight on Brazil, for example (see Chapter 6) illustrates how government can productively interact with public and private sector stakeholders to help drive forward the nation-brand strategy. However, as Jack Yan has stressed, 'governments are voted for very short terms, much shorter than what a branding campaign necessitates … In addition, governments have not always been stellar exhibitors of promotion', (see practitioner insight, Chapter 7).

Country Case Insight – Hungary

Country promotion and image management – The case of Hungary

Gyorgy Szondi
Senior Lecturer, Leeds Business School

Hungary has become a successful destination brand but has been less successful at more comprehensive country branding, which involves the systematic promotion of economic, commercial and political interests at home and abroad. Developing a coherent and strategic country brand can take decades and require a harmoniously co-ordinated approach; however, many country-branding initiatives fall short on this criterion, including Hungary too.

When analysing the evolution and development of country branding, it is crucial to understand and examine the context in which country branding emerged. In Central Europe, the context has been potential EU membership as well as distancing the countries from the old images of communism by developing a 'Euro-confirm' identity, which is sellable in and to the Western world.

In 1998, the Hungarian government set up the *Country Image Centre* to manage Hungary's reputation abroad. The Centre was responsible for developing a concept for Hungary's new image and building this new image both inside and outside the country. The Centre's aim was to survey and evaluate the image of Hungary both domestically and internationally, to search for Hungary's exceptional values and strengths, and to communicate these with the help of other organizations.

Country promotion and image management have become a highly sensitive issue in Hungary since the launch of the Country Image Centre. It was heavily criticized by the opposition given that the Centre was more concerned with promoting the government rather than the country itself – eventually, the Centre was abolished once the new government was formed in 2002. This is a common phenomenon in Eastern Europe, where country branding and reputation management becomes the victim of domestic politics, especially when there is no agreement among the different political parties about how or by whom the country's reputation should be managed abroad.

In Hungary as well as in many other Central European countries, the newly elected governments have usually erased the efforts of the previous government, resulting in discontinuity of country promotion. Soon after, however, the new government also realizes that there is an 'image problem' abroad and tries to set up institutions and develop new strategies to deal with them. Other institutions, such as the 19 Hungarian Cultural Institutions worldwide, the Hungarian Investment and Trade Development Agency, the Hungarian National Tourism Office (HNTO), and the Ministry of Foreign Affairs together with the Ministry of Culture and Education have had their own share in promoting Hungary abroad; however, strategies and messages about the country are rarely synthesized or co-ordinated.

Not only governmental organizations but also for-profit organizations can also contribute to a successful country brand. In 1999, four Hungarian companies founded the Hungaricum Club with the aim of creating a 'calling card' for Hungary. The founders' aim was to contribute to Hungary's image by their own means and through their joint appearance and to 'further Hungary's progress towards membership of the European Union, while retaining their traditional identities as Hungarian brands'. Members of the Club put together a boxed set called *A Taste of Hungary* featuring selected samples of their products, Herend Porcelain, Pick Salami, Tokaj Aszu Wines, Zwack Unicum liqueur and the Halas sewn lace, all linked to traditional dining. These are typical Hungarian products, which have come to symbolise the country and are important cultural artefacts.

Hungarian country branding did not follow the so-called 'land of contrast' approach, where the contrast between the country's past and present and paradox of country characteristics serve as the central theme. Rather than following the same clichés advised by Western branding consultancies, Hungary's approach was different: to promote the country by real 'faces' and emphasize the human dimension in branding as opposed to other countries' approaches, which relied more on the natural, physical characteristics of the country. In 2005, the Hungarian National Tourism Organisation developed a new brand identity for Hungary, with the slogan 'Talent for entertaining'. This idea was developed by a public relations agency, based on research among those foreign citizens who often choose Hungary as a holiday destination. The research revealed that Hungary is most often associated with hospitality and talented people, which is reflected in the slogan. The core idea of the campaign involved the personalization of the strategic tourism products of Hungary and the promotion of the country by 11 recognized Hungarian celebrities, who are professionals in their own field. This campaign was aimed at foreign audiences only, because a different campaign targeted domestic tourism with different slogans and visuals. The 'Talent for . . . ' initiative followed an earlier campaign where the American actor, Tony Curtis – whose parents were Hungarians – was promoting Hungary in the USA.

To develop a more coherent country brand for Hungary, the so-called 'Hungary Roundtable' was set up in 2005 where the Hungarian National Tourism Organisation played a co-ordinating role. The 'Talent for . . . ' theme has been suggested as the core of the Hungarian country brand around which several sub-brands could be developed and tailored towards the different stakeholder groups. This initiative, however, came to a halt with the national elections in 2006, although the organizations involved are determined to reinvigorate the initiative.

The majority of Central European countries maintain modern and up-to-date country websites, which serve as a 'one-stop shop' about the country. The http://www.hungary.hu website is run by the government and serves as an important country branding as well as public diplomacy tool, providing general information about Hungary. The http://www.hungary.com website is run by the HNTO and specializes in information related to tourism.

According to the GMI Nation Brand Index, published at the end of 2005, Hungary's brand value was estimated at US $78 billion and the country occupied the 21st position of the 35 countries surveyed. The Brand Index, commissioned by Hungarian National Tourist Office, confirms the findings of previous research done by the HNTO, thus revealing little new information. Its most important value is that it puts Hungary well ahead of its competitors; namely the Czech Republic (29th place) and Poland (30th place). The Brand Index survey evaluated Hungary to be in a 'pretty good shape'. If one can rely on the Index, this can be considered a good result because Hungary is one of the very few CEE countries that has not employed a foreign (usually British) branding agency or consultant but has used only its own resources. Hungary has had a long experience in destination branding, dating back to communist times when the country was branded as the 'happiest barrack' of the Eastern block and Hungary had a relatively positive image, which the country did not capitalize upon after the fall of the Berlin Wall.

Another characteristic of Hungary's country branding is the increasing role of public relations over advertising. Third party endorsement, events management, efficient media relations, study tours for the foreign press, road shows organized by embassies to attract investment, efficient crisis and issues management are among the most frequently used public relations tools. Public relations is integrating the communication activities and has become crucial in developing and maintaining relationships with key stakeholders and publics.

Attracting investment into a country is another important goal of country branding. In 2007, China chose Hungary as its gateway to Europe, opting to build a US $1 billion commercial hub in Budapest to allow Chinese companies to market and sell their goods across the European Union. Central Hungary came second in the *Financial Times' fDi* magazine's prestigious 'Region of the Future 2006/07' award, in which Vilnius and Kaunas took the prize. In the Central Hungary region alone, over 100 foreign direct investment deals were signed in 2004 and the region boasted more than 1255 public and private Research and Developments units. FDI promotion was one of the judging criteria where Vilnius and Kaunas excelled but Central Hungary was weak.

A country can have a successful brand, but it can be threatened by politics or politicians. Hungary's socialist Prime Minister Ferenc Gyurcsany made the international headlines a few times during 2005 and 2006. When the Hungarian national soccer team played a friendly game against Saudi Arabia in February 2005, he praised the Hungarian players' performance: 'I think that there were very many terrorists also among the Saudi soccer players, and our sons fought with death-defying bravery against these terrorists, so a draw away from home is a fantastic result'. This quote received worldwide publicity and damaged not only Gyurcsany's reputation but that of Hungary among Arab states too. The Saudi ambassador left Hungary and the government begged him to return to Hungary and had to apologize. In a leaked video tape in 2006, Gyurcsany admitted that he and his socialist government 'lied in the morning, and lied in the evening' for years, which created a wave of protests against the government and a moral crisis in Hungarian politics. Protests reached a climax at the fiftieth anniversary of the 1956 Hungarian revolution, where serious fights broke out between protesters and the police, making international headlines again and showing Hungary in a bad light. No branding initiative can protect a country against such actions and comments.

As this case has demonstrated, Hungary still has a long way to go to achieving a coherent, well-synthesized and strategic country brand; however, the pieces of the puzzle are slowly coming together.

*****

■ Summary

In this chapter, we have looked at the pragmatic challenges to the nation branding concept. In terms of inclusiveness, nation-brands may aspire to a fully inclusive approach whereby all the nation-brand's stakeholders are involved in the country's nation-branding strategy; alternatively, a programme-specific approach may be adopted, as in the case of campaigns such as 'Brazil IT', 'IN' and 'The New France'. The concept of brand architecture has been discussed and related to the concept of the nation-brand. It has been noted that nation branding is inevitably a highly politicized activity, which requires the active commitment of government if the nation-brand's goals are to be achieved.

■ References

1. Ind, N. (2003) *Living The Brand: How to Transform Every Member of Your Organization into a Brand Champion*, Second Edition, Kogan Page, UK.
2. Barrow, S. and Mosley, R. (2005) *The Employer Brand: Bringing the Best of Brand Management to People at Work*, John Wiley & Sons, Ltd, UK.
3. Hung, S.-C. (2002) Mobilising networks to achieve strategic difference. *Long Range Planning*, **35**, 591–613.
4. *Brand Strategy* (2007) Roundtable: Russian reputation, February, pp. 44–47.
5. Hankinson, G. (2007) The management of destination brands: Five guiding principles based on recent developments in corporate branding theory. *Journal of Brand Management*, **14**, 240–254.
6. Burnett, J. and Moriarty, S. (1998) *Introduction to Marketing Communications: An Integrated Approach*, Prentice Hall, USA.
7. Dooley, G. and Bowie, D. (2005) Place brand architecture: Strategic management of the brand portfolio, *Place Branding*, **1**, 402–419.
8. Frasher, S., Hall, M., Hildreth, J., and Sorgi, M. (2003) A Brand for the Nation of Latvia, Oxford Said Business School, available at www.politika.lv (accessed 17/10/06).
9. Aaker, D.A. and Joachimsthaler, E. (2000) *Brand Leadership*, The Free Press, New York, USA.
10. Temporal, P. (2002) *Advanced Brand Management: From Vision to Valuation*, John Wiley & Sons, Ltd, Asia.
11. Olins, W. (1989) *Corporate Identity*, Thames and Hudson, UK.
12. Douglas, S.P., Craig, C.S., and Nijssen, E.J. (2001) Integrating branding strategy across markets: Building international brand architecture. *Journal of International Marketing*, **9**, 97–114.
13. Dooley, G. and Bowie, D. (2005) Place brand architecture: Strategic management of the brand portfolio, *Place Branding*, **1**, 402–419.

PART 4

Current practice and future horizons for nation branding

CHAPTER 9

Elements of nation-branding strategy

Country Case Insight – Japan

The directions and the key elements of branding Japan

Satoshi Akutsu
Associate Professor, Hitotsubashi University

■ 1. Introduction

In 2004, the Task Force on Contents in the Intellectual Property Policy Headquarters (Policy Headquarters) organized the Japan Brand Working Group to discuss the directions and the key elements of branding Japan.

The goal of this nation-branding effort is to 'improve the image and reputation of Japan and turn it into a nation that is loved and respected by people throughout the world'.[1] Thus, naturally, the focus is on leveraging the lifestyle and the overall power of Japan's cultural assets. The Working Group's discussion (as well as the report) focuses on three areas of emphasis: food culture, fashion and local brands.

■ 2. Background

In 2002, Japan took the first significant step towards becoming an intellectual property-based nation (*chizai-rikkoku*). Specifically, then Prime Minister Junichiro Koizumi declared in his policy speech to the Diet that Japan had set the new goal of becoming more competitive through the creation, protection and strategic utilization of intellectual property. Following the speech, the government established the Strategic Council on Intellectual Property, comprising the prime minister, related ministers and experts from the private sector. The council recommended the enactment of the Basic Law on Intellectual Property, a bill that was then submitted to the Diet and subsequently passed. In accordance with the new law, the Policy Headquarters was established in 2003. Since then, a cohesive intellectual property policy has been formulated and implemented in Japan to achieve the above goal.

Shortly afterwards, the Policy Headquarters adopted the *Intellectual Property Strategic Program* 2003, a strategic program for the creation, protection and effective utilization of intellectual property. This program, which originally consisted of about 270 measures, has been renewed each year since then, with the number of additional measures increasing annually.

---

[1] Intellectual Property Strategy Headquarters (2006), *Intellectual Property Strategic Program 2006*.

These measures encourage a wide range of creative activities ranging from scientific inventions and technology development to art and design. Particular emphasis has been put on the creation and management of intangible assets such as technology, design, brands and media contents. To develop these measures, the Policy Headquarters established the Task Force on Contents, as well as three other task forces.[2] The Task Force on Contents primarily discusses issues pertaining to media contents and the Japan brand.

Established in 2003, the Task Force on Contents first focused its discussion on the management of media contents, such as music, movies, game software and animation.[3] It then expanded the scope of its agenda to include other key resources of Japan branding, namely, intellectual and cultural assets related to food culture, local brands and fashion. The Japan Brand Working Group was organized within the task force in 2004 to conduct more in-depth discussions on the three areas of food culture, local brands and fashion, as well as policy issues concerning ways to build an attractive Japan brand, which would lead to more specific measures for Japan branding.[4]

■ 3. Development of Japan Brand Initiatives

The Policy Headquarters has provided the vision of a strong Japan brand to be built strategically by strengthening the contents business, nurturing unique and attractive lifestyles as reflected in the food culture, local brands and fashion and assimilating the brand image in collaboration with the tourism industry, as well as through cultural diplomacy. A key premise here is that Japan aims to become an intellectual property-based nation, attractive and influential in entertainment contents, lifestyle and culture in general.

The Policy Headquarters functions as the hub of Japan branding efforts. Its annual *Strategic Program* report has been a guiding principle for related government offices as well as private organizations. The Task Force on Contents plays a leadership role in the discussion, providing guidance for the direction of Japan branding. In its first report, *Content Business Development Policy*, it proposed the goal of making Japan a world-class content superpower and suggested that the promotion of content business

---

[2] The three other task forces are the Task Force on Strengthening of the Foundation for Rights Protection, the Task Force on the Protection of Patents of Medical-Related Acts and the Task Force on the Intellectual Creation Cycle.

[3] The summary of the early discussion and a set of subsequent measures have been reported in the *Promotion Policy of Contents Business*.

[4] The Task Force on Contents had organized two more working groups by 2007 to provide more in-depth discussion of media contents; the Digital Contents Working Group and the Planning Working Group.

be made a core national policy. The task force also devised measures for achieving this goal. The Japan Brand Working Group compiled the report entitled, *Promotion of Japan Brand Strategy*, in which it sets three goals. These three goals are (1) fostering a rich food culture, (2) establishing diverse and reliable local brands and (3) establishing Japanese fashion as a global brand. The working group has soon added a fourth goal of adopting a strategic approach for publicizing Japan's attractive features. Again, each of these goals is accompanied by a set of measures. The report contains 12 proposals in all.

Although the Japan Brand Working Group, the Task Force on Contents and the Policy Headquarters as a whole, set goals and adopt measures, actual implementation must be undertaken by various related organizations through government offices and representative organizations in the private sector. Indeed, the annual *Strategic Program* has significantly influenced several government offices and prominent organizations in Japan and has shaped their thinking and activities accordingly. Exhibit 1 shows a chronological table of the Japan brand-related initiatives of these government offices, along with the achievements of the Policy Headquarters.

As shown in Exhibit 1, one early initiative taken by the ministries was the formulation of Global Tourism Strategy in 2002 by the Ministry of

Exhibit 1	A Chronological Table of Japan Brand-Related Initiatives	
	Background, activities and results of Policy Headquarters (especially Task Force on Contents)	**Initiatives by government offices**
2002		
February	Policy speech by Prime Minister Koizumi	
February	Strategic Council on Intellectual Property inaugurated	
July	Fifth meeting of Strategic Council on Intellectual Property	
	Intellectual Property Policy Outline adopted	
December		Formulation of Global Tourism Strategy by the Ministry of Land, Infrastructure and Transport
2003		
March	Basic Law on Intellectual Property put into force	
	Intellectual Property Policy Headquarters inaugurated	
	Secretariat of Intellectual Property Policy Headquarters established within the Cabinet Secretariat	

(Continued)

Exhibit 1 (Continued)

	Background, activities and results of Policy Headquarters (especially Task Force on Contents)	Initiatives by government offices
July	Fifth meeting of Intellectual Property Policy Headquarters	
	Strategic Program for the–Creation, Protection and Effective Utilization of Intellectual Property adopted	
	The Task Force on Contents established	
2004 April	Report of the Task Force on Contents compiled Content Business Development Policy	
May	Eighth meeting of Intellectual Property Policy Headquarters	
	Intellectual Property Strategic Program 2004 adopted	
November	First meeting of the Task Force on Contents' Japan Brand Working Group	
2005 February	Report of the Task Force on Contents' Japan Brand Working Group compiled	
	Promotion of Japan Brand Strategy	
April		The National Conference for the Export of Agricultural, Forestry and Fishery Products was inaugurated by Ministry of Agriculture, Forestry and Fishery
May		Establishment of an advisory panel to the Brand Promotion Council for a New Japanese Style
		(Japanesque*Modern) at the Ministry of Economy, Trade and Industry
June	Eleventh meeting of Intellectual Property Policy Headquarters	
	Intellectual Property Strategic Program 2005 adopted	
July		
November	First meeting of the Task Force on Contents' Digital Content Working Group	
December		Prime Minister Koizumi called for the first meeting of the Council on the Promotion of Cultural Diplomacy

(Continued)

Exhibit 1 (Continued)		
	Background, activities and results of Policy Headquarters (especially Task Force on Contents)	**Initiatives by government offices**
2006 **January**		Japanesque Modern Committee was established and the Neo-Japanesque Conference was inaugurated
February	Report of the Task Force on Contents compiled Strategy for the Development of Digital Contents	
March		
April		
June	Fourteenth meeting of Intellectual Property Policy Headquarters	
	Intellectual Property Strategic Program 2006 adopted	
September	First meeting of the Task Force on Contents' Planning Working Group	
September	First Policy speech by Prime Minister Abe	

Source: Compiled by the author based on *Intellectual Property Strategic Program 2006*.

Land, Infrastructure, and Transport, which was incorporated into the widely publicized 'Visit Japan Campaign'. It is followed by the Neo-Japanesque Conference sponsored by the Ministry of Economy, Trade and Industry and the National Conference for Export of Agricultural, Forestry and Fishery Products, organized by the Ministry of Agriculture, Forestry and Fishery. Prime Minister Koizumi himself called for the first meeting of the Council on the Promotion of Cultural Diplomacy and continued to be a high-profile leader of the Japan branding efforts. Although the government took the lead in initiating these actions and conferences, the private sector and ordinary citizens played a major role by discussing the issues, setting the direction and implementing the proposed actions.

In concert with the initiatives by government offices, leading business organizations such as the Japan Business Federation (*Nippon Keidanren*) and the Japan Association of Corporate Executives (*Keizai Doyukai*) have established committees, sections and the like to discuss matters related to the Japan branding. The Japan Business Federation has contributed to the annual *Strategic Program* by providing opinions and suggestions from a business perspective. The Japan Association of Corporate Executives submitted a policy proposal on Japan's nation-branding strategy, drawing attention to the urgent need to create a set of appealing Japan Brand identities.

■ 4. Key Elements of the Japan Branding Strategy

Much progress has been made in the implementation of Japan Brand-related measures, initiatives and activities. Key achievements critical to Japan branding initiatives aspire to two major goals (with respective sub-goals) set by Policy Headquarters, as summarized in Exhibit 2. The two major goals are (1) making Japan a world-class content superpower and (2) implementing the Japan brand strategy based on the Japanese lifestyle. The first goal can be further divided into the sub-goals of making

Exhibit 2 Japan Brand-Related Goals and Achievements by FY2006

Goals		Details	Achievements
Making Japan a World-Class Content Superpower	Making Japan a content-user superpower	• Use of IP multicasting • Adopting protection systems • Efforts to establish content archives	
	Making Japan a content-creator superpower	• Assuring fair returns for creators • Helping creators to exercise their Abilities • Developing human resources in the contents field • Honouring outstanding content	• The Visual Industry Promotion Organization (December 2004) was established as an organization for the development of content-related human resources • The Film Production Course at the Tokyo National University of Fine Arts and Music was established in collaboration with the government of Yokohama City (April 2005)
	Making Japan a content-business superpower	• Strengthening the functions of content producers • Exporting contents • Solving problems related to copyrights • Promoting live entertainment	The Copyright Law was revised (put into force in January 2005)

(Continued)

Exhibit 2 (Continued)

Goals	Details		Achievements
	Accomplishing the roadmap for reforms Appropriately applying the Law on Promotion of the Creation, Protection, and Exploitation of Content		The Act on Creation, Protection, and Exploitation of Content was put into force (in June and partially in September 2004)
Implementing the Japan Brand Strategy Based on the Japanese Lifestyle	Fostering a rich food culture	• Spreading Japanese food culture and foodstuff around the globe • Developing diverse human resources in the culinary world (e.g. Established food-related faculties and schools at universities) • Promoting *Shokuiku* [1][5]	The Council on the Promotion of Food Culture Study issued a report on the 'Promotion of the Japanese Food Culture' (July 2005)
	Establishing diverse and reliable local brands	• Creating and spreading attractive local brands • Developing and publicizing standards for local brands	The Trademark Law was revised, with the aim of protecting local brands more appropriately (put into force in April 2006)
	Establishing Japanese Fashion as a global brand	• Making information available worldwide (Fashion Week, Japanese street fashion) • Increasing the international competitiveness of the Japanese Fashion Industry • Discovering and developing fashion-related human resources	The Japanese fashion Week in Tokyo was held (October 2005, March 2006)

(Continued)

Exhibit 2   (Continued)

Goals	Details	Achievements
Strategically publicizing the attractiveness of Japan	• Making information available in collaboration with Cultural Diplomacy and the Tourism Industry	• The Council on the Promotion of Cultural Diplomacy issued report 'On the Creation of Japan as a Peaceful Nation of Cultural Exchange' (July 2005)
	• Promoting a new Japan Brand, 'Neo-Japanesque'	• Japanesque Modern Committee selected items for the inaugural Japanesque Modern Collection. (October 2006)

[5] Generally, '*Shokuiku*' is defined as 'Promotion of learning on the healthy diet from an early stage, in particular on the choice of foods, so as to secure the healthy living over the course of one's life.' (http://www.nih.go.jp/eiken/english/research/project_shokuiku.html)

Source: Compiled by the author based on the *Intellectual Property Strategic Program 2006*.

Japan a world-class (i) content-user, (ii) content-creator and (iii) content-business superpower, as well as (iv) accomplishing the roadmap for reform and (v) appropriately applying the law on the promotion of the creation, protection and exploitation of content. Similarly, the second goal is divided into the aforementioned four sub-goals.

Whereas the first goal suggests a rather unique emphasis of Japan's brand identity, the second goal seems more standard as a nation brand element, reflecting its comprehensive nature. As discussed, the Policy Headquarters had become aware of Japan brand strategy when it specified the second goal. The first goal originally had been a future vision, but eventually became the identity to which the Japan brand aspired. As such, many of the visible achievements resulting from the Japan brand strategy so far relate to the second goal.

Noticeable achievements related to the food culture were actions taken by the Council on the Promotion of the Food Culture Study, which mainly consists of parties from the private sector. Regarding progress on local brands, the trademark law was revised to better protect local brands, and local governments began providing increased support for local brands. For example, Fukushima prefecture established the Fukushima Brand Certification Committee in 2006 to systematically support local brands. Many other prefectures have engaged in similar initiatives. To promote Japanese fashion, the Fashion Strategic Council was inaugurated, and its executive committee held the Japanese Fashion Week in Tokyo in October 2005 and March 2006.

■ 5. Future direction

As its background suggests, issues for branding Japan have been discussed as part of broader discussion of intellectual property development and management at the Policy Headquarters. Although the Policy Headquarters serves as the policy-making unit for national branding, its authority is limited, and therefore, it could not effectively take responsibility for the overall management of the national identity and Japan branding as a dedicated central body would. The limitations of the current setup need to be acknowledged, and the following tasks for the future need to be addressed.

The Policy Headquarters aims to create a new Japan brand associated not only with high-quality products and manufacturing but also with intellectual and cultural contents and their creation. Although being a world-class content superpower, in particular, seems a key identity for the Japan brand, they suggest that more comprehensive and open discussion of Japan's brand identity may be required. On the other hand, building a comprehensive nation brand requires a wide range of branding efforts, and thus contributions from various agents – public and private, domestic and foreign – are necessary. These contributions need to be compiled, organized and coordinated by some responsible authority. The authority may want to open a Japan brand portal website to accomplish this task efficiently.

Just like a company brand, the equity of a nation brand resides in the minds of its audiences. Somebody must keep track of the equity of the Japan brand and manage this brand effectively, using an analytical approach. Management can be improved by developing the scale and the measurement method, by carefully selecting and/or effectively collecting data and by devising analytical models. It may be necessary to create an institute dedicated to carrying out this task, even if data collection on a global basis is to be handled by the existing agencies and institutes, such as the overseas agencies of the Ministry of Foreign Affairs.

*****

■ Introduction

There is no universal template for nation-branding strategy, as nations have only relatively recently engaged in nation branding and are exploring different strategies for achieving their nation-brand goals. However, there are certain basic principles of strategy that we shall look at in this chapter, relating these principles to the context of nation branding. Internal and external analyses, for example, are important bases for strategy formulation, and we outline techniques and issues in this regard. Specific elements of nation-branding strategy are also discussed, including advertising, customer and citizen relationship management and diaspora mobilization.

In his country case insight on the directions and the key elements of branding Japan, Professor Satoshi Akutsu discusses the work of the Japan Brand Working Group and describes the Working Group's focus on three key areas – food culture, fashion and local brands – as part of an overall nation-branding effort to improve the image and reputation of Japan. In the second country case insight in this chapter, the leading international branding consultancy Interbrand give an account of their work on developing a nation-brand for Estonia, the main objectives of which were to enable Estonia to achieve greater success in attracting FDI, to expand its tourist base beyond Sweden and Finland and to broaden European markets for its exports.

■ Principles of strategy

The basic principles of strategy centre upon three key questions for the firm, or in our case, the nation. First, where are we now? Second, where do we want to go? Third, how do we get there? The formulation and implementation of strategy is a complex task, yet these three guiding questions provide a framework within which strategy can be developed. Strategy has been defined as 'the direction and scope of an organisation over the long term, which achieves advantage in a changing environment through its configuration of resources and competences with the aim of fulfilling stakeholder expectations' [2]. Nations, like companies, must decide on their long-term direction and scope; for nations, this will involve strategic decisions regarding the configuration of resources and competences to achieve goals in the areas of FDI, export promotion, tourism, talent attraction and so on. Nations will rarely be able to excel in all of these competitive domains, and therefore, strategic decisions must be made regarding the nation-brand's direction.

Where are we now? Strategic analysis

To assess the nation-brand's current competitive position, it is necessary to conduct both internal and external analyses. The main thrust of the internal analysis is to evaluate the nation-brand's capabilities across a range of sector-specific indicators. External analysis, on the other hand, focuses on the nation-brand's competitors and also on the wider environmental forces that affect the nation-brand's activities.

Internal analysis

Internal analysis for the nation-brand serves to evaluate the nation's capabilities across the different arenas it competes within. The analysis needs to be conducted on a sectoral basis in order to identify existing capabilities, evaluate the strength of these capabilities and then derive appropriate action points based on the nation-brand capability analysis.

The main sectors that nation-brands compete in include tourism, FDI, export promotion and talent attraction. The internal analysis required by nation-brands competing in these sectors is outlined below.

Tourism: Many nations are heavily dependent upon tourism. Remote, landlocked states in particular find it difficult to compete in the other arenas of nation-brand strategy and therefore turn to tourism as a key component of economic development (see academic perspective on the repositioning of Nepal, Chapter 2). Other nations, blessed with attractive climates and sights, but poor in other resources, also rely heavily on tourism as a reliable revenue stream. An indicative, though not exhaustive, range of key success factors for nation-brands' performance in the tourism sector are shown in Table 9.1.

The key success factors in Table 9.1 are clearly beyond the control of national tourism organizations; yet, tourism boards can and do take initiatives to try and drive up overall levels of customer service levels, for example. Amongst the other key success factors, reasonable levels of safety and law and order are a pre-requisite for attracting mainstream tourism; value for money is an important attribute; whilst accessibility can represent a considerable obstacle for otherwise highly attractive destinations – Australia and New Zealand, for example, enjoy positive perceptions as a tourist destination amongst UK consumers yet the distance involved in travelling there is a considerable deterrent. For other countries, such as Iceland and other nordic states, their remoteness may be more perceptual than real; in such a case, there is clearly potential for effective nation branding to overturn misperceptions of remoteness.

FDI: Globalization has sharpened the competition between nations to attract inward investment. In response to this, nations need to put in place a long term strategy to ensure that their levels of FDI attraction make a significant contribution to the nation's economy (see country case on France, Chapter 10). Some of the key success factors in attracting FDI are shown in Table 9.2.

Without a stable economic and political environment, there is little likelihood of attracting FDI. Companies looking to make long-term investments in foreign nations will be put off by a volatile political situation or a mismanaged economy. A skilled workforce is attractive in that it minimizes the need for companies to pay for the training of their workforces in foreign locations and offers the prospect of higher productivity

Table 9.1 Nation-brand internal analysis – *tourism*

Key success factors	Nation-brand capability									
Customer service levels	1	2	3	4	5	6	7	8	9	10
Safety	1	2	3	4	5	6	7	8	9	10
Value for money	1	2	3	4	5	6	7	8	9	10
Accessibility	1	2	3	4	5	6	7	8	9	10

Table 9.2 Nation-brand internal analysis – *FDI*

Key success factors	Nation-brand capability									
Stable economic and political environment	1	2	3	4	5	6	7	8	9	10
Skilled workforce	1	2	3	4	5	6	7	8	9	10
Streamlined administrative procedures	1	2	3	4	5	6	7	8	9	10
Infrastructure	1	2	3	4	5	6	7	8	9	10

than less-skilled workforces in other nations. Administrative procedures can be so complex, bureaucratic and slow in some nations that companies will look elsewhere rather than submit to the uncertainty of a wait of several months for approval to do business in a nation whose business environment is strangled by cumbersome administrative processes. Finally, nations need to invest in efficient, modern infrastructure if they are to compete effectively for highly sought-after FDI.

Export promotion: A key objective of nation-branding strategy is to boost the nation's level of export performance. Country case insights on Chile, Iceland and Estonia, for example, have illustrated the ways in which these nations have sought to improve their export performance (see Chapters 3, 8 and 9). Some of the key success factors for export promotion are shown in Table 9.3

An indicative range of key success factors for export promotion includes the need to build high-quality brands, establish effective COO positioning through sound management of country image perceptions, the strategic development of target markets and high levels of innovation.

Talent attraction: The two major objectives of talent attraction are to attract skilled workers and to attract foreign students to the country's higher education system. Some of the key success factors for talent attraction are shown in Table 9.4.

The attraction of suitable numbers of skilled workers will depend upon various criteria, including favourable visa and residency regulations, opportunity for career progression and an attractive lifestyle. For potential students, the country's reputation for higher education plays an important role, particularly in the highly competitive market for Masters and MBA students.

Table 9.3 Nation-brand internal analysis – *export promotion*

Key success factors	Nation-brand capability									
High quality brands	1	2	3	4	5	6	7	8	9	10
Effective COO positioning	1	2	3	4	5	6	7	8	9	10
Strategic development of target markets	1	2	3	4	5	6	7	8	9	10
Innovation	1	2	3	4	5	6	7	8	9	10

Table 9.4 Nation-brand internal analysis – *talent attraction*

Key success factors	Nation-brand capability									
Favourable residency criteria (for visa, passport, etc.)	1	2	3	4	5	6	7	8	9	10
Attractive lifestyle	1	2	3	4	5	6	7	8	9	10
Opportunity for career progression	1	2	3	4	5	6	7	8	9	10
Reputation for higher education	1	2	3	4	5	6	7	8	9	10

External analysis

External analysis takes two main forms – *competitor* analysis and *environmental* analysis.

Competitor analysis focuses on a number of key questions, which have been identified as follows: Who are our competitors? What are their strengths and weaknesses? What are their strategic objectives and thrust? What are their strategies? What are their response patterns? [3]. Nation-brands need to conduct this type of competitor analysis for each of the arenas within which they are competing. This can encompass tourism, FDI, export promotion, talent attraction and any further nation-branding domains. The competitor set will vary according to which competitive arena is under analysis – a nation that is a key competitor in the tourism sector may barely figure at all as a competitor for FDI, for example. The nation-brand competitor analysis matrix provides a tool for analyzing the nation-brand's competitive set across the key dimensions of nation-branding activity such as tourism, FDI, export promotion and talent attraction (Table 9.5).

Table 9.5 Nation-brand competitor analysis matrix

	Strengths	Weaknesses	Strategic goals	Current strategies
Tourism				
Country A				
Country B				
FDI				
Country C				
Country D				
Export promotion				
Country E				
Country F				
Talent attraction				
Country G				
Country H				

The nation-brand competitor analysis matrix allows for the concise presentation of a large number of complex variables. It can be used not only for analysis of the nation-brand's key competitors but also as a basis for strategy development.

Where do we want to go? Strategic planning

Strategic planning involves setting specific, measurable goals and targets. It has been suggested that 'few businesses pursue a single objective; instead they have a mixture, which typically includes profitability, sales growth, market share improvement, risk containment, innovativeness. . . ' [4]. Likewise, nations will pursue multiple objectives, and these objectives should underpin strategy formulation. One of the most widely used tools in strategic planning is Ansoff's matrix, which identifies potential directions for the development of strategy based on permutations of existing or new products and existing or new markets [5]. In the context of nation branding, Ansoff's matrix can be used to identify strategic directions across the full range of nation-brand activities.

How do we get there? Strategic implementation

After the preceding stages of analysis and strategic planning, the final and obviously crucial stage in strategy lies in the implementation of the chosen strategy. Key challenges in strategy implementation include ensuring control, managing knowledge, coping with change, designing appropriate structures and processes and managing internal and external relationships [1]. It is perhaps in the area of implementation that nation branding faces its biggest challenge, given that the nation-brand stakeholders may not be as easily structured and managed as the various business units of a commercial organization. Switzerland is one country that has addressed the challenge of strategic implementation through establishing a coordinating body, Presence Switzerland, that performs many of the strategy implementation roles outlined above, for example, managing knowledge, coping with change and managing internal and external relationships (see country case insight, Chapter 4).

Having provided an overview of the fundamental issues in strategic analysis, planning and implementation, we shall now focus on some of the specific elements that nation-branding strategy may encompass.

■ Nation-brand advertising

Nation branding does not consist merely of running advertising campaigns. Advertising can obviously be a powerful tool, but it is only one element of a nation-brand's overall strategy. In fact, if a nation has severely limited financial resources, it would probably be far better off activating its diaspora rather than placing its hope in an advertising campaign. However, if the funds are available, then advertising should be used as part of an integrated strategy to achieve specific, clearly stated goals.

Advertising can deliver numerous benefits to brands. It can generate new markets for a brand; revitalize a declining brand; change consumer behaviour and generate rapid sales increases [6]. There are, however, a number of common mistakes in advertising that nation-brands need to be aware of before handing over significant resources to advertising agencies. Such mistakes have been identified as including mistaken assumptions about consumer knowledge; failure to break through the advertising clutter; distracting, overpowering creative in ads; under-branded ads; failure to use supporting media; changing campaigns too frequently and substituting ad frequency for ad quality [7]. The foregoing mistakes in advertising have been found in advertising for FMCG brands and do not necessarily appear in such nation-branding advertising as has been produced to date. For example, the mistake concerning the overpowering creative element of an ad can certainly be seen in product-brand advertising, where the viewer of the ad may find the ad itself entertaining yet have no idea what brand the ad was for. This phenomenon has not yet afflicted nation-branding advertising, where a far more common mistake is to produce bland, information-heavy ads that fail to break through the advertising clutter.

If some advertising is going to be bought as part of a country's overall nation-brand strategy, those involved in procuring the advertising need to have at least a basic knowledge of the advertising industry and the way that advertising agencies work. Without a basic level of advertising literacy, precious resources could be wasted through failing to develop a mutually beneficial relationship with the advertising agency selected to produce the campaign. People in the nation-brand team need to be familiar with what is meant by a client brief, creative teams, the concept of brand positioning and so on. Individuals with a background or qualification in marketing will know all about such things, but it cannot be assumed that people with non-marketing backgrounds, government officials or other stakeholders in the nation-brand team will be equally knowledgeable in this area. The concept of brand positioning has already been covered (see Chapter 2), so we will focus here on the other key advertising-related issues.

The client brief is issued by the client to the advertising agencies it is inviting to pitch for its business, in the form of a written brief which details the client's requirements; after an advertising agency has been appointed, the brief will normally be refined in order to establish clear lines of communication and accountability between client and agency [8]. The creative team within the ad agency will normally comprise an art director and a copywriter, whose role is to produce creative work that will grab the target audience's attention and deliver the campaign's specified goals. The art director will be responsible for the visual element of the advertisement, whilst the copywriter will provide any text that the ad will use.

On a day-to-day basis, however, the client will not normally be in contact with the agency's creative team. Rather, the agency will communicate with the client through an account manager whose role is to ensure a smooth relationship between client and agency throughout the duration of the planning and implementation process. The quality of the work produced by the agency is therefore dependent not only on the agency's own creativity but also on the client's ability to clearly communicate its needs to the agency. Clients can influence the creativity of their ad agency, for example, by 'setting direction' through their initial brief to the agency and also as they interact with the agency during the advertising planning process and also by 'resource allocation' in terms of providing the ad agency with access to the client's top management in order to provide strategic insights to the campaign and also by providing access to previously conducted consumer research data [9].

Whereas the *client brief* will detail the strategic objectives to be met by the advertising campaign, the client will also need to produce a so-called *creative brief* that focuses more closely on exactly what the ad is going to say, to whom and the tone that is going to be used. It is important to ensure that an appropriate tone is used in the ad's message. If the wrong tone is used, the audience may feel alienated or even offended. The advertising campaign promoting Australian tourism that used the tagline 'Where the bloody hell are you?' clearly runs the risk of offending its audience, who may find the slogan rude and aggressive. A different type of nation-branding advertising, aimed at attracting FDI rather than tourists, was carried out by 'The New France' campaign, which launched in 2004 and which followed up the first wave of advertising with a second wave in 2005, with 77 ads appearing in 19 publications; the effect of this campaign was evaluated based on a survey of the target audience – company managers in four of the target countries – and taking into consideration the survey results, the advertising approach in one of the target countries was switched to focus on sector-based magazines rather than financial publications (see country case insight on France, Chapter 10). This illustrates the importance of evaluating the effectiveness of an advertising campaign and then fine-tuning the campaign based on the results of the evaluation.

A full-service advertising agency will not only produce the advertising for the client but also buy the media space within which the advertising will appear. However, there are many dedicated media buying agencies that exist independently of the creative advertising agencies, and in some cases, it may be cost-effective to hire the services of such a specialized media buying agency. It is a complex task to evaluate the numerous different media channels and vehicles available for any one advertising campaign. Media *channels* include TV, newspapers and magazines, Internet, radio, outdoor and so on. Media *vehicles* include the different options that exist within each media – for example, within newspapers as a media channel, the available vehicles are represented by the individual newspaper brands within that sector such as the *Financial Times, Wall Street Journal* and so on. Full-service ad agencies or specialized media buying agencies will normally use media planning software to determine the optimum mix of advertising media in order to achieve the campaign's stated goals. Media planning software works in the following way: first, the user develops a media database of possible advertising vehicles, specifying their ratings and cost; second, the user selects the criterion for schedule optimization, e.g. reach, frequency; third, the user specifies constraints, e.g. a budget constraint for the media planning period; and finally, the software algorithm seeks out the optimum media schedule according to the specified objectives and constraints [10].

The structure of the advertising industry has been in flux over recent years and clients will usually have a choice between opting for a full-service agency or specialized creative agencies and media buying agencies. It has been argued, for example, by the head of WPP's media network, Mindshare, that the media agency is best placed to orchestrate a brand's communication efforts [11].

■ Customer and citizen relationship management

CRM is a well-established practice in the business world, where the acronym is widely considered to stand for 'customer relationship management'. The application of the CRM concept to nation branding is a much more recent development, where the term 'citizen relationship management' has been used [12]. The concept of citizen relationship management suggests that governments need to engage with and respond to their citizens in a similar way in which companies do with their customers. Understanding citizens' needs and communicating with citizens in an appropriate manner at an appropriate frequency represent CRM principles that nation-branding strategy may usefully adopt. CRM as a process that 'involves the application of technology to help manage interactions and transactions with customers, so that organisations can optimise their returns across their customer portfolio' (Francis Buttle, academic perspective, Chapter 3) also has direct applicability to nation-brands that have a customer portfolio spread across sectors as diverse as tourism, FDI, export promotion, and talent attraction.

Citizen relationship management may be seen in the case of Russia's 'Church diplomacy' project as well as in its social projects (see country case insight on Russia, Chapter 5) and in the nation-branding efforts of Estonia, where it is hoped that the brand's aim of establishing broader international recognition will motivate Estonia's own citizens (see country case insight on Estonia, Chapter 9).

■ Nation-brand ambassadors

Companies in many sectors employ brand ambassadors in order to provide a human face to their activities. Currency exchange firm Travelex, for example, signed up England rugby star Jonny Wilkinson as a brand ambassador for a 2-year period; Travelex had previously signed up Australian cricketer Adam Gilchrist as a brand ambassador in 2003 [13]. Other companies appoint brand ambassadors internally. These brand ambassadors are highly enthusiastic individuals imbued with a deep knowledge of their company, and they also possess the ability to communicate the company's brand values effectively to targeted audiences.

Nations, on the other hand, traditionally employ ambassadors in a more discreet role, so discreet that few people outside of diplomatic circles will know much, if anything, about them. Famous sporting or cultural figures may perform an unplanned, unscripted form of nation-brand ambassador role, without any official endorsement from their nation or any agreement by the individual concerned that they are in fact a type of ambassador for their nation. Likewise, the behaviour of individual citizens when in foreign countries can be interpreted as being representative of their home nation (see country case insight on Russia, Chapter 5). When this behaviour is bad, as in the case of English football hooliganism during the 1980s, it can tarnish the overall country image. It is clearly unrealistic to expect every citizen in a population of millions to act as a nation-brand ambassador, yet it may be possible to identify certain individuals who are qualified and willing to play such a role.

■ Diaspora mobilization

Nations that fail to have a strategy for activating their diaspora network are squandering a unique and precious resource. The existence of diaspora networks spread across the globe represents a potentially immense asset for the nation, not only in terms of remittances sent by diaspora members but also in terms of stimulating FDI through interventions by well-placed senior executives in international firms. Furthermore, the reputation-building capacity of diaspora networks represents another key opportunity to enhance the nation-brand.

Some observers remain unconvinced that remittances by migrants can have a significant impact on a nation's development, although they acknowledge that such remittances play an important role in poverty alleviation [14]. Rather than the financial flows inherent in remittances, it has been suggested that a more important role of diasporas is their knowledge and institution-building capacity [15]. Kuznetsov [16] has described successful diaspora networks as combining three main features: first, networks bring together people with strong intrinsic motivation; second, members play both direct roles (implementing projects in the home country) and indirect roles (serving as bridges and antennae for the development of projects in the home country) and third, successful initiatives move from discussions on how to get involved with the home country to transactions, i.e. tangible outcomes. There is huge variation in the impact that different nations' diasporas have had – the diasporas of China and India, for instance, have had a considerable positive impact on their home countries, whereas Armenia has failed to benefit from its wealthy diaspora [17]. This highlights the necessity of integrating diaspora networks into overall nation-brand strategy.

Diaspora networks are not necessarily monolithic and homogeneous. For example, there are many diaspora networks that take the form of professional associations dedicated to helping members advance in their professional field – such networks include the Association of Doctors of Armenian Origin in the United States, the Association of Engineers from Latin America or Indus Entrepreneurs [18]. South Africa has two diaspora networks, the South African Network of Skills Abroad, a network that links expatriate and South Africa-based academics, researchers and practitioners working in science and technology; and the South African Diaspora Network, which focuses on developing knowledge and entrepreneurial connections between South African firms and well-connected, strategically placed individuals in the UK [19]. Government support for such networks should focus on achieving synergies between the different diaspora networks and simultaneously avoiding duplication of effort and activity by complementary networks.

■ Nation days

The celebration of nation days represents another potential element of nation-brand strategy, both internally as a means of generating interest and pride domestically from the nation's citizens and also externally as a focal point for events to promote the nation-brand. The natural place to hold such nation day celebrations outside of the home country is in locations where there is a significant diaspora presence. Ireland and Scotland, for example, have done this through their respective nation day celebrations in New York, a city that is home to large numbers of Irish and Scottish diaspora. The Irish celebration is based on St. Patrick's Day, whilst the Scottish celebration is based on what started as 'Tartan Day' but which has since expanded to 'Tartan Week'. It has been suggested that 'whilst both are phenomena that rely on a certain amount of constructed heritage, the Tartan Day events are recent and politically created, whereas St. Patrick's Day has several centuries of what may be regarded as "genuine" heritage' [20]. The question of how 'genuine' heritage is relates to the concept of 'invented tradition' that has been widely debated in the field of national identity (see Chapter 5).

■ The naming of nation-brands

The country case insight on Iceland (see Chapter 8) illustrates the potential effect of a nation's name on its country image perceptions. Nations rarely tamper with their names and when they do so, it is often to signal a powerful symbolic event such as the birth of a nation gaining its freedom from a former colonial power. This can be seen in the case of many African states, for example, the name Ghana replacing Gold Coast when that country achieved independence from the UK. Sometimes there can be widespread misunderstanding of a nation's name – many people considered the old Soviet Union to be 'Russia', for example (see country case insight on Russia, Chapter 5), and there is still a widespread misperception that the UK and England are interchangeable terms. A further dimension of the naming of nation-brands is that some nations have two different names in use – Greece/Hellas, Holland/Netherlands and so on. To avoid potential confusion, when nation-brand architecture is being developed (see Chapter 8), there will need to be a strategic decision taken on which name is to be used as the 'umbrella brand'.

■ Nation-brand tracking studies

The effectiveness of nation-branding strategy needs to be assessed on an ongoing basis. Various types of tracking studies can be conducted, and there are numerous indexes available that can be used to determine different facets of nation-brand performance. A widely publicized survey in the field of nation branding is the Anholt-GMI Nations Brands Index, an analytical ranking of the world's nation-brands that appears on a quarterly basis. There are also other indexes available that, although not designed with nation branding in mind, represent useful indicators of national performance that nations could use to enhance their country image perceptions – on condition, of course, that the nation performs well in these indexes. One such index is the Environmental Sustainability Index, which measures the quality of nations' environmental stewardship (see Chapter 7); another index is the World Economic Forum's Global Competitiveness Index, which assesses a nation's competitiveness in terms of its institutions, infrastructure, macroeconomy, health and primary education, higher education and training, market efficiency, technological readiness, business sophistication and innovation. If a nation scores highly on these criteria, then it should highlight and communicate its positive performance in order to achieve strategic objectives such as increasing FDI, talent attraction, and so on.

Country Case Insight – Estonia

Interbrand, a leading international branding consultancy

■ 1. Foreword

This project was commissioned by Enterprise Estonia and undertaken in 2001–2002 to promote the Republic of Estonia abroad. Its objectives were to enable Estonia to achieve greater success in attracting foreign-direct investment, to expand its tourist base beyond Sweden and Finland and to broaden European markets for its exports.

■ 2. Introducing Estonia

In 2001, when this project was in its early stages, Estonia was relatively undefined and poorly understood among Europeans at large and, indeed, the rest of the world. In reality, Estonia has a great many things to offer. To attract the world's attention, however, it needed to say something interesting about itself.

Simply announcing one's existence, however, will not in most cases attract investment or tourism; people need to be given motivating reasons for choosing to do business with a country. By explaining in a clear, reasoned and targeted manner why Estonia is a great location for a holiday or office or factory, Estonia can cleverly position herself ahead of other countries. By doing so over time, and by ensuring consistency in message and appearance, Estonia will establish a set of recognizable brand attributes.

Second, Estonia is at a unique moment in her history. Its re-emergence on the European stage has given Estonia a critical and rare opportunity to make a first impression on millions of European business people and potential tourists. For most of them, the name 'Estonia' will be unfamiliar, or, if they have any impressions at all, they will more likely than not be vague or even negative regarding Estonia's occupied past or perceived poor climate. By informing people in a compelling and distinctive way, we can begin to generate interest and forge a desirable reputation for the country.

Finally, by proving that the country has a lot to say and a lot to offer, there is a real opportunity to 'punch above its weight' in European and world affairs. Estonia's perspective, opinion and voice will ultimately represent and deliver far more than a population of 1.4 million people could have achieved in the absence of 'brand recognition'. Being recognized and seen to stand for the tangible and the relevant enables small countries to surpass expectations in creating demand for exports, attracting strong foreign direct investment and building and promoting a thriving tourist industry. In addition, the brand should establish broader international recognition that will motivate Estonia's own citizens.

■ 3. Defining the project

Despite an absence of any managed effort in the past, Estonia's brand identity has been reasonably well understood within the Nordic region, yet it is less robust than those of other Nordic nations. It is relatively indistinct among the EU applicant states (even in comparison to some less-well-prepared nations) and is largely unknown or not understood outside Europe and Russia.

To successfully develop and promote Estonia's image abroad, a rigorous, six-month brand-development process was commissioned and undertaken. The initial segment of the project focused on understanding the way people think about Estonia now and defining how they should view it in the future, through an understanding of contemporary Estonia. This research involved extensive reading and desk research, 70 in-depth interviews with Estonian political, cultural and opinion-leaders, entrepreneurs and journalists, a comprehensive audit of Estonia's existing visual identity, focus-groups with Estonian and non-Estonian business people, 250 telephone interviews within Estonia and a further 1476 with tourists, investors and importers in the UK, Germany, Finland, Sweden and Russia, team participation in several public panels and conferences on national identity and, lastly, input from artists, designers, marketing professionals, researchers and public and private officials in Estonia.

This comprehensive understanding fed into the development of the Brand Estonia strategy; recommendations for the brand's core messages and eventual verbal and visual expression.

■ 4. Learning from research

At a qualitative level, the themes uncovered in the process of researching and understanding internal and external perspectives regarding Estonia were remarkably consistent across different audiences. Through the quantitative component, however, internal perceptions were seen to be rather more positive than those of external audiences – particularly among people with little real experience of Estonia or who were geographically further away (e.g. in the UK and Germany).

In summary, it is clear that while Estonia offers great potential for distinctive and positive experiences among both tourist and business audiences, there is much more that can be done to communicate and deliver this. However, one of the most obvious lessons from the research is a clear impression of change and contrast within the country that, in turn, affords many opportunities. People who do not know the country, or are encountering it for the first time, seem positively surprised. Such notions of contrast, surprise and change seem to be striking identifying elements in what now characterizes contemporary Estonia. This evidence of change and transformation provides powerful drivers in the branding of Estonia. These elements are not only well recognized by people who know the country but also illustrate real, positive benefits to those who will perceive Estonia from abroad. How these ideas will manifest themselves will be discussed below in the context of the brand strategy.

■ 5. Building a brand strategy for Estonia

Because Estonia's potential audiences are so diverse, a brand model has been developed, which takes this diversity into account. Within this model, a series of co-ordinated and reinforcing messages or 'stories' can be used by the different public- and private-sector organizations in the country when speaking to specific audiences.

The brand model contains a number of interrelating components that include essence that defines the country when seen as a brand, a series of Brand stories or Narratives to explain and explore the breadth thereof and a translation of those stories into specific messages for tourism, exports and inward investment.

Ultimately, the brand model provides a systematic means to communicate positive and valuable ideas about the country, particularly to foreign audiences, in a way that will position Estonia favourably and competitively. It is the reference point for the differentiated, creative expressions of the brand, and thus naturally drives the 'look and feel' of Brand Estonia's communications.

The Brand model

The Brand essence

The brand essence has been captured in two words: positively transforming. Over the past decade, Estonia has proven herself capable of revolutionary, positive and welcome change against all odds.

The Brand narratives

A series of Estonian brand stories or narratives provides a relevant and motivating way of articulating the essence – positively transforming – to the world.

1. *A fresh perspective*: To the outsider, Estonia's culture and landscape differs vastly from what they are accustomed to. Although aspects of Estonia will be familiar through reference to other European societies – architecture, cuisine, language, landscape and music to name a few – their uses and the forms they take will often be innovative or surprising to newcomers.

2. *A radical, reforming and transforming attitude*: Because Estonia has had to learn first hand how to participate in the contemporary, political economy, she has had to take risks, to innovate and use creativity to solve substantial problems in order to leapfrog ahead and put the country squarely on the politico-economic map.

3. *A Nordic temperament and environment*: Estonia has always been part of the web of Northern Europe. Yet, an accident of history links Estonia in the minds of most people with the East instead of the West. Although some specific elements of Estonia's social and economic structure do diverge from the established 'Nordic' pattern, the country is very much a part of the Nordic socio-geographic region in temperament and environment.

4. *A resourceful self-starter by nature*: To attain the advanced level of political and economic development Estonia enjoys, the country has to acquire the utmost confidence in itself and its abilities. The Estonian labour force is educated, advanced in skills and adept in languages, and its solutions to the most pressing of contemporary issues in business and governance have proved effective time and again.

5. *A European society*: Despite so much change in so little time, Estonia has not forgotten its roots and its place in the world. The Estonian language and folk culture have survived despite a millennium of foreign occupation, socio-linguistic influence and outright suppression, as if the society of the past knew that these elements had to be preserved for a future generation that would fully enjoy the freedom to be themselves, by themselves.

Translating the Brand Stories for different audiences

To make the Brand Stories as motivating and relevant as possible, these stories may also be translated into specific messages aimed at each of Brand Estonia's target audiences: tourists, investors and importers.

■ 6. Managing the brand and bringing it to life

Each of these stories translates into verbal and visual brand-communication pieces or brand manifestations – posters, brochures, website, environmental design and so on, to be seen in places such as the airport, police vans and sides of taxi cabs. (2007 Postscript: Since the project was rolled out, t-shirts with 'Welcome to Estonia' emblazoned on them have become something of a cult statement, with students seen wearing them in nightclubs around Europe and America.)

Why is this so important? As well as the more obvious communication points that a new brand needs to touch, public infrastructure and public services are the most noticeable and memorable national symbols for visitors and those who come to work in a country. Taxi-cabs are also important in portraying a location: one only has to think of London's black and New York's yellow cabs, both of which are 'postcard' images and give a real sense of place. Managers of public infrastructure may thus choose to ignore the obvious role they play in characterizing the country, or whole-heartedly adopt the spirit of Brand Estonia to assist in positively transforming the way they are seen.

To establish Estonia's identity firmly among potential tourists, investors, and importers-as well as politicians, officials, journalists, writers, artists and everyday people throughout Europe and the world – Brand Estonia will need to be brought to life in a way that reflects the country's heritage, unique qualities and, above all, what Estonia has to offer the world.

*****

■ Summary

Nation-branding strategy is a complex undertaking. The principles of strategic analysis, planning and implementation apply to nations as they do to companies, although the specific elements of nation-branding strategy will differ considerably from those encountered by commercial organizations. Nation-brands need to conduct internal and external analysis in order to assess the current competitive position, from which they can formulate and implement strategy in an appropriate direction. The country case insights on Japan and Estonia that appear in this chapter show how those two nations have gone about developing their respective nation-branding strategies.

■ References

1. Johnson, G., Scholes, K. and Whittington, R. (2005) *Exploring Corporate Strategy: Text and Cases*, Seventh Edition, FT Prentice Hall, UK.
2. Johnson, G., Scholes, K. and Whittington, R. (2005) *Exploring Corporate Strategy: Text and Cases*, Seventh Edition, FT Prentice Hall, UK.
3. Jobber, D. (2004) *Principles and Practice of Marketing*, Fourth Edition, McGraw-Hill, UK.

4. Wilson, R.M.S. and Gilligan, C. (2005) *Strategic Marketing Management: Planning, Implementation & Control*, Third Edition, Elsevier Butterworth Heinemann, UK.

5. Ansoff, H. (1988) *Corporate Strategy*, Penguin, UK.

6. IPA Effectiveness Awards (1998) http://www.ipa.co.uk (accessed 08/03/02).

7. Keller, K.L. (2003) *Strategic Brand Management: Building, Measuring, and Managing Brand Equity*, Second Edition, Prentice Hall, USA.

8. Hackley, C. (2005) *Advertising and Promotion: Communicating Brands*, Sage Publications, UK.

9. Koslow, S., Sasser, S.L., and Riordan, E.A. (2006) Do Marketers Get The Advertising They Need Or The Advertising They Deserve? *Journal of Advertising*, **35/3**, 81–101.

10. Shimp, T.A. (2003) *Advertising, Promotion, & Supplemental Aspects of Integrated Marketing Communications*, Sixth Edition, Thomson South-Western, USA.

11. Marquis, S. (2007) Buyers storm the creatives' citadel. *The Guardian*, Media-Guardian, Monday April 23, p. 10.

12. Sheth, J. (2006) Keynote Speech, *Academy of Marketing Conference*, July.

13. Barrand, D. (2005) Travelex secures Jonny Wilkinson as ambassador. *Marketing*, May 18, p. 4.

14. Kuznetsov, Y. and Sabel, C. (2006) International Migration of Talent, Diaspora Networks, and Development: Overview of Main Issues, in *Diaspora Networks and the International Migration of Skills: How Countries Can Draw on Their Talent Abroad* (Y. Kuznetsov, ed.), WBI Development Studies, pp. 3–19.

15. Kapur, D. and McHale, J. (2005) *Give Us Your Best and Brightets. The Global Hunt for Talent and Its Impact on the Developing World*, Center for Global Development, Washington D.C., USA.

16. Kuznetsov, Y. (2006) Leveraging Diasporas of Talent: Towards a New Policy Agenda, in *Diaspora Networks and the International Migration of Skills: How Countries Can Draw on Their Talent Abroad* (Y. Kuznetsov, ed.), WBI Development Studies, pp. 221–237.

17. Kuznetsov, Y. and Sabel, C. (2006) International Migration of Talent, Diaspora Networks, and Development: Overview of Main Issues, in *Diaspora Networks and the International Migration of Skills: How Countries Can Draw on Their Talent Abroad* (Y. Kuznetsov, ed.), WBI Development Studies, pp. 3–19.

18. Kuznetsov, Y. and Sabel, C. (2006) International Migration of Talent, Diaspora Networks, and Development: Overview of Main Issues, in *Diaspora Networks and the International Migration of Skills: How Countries Can Draw on Their Talent Abroad* (Y. Kuznetsov, ed.), WBI Development Studies, pp. 3–19.

19. Marks, J. (2006) South Africa: Evolving Diaspora, Promising Initiatives, in *Diaspora Networks and the International Migration of Skills: How Countries Can Draw on Their Talent Abroad* (Y. Kuznetsov, ed.) WBI Development Studies, pp. 171–186.

20. Nunan, D. (2005) Marketing to Diasporas: A comparison of nation branding strategies employed by Scotland and Ireland, unpublished MSc Dissertation, University of Strathclyde.

Future horizons
for nation
branding

Country Case Insight – France

The new France – Breaking through the perception barrier

Philippe Favre

French Ambassador for International Investment, Chairman and CEO of Invest in France Agency

■ 1. Myth versus reality

Now the world's fifth-largest economy, France is a modern and dynamic country located at the heart of the largest market in the world – Europe. It has reinvented itself over the past few years with significant privatizations and reforms across key sectors to be more competitive on an international scale. Business formalities have been simplified, and work-time regulations have been improved to attract foreign investors, while its first-class infrastructure and talented workforce are other advantages that have helped raise France's allure worldwide.

Despite these realities, some people around the globe – in the USA and the UK in particular – continue to have stereotyped images of the nation that overshadow its business leadership and thriving economy: France is still viewed as the tourist capital of the world, best known for its fine wine, food and fashion. Its leading-edge technology and innovation in healthcare, already familiar to investors in China and Japan, are overlooked by companies in the USA and the UK, who are preoccupied with outdated perceptions that go against the modern actuality of France.

■ 2. Changing the world's opinion

The French government recognized that correcting the discrepancy between the myth and the reality of France's image was important to the success of its economy and inward investment levels. But, how does a nation convince the world that it would make a savvy business partner and sell itself to foreign investors?

In France's case, it had the help of the Invest in France Agency (IFA), a government organization responsible for promoting international investment and helping foreign investors succeed in France. As part of its mission, IFA has helped erase misconceptions about France over the past

3 years with the rollout of an image campaign entitled 'The New France. Where the smart money goes'.

With a total budget of €35 million, the campaign was developed and run by IFA in collaboration with several French government bodies, including the international business development agency, UBIFrance; the national tourist office, Maison de la France; the information service department; the Ministry of Foreign Affairs; the French Economic Mission; the national agricultural marketing and communications consultant, Sopexa; the education promotion agency, EDUFrance; the Treasury Directorate and the French State Council. Pierre Dauzier, communications expert and ex-president of the advertising company Havas, headed the group along with the president of IFA.

■ 3. Goals and strategy

The main goal of the campaign was to raise France's economic profile among five leading target investment countries: the USA, the UK, Germany, Japan and China. IFA aimed to improve foreign investor opinions of France to attract new business and increase inward investment. Creating solid relationships with foreign investors for long-term dialogue was another important objective. To be most effective, steering committees and press agents were designated in each of the target countries to create tailored communications for the different international audiences.

The campaign strategy was focused on boosting visibility and credibility to best highlight France's numerous social and economic benefits. Tangible facts and testimonials from international corporations already doing business in France helped gain authority with investors in the USA and the UK, where opinions were unfavourable. Senior executives from 12 reputable global companies, including FedEx, Toyota, Xerox, GE and Sony, described their success firsthand to underline the ease of setting up, the access to qualified talent and the convenience of a central location, positioning France as a land of new opportunity.

In Germany, Japan and China, where France's image was already in good standing, the purpose was to reinforce its core strengths in 10 key industries, including telecommunications, technology, pharmaceuticals and aeronautics. Targeted sector reports, sector advertisements, success stories and testimonials were valuable in showing France's leadership, innovation and productiveness in a concrete manner.

To further emphasize France's attractiveness in all target countries, over 35 arguments were produced to point out its flexible labour laws, superior healthcare system and diverse business clusters, whereas statistical benchmarks were effective in displaying its competitiveness in categories such as real-estate costs, employee salaries and tax rates.

High-impact advertisements spread the message of France's appeal in the USA, the UK, Germany and Japan. In total, over 185 advertisements endorsed 'The New France' in top economic news publications, including *The Financial Times*, *The Wall Street Journal*, *Handelsblatt* and *Nikkei*. Billboard advertisements also appeared throughout major airports in the USA, the UK, Japan and China, as well as in Roissy Charles de Gaulle airport in Paris.

In addition, sector videos, a comprehensive multi-lingual communications kit and a book available in five languages entitled *France means business* (10 000 copies distributed in 60 countries) served as campaign support materials. A microsite, www.thenewfrance.com, relaying testimonials and information on doing business in France was launched in complement to the project.

Outside of the print and press arenas, IFA executives met with economic leaders and potential investors at nearly 150 high-profile events during the campaign, including the World Economic Forum in Davos, the Forbes CEO Conference, the BusinessWeek Leadership Forum and the Fortune Innovation Forum. This provided a valuable opportunity to speak to the target audience face-to-face and directly showcase France's profile in an international environment.

■ 4. Campaign rollout

'The New France' campaign was rolled out in phases over the past 3 years, using a combination of strategic advertising, public relations, printed press and web media. The launch in October 2004 started with an intensive print advertising campaign with 51 advertisements in 21 international economic publications in the USA, the UK, Germany and Japan. The microsite was introduced at the end of the year.

An expanded, multi-tiered plan followed in 2005, with a total of 77 advertisements appearing in 19 publications. After a first wave of print advertisements, a survey was conducted by the research group TNS Sofres to measure the campaign's effectiveness among company managers in four of the target countries. Based on the outcome, IFA switched its advertising approach in Germany to focus on sector-based magazines instead of financial publications. The second half of 2005 saw the release of more print advertisements and large billboard advertisements in international airports. The campaign also made its way onto the Internet in the form of banner advertisements on leading economic websites.

In 2006, the promotion of France intensified with 59 advertisements appearing in 17 well-known financial publications in the USA, the UK and Japan. Also, IFA's website, www.investinfrance.org, became a focal point in communicating consistent information about investing in France.

This year, IFA plans to increase its presence on the Internet by creating a dedicated B2B site to better respond to investor demands. The website will be used increasingly as a primary tool to offer a wider range of updated and useful information to investors.

■ 5. What were the results?

Today, France's image is in good shape. It was recently ranked fourth among the most popular countries in the world, according to a BBC World Service survey, and 'The New France' campaign has generated positive results. The TNS Sofres survey, conducted during the course of the campaign, revealed that 55% of respondents in the USA, the UK, Germany and Japan felt the campaign clearly demonstrated France's strengths, and another 61% in the USA, the UK and Japan said it made them view France in a new light.

On the inward investment front, France had an exceptional year in 2006, with 40 000 new jobs created from foreign investment projects, a 33% hike over 2005. It now ranks third in the world for foreign direct investment according to UNCTAD, and the USA is its leading investor, with corporate investments valued at US $171 billion.

France is an ambitious leader in the world marketplace. Its economic profile will continue to grow even stronger in the near future as more and more foreign investors learn about the many opportunities 'The New France' has to offer. And the potential investor base is widening quickly with IFA aiming to meet 6 500 companies around the world and 800 subsidiaries of foreign companies in France in 2007.

*****

■ Introduction

In this chapter, we view the future horizons for nation branding, identifying a number of trends that could characterize nation branding in the coming years. These trends range from the increasing impact of consumer-generated media to the potential of nation branding to act as a catalyst for sustainable development and competitive parity. The country case insight on France that appears in this chapter shows how nation branding can contribute to attracting FDI to a country, whilst Prof. Stephen Brown's academic perspective discusses the challenges in branding a nation whose nation-state status is debatable. In his practitioner insight, Chris Macrae offers a perspective that challenges the concept of nation-brands as possessing standalone power in an increasingly connecting world.

■ A shift away from anglocentric paradigms

As the twenty-first century unfolds, and the BRIC nations emerge as global economic superpowers, joined by other nations taking a more prominent place on the global stage, we can expect to see a shift away from existing anglocentric paradigms of brand management towards new paradigms that reflect the new world order. What exact form the new paradigms take is yet to be seen. Jack Yan has predicted that 'by the second part of the twenty-first century, India will probably be the source from which the West will learn how to nation brand' (see practitioner insight, Chapter 7). Simon Anholt has described how his work, initially brand-focused, now involves building and training high-level teams of national decision-makers in the principles of competitive identity (see practitioner insight, Chapter 1). The immense scope of nation branding and the universal need for countries to compete effectively in a globalized economy render it unlikely that the fundamentally Western-based paradigm of brand management will remain dominant over the coming decades. Exciting new perspectives can be expected as more and more nations find original, context-specific solutions to their own unique challenges.

■ Improved coordination of nation-branding strategy

The concepts and issues involved in nation branding are not difficult to grasp intellectually. The challenge is in delineating the areas of activity that the nation-brand strategy needs to encompass and then ensuring that there is adequate coordination of the different organizations and individuals involved in the overall strategy's component parts. This imperative has been alluded to by Prof. Akutsu in his country case insight on Japan (Chapter 9). The paramount need for coordination is a recurring theme in many of the country cases, academic perspectives and practitioner insights that appear in this book. For example, Vladimir Lebedenko describes how in the 1990s, left to its own devices, the image of Russia just drifted (see country case insight on Russia, Chapter 5); Prof. Martial Pasquier refers to the fragmented manner in which Switzerland's image had been managed before the setting up of the 'Presence Switzerland' coordinating organ (see country case insight, Chapter 4); and Philippe Favre demonstrates how the image of France as a business destination has been improved through a campaign coordinating the activities of over ten different government bodies (see country case insight, Chapter 10). In these and other cases, clear benefits have been derived through establishing and implementing the principle of a coordinated approach to nation-branding strategy.

■ Growing adoption of brand management techniques

Although in the long term, one can foresee the emergence of alternative paradigms to the brand management paradigm, in the short to medium term, it is likely that nations will become more savvy with regard to using the tools and techniques of brand management in order to promote their nation's competitiveness in the global economy. Established principles such as brand identity, brand image and brand positioning are useful for clarifying the bases of nation-brand strategy and for guiding the development and implementation of coordinated campaigns. Another branding concept for which nations may investigate potential applications is the practice of co-branding. Co-branding is commonly seen in business, where two brands owned by different companies join together in order to benefit from each other's existing brand equity. Co-branding can be seen in the domain of nation branding in the joint bids that two countries make to host high-profile sporting events, for example the Austria–Switzerland bid to host the 2008 European Football Championship and the Poland–Ukraine bid to host the same tournament in 2012. Another example of co-branding being practised as an element of nation-brand strategy can be seen in print magazine advertisements forming part of the 'Malaysia Truly Asia' campaign, where the participating 'brands' are Visit Malaysia 2007, Tourism Malaysia, Malaysia Airlines and, perhaps surprisingly, Manchester United FC.

In terms of basic marketing literacy, the marketing principles of segmentation and targeting of markets and audiences are useful – and easily understood – techniques for ensuring that resources are not wasted on poorly targeted activities and communications. Those politicians, government officials and other public servants who are involved in nation-branding strategy should also be trained to at least a basic level in the principles of branding, so that they can not only contribute effectively to the achievement of nation-branding goals but also in order to ensure that public money is not squandered on hiring inept or under-performing advertising agencies, branding consultants and so on.

It would also be useful for government and public agencies involved in nation branding to have some knowledge of marketing metrics, the ways in which marketing's return on investment can be measured. Tim Ambler, a Senior Fellow at London Business School, has stated that 'clear goals and metrics are what separate the professional from the amateur', and he goes on to suggest that following ten questions that companies should ask themselves about their marketing performance: (1) Does the senior executive team regularly and formally assess marketing performance? (2) What does the senior executive team understand by the term 'customer value'? (3) How much time does the senior executive team give to marketing issues? (4) Does the business/marketing plan show the non-financial corporate goals and link them to market goals? (5) Does the plan show the comparison of your marketing performance with competitors or the market as a whole? (6) What is your main marketing asset called? (7) Does the senior executive team's performance review involve a quantified view of the main marketing asset and how it has changed? (8) Has the senior executive team quantified what 'success' would look like 5 or 10 years in the future? (9) Does your strategy have quantified milestones to indicate progress towards that success? (10) Are the marketing performance indicators that are seen by the senior executive team aligned with these quantified milestones? [1]. Although designed for senior executives in the corporate world, the above metrics can also be applied to the marketing activities conducted for nation-branding campaigns. In fact, if such metrics are not applied, then there will be a lack of accountability that will hamper the effective evaluation of the marketing-specific elements of the nation-brand strategy.

Being familiarized with marketing and branding techniques, even at a basic introductory level, will equip those involved in nation-branding activities with the tools and insight to increase their personal and team effectiveness. However, these marketing and branding techniques should not be viewed as a means to gloss over unethical behaviour. The essence of nation branding should be to coordinate the nation's key stakeholders in pursuit of goals that will benefit the whole nation; it is not a PR exercise for spinning away the nation's social, commercial, political or military faults. Nation branding aims to enhance a nation's image and reputation in order to allow benefits to flow in terms of boosting FDI, tourism, export promotion and so on. This can only occur if the nation's actions are respectable and well communicated – in a wide sense, it has been suggested that 'a strong reputation follows from performing reputable acts, explaining them forcefully, and listening carefully' [2].

Practitioner Insight

The coming crisis in the geography-chained market of nations

Chris Macrae

Consultant and Writer

In analysing the climate crisis, Sir Nicholas Stern has named energy as the greatest ever failure of markets. I beg to differ. I am concerned by the prospect that the geography-chained market of nations will turn out to be an even bigger failure. This is increasingly putting the sustainability of future generations at risk. However democratic it claims to be, the twentieth century's separated nation brand is now in danger of becoming a failing system. It is inappropriate to value such stand-alone power in an increasingly connecting world. Will we, the globe's people, turn up to be just in time to simultaneously reform communications, bridge cultures and develop world citizen networks so as to counter this threat to all our future generations' sustainability?

In terms of sustainability, there is a risk that aid policy if it is only tangible may actually enslave developing nations even more into commodity status. Whilst we may or may not have a complete plan about how we may provide an intangible aid policy, nation branding provides us with some potential means to advance the social and economic welfare of developing nations. Although a brand is an incredibly powerful instrument, it can be used to good or bad purposes. And I now essentially agree with Naomi Klein that most global organizations currently, by mistake or otherwise, are using the instrument of branding to bad purposes. But that is why nation branding is almost marketing's last chance to try and find at least some context that we can be proud of. Brands are powerful instruments and could be used for good.

For me, a problem with nation branding is you always have to find a language that different people are happy with. In my view, it is totally inappropriate *not* to think of a nation as a brand, because ultimately we are saying that everyone's democratic permission to be productive depends on how well the nation is branded – or whatever you call this construct, which essentially is responsible for some nations being seen to be only commodity providers and others to be seen as leaders of something. Nation branding needs to be the way that you coordinate your whole socio-economic policy. It links through to all the other constructs that people have used to plan nations, but it provides a sort of missing link. I do not care if we call it nation branding, nation knowledge, or knowledge of your future or something else, as long as we get one of these human-connecting constructs into the planning of nations. Of course, what this also means is that the democratic idea of what the nation should be about is something that everyone in the nation should be participating in. We also need a consistency about this, so that the core elements do not become party political and change every 2 years.

*****

■ Online nation branding

Online branding is an integral part of most businesses in the digital age. The Internet has become recognized as a great equalizer, allowing any brand, however small, to become global simply by having a website. Chris Anderson, former Editor-in-Chief at *Wired* magazine and author of *The Long Tail* [3], has described how the Internet is allowing niche brands to build a market that is even greater than that of the big, blockbuster brands and even though word-of-mouth marketing may be the only marketing available to these niche brands, 'it's never been a better time and the tools have never been more powerful' [4]. This is an encouraging observation for smaller, emerging or less-developed nations that cannot realistically hope to compete with the global economic superpowers in terms of financial firepower to fund their nation branding. Online branding offers such nations the opportunity to establish themselves as niche brands in a way that would not be possible through using more conventional branding techniques such as print advertising, for example whose cost puts it beyond the budget of many less-wealthy nations. Online branding can stimulate positive word-of-mouth through techniques such as seeding trials, viral advertising, brand advocacy programmes and influencer outreach initiatives [5]. As well as these specific techniques, there are also new virtual worlds appearing such as Second Life, in which nations will rapidly need to establish a presence if they are not to be left behind by more prescient rivals.

Online branding is obviously also important for larger, relatively wealthy nations, and 'The New France' campaign illustrates how an online presence has been integrated into that overall campaign through the development of the IFA's own site, www.investinfrance.org, a microsite relaying testimonials and information on doing business in France, www.thenewfrance.com, as well as a dedicated B2B site to be created before the end of 2007 (see country case insight on France, Chapter 10).

■ Increasing impact of consumer-generated media

A key phenomenon in the digital age has been the emergence of consumer-generated media. The liberating, equalizing nature of the Internet has empowered consumers in terms of their ability to make their voice heard in comparison with previous eras when it was brand owners who had a near monopoly on communications. The business-to-consumer monologue has transformed into a dialogue in which the co-creation of brand value occurs through interaction between the brand and the consumer. This implies a certain willingness on the part of brand owners to reduce their control over the brand, for example by inviting consumers to suggest creative themes and executions for future advertising campaigns. There are probably few nations that would consider such a radical redistribution of brand influence away from the brand owner and towards the consumer; yet, there is evident potential for nation-brands to emulate some of the brand value co-creation strategies currently employed by PSC brands. The social networking site, myspace.com, for example has already been used by the US Marine Corps for recruitment and brand-building [6]. Nation-brands should likewise consider the possibilities of such social networking sites as a possible component of their overall strategy.

Companies are taking an increasing interest in the 'blogosphere', and nation-brands can be expected to follow suit by devising strategies to engage with the ever-increasing numbers of bloggers, many of whom are writing about issues that affect nation-brands. The most obvious example is individuals who publish blogs on their experiences as a tourist visiting various nations.

■ Internal nation branding

Internal branding is one area in which governments have been slow to engage compared with other aspects of nation-branding strategy. Internal nation branding will gain in importance as nations realize that the necessary behaviours for successful implementation of strategy result from the commitment levels that individuals exhibit towards the strategy in question. For nation branding, the two audiences for internal branding are, on the one hand, the stakeholder organizations and individuals involved in the development and implementation of nation branding strategy and, on the other hand, the domestic population, the entirety of the nation's citizens. In a firm context, Burmann and Zeplin [7] have identified three key levers for generating brand commitment: brand-centred human resources management, brand communication and brand leadership. In a nation-branding context, responsibility for these three key levers needs to be allocated to specified individuals or agencies, the exact identity of which will depend upon the specific structure within which the nation-brand has been developed. Some of the steps to effective internal branding used by Yahoo! can equally be applied to internal nation branding: for example do not work in silos, think like a marketer, use powerful keywords that embody your brand promise and so on [8].

■ Sonic nation branding

Sonic branding is a relatively recent addition to the array of techniques available to brand managers. There are three components of sonic branding – voices, music and sound effects [9]. Sonic branding can take the form of a sonic logo that plays on every advertisement for a brand, or it can take on a wider application through the consistent use of sound and music across every aspect of the business, as is practised by companies such as Honda, Intel and Easyjet [10]. Siemens, for example has added a seventh element to its branding, with sound now joining logo, claim, typeface, colours, layout and style amongst the basic building blocks of its brand; the company is using sound through the creation of an audio signature, or sonic logo, and also some mood sound [11]. It has been claimed that sonic branding implants a memory in the aural pathways of listeners' brains that is so powerful that it is virtually impossible to forget and that sonic branding is now a key weapon in competition for market share [12].

Although the strategic use of sound in branding has only recently been adopted by companies, the power of music to affect consumer behaviour has been widely researched for several years in the service sector, particularly in the retail and restaurant sectors [13,14]. Some studies have indicated that musical tempo can affect consumer behaviour – supermarket shoppers have shown increased purchase levels when slow tempo music was being played compared with fast tempo music [15], whilst fast tempo music significantly increased diner eating speed [16] and fast tempo renditions of piano tunes were found to increase drinking speed compared with slow tempo versions [17]. These studies usefully demonstrate the power of music to affect specific aspects of consumer behaviour, but of more direct relevance to nation branding is one of the best-known studies in the area of the use of music in marketing, the so-called 'wine-aisle experiment'.

The 'wine-aisle experiment' [18] took place over a period of 2 weeks during which the music played in the wine section of a supermarket was alternated on a daily basis between French and German styles – the study's findings indicated that when French music was played, the French wine would outsell its German counterpart and vice-versa, even though customers did not seem to be consciously aware of the music being played. Export promotion agencies and provenance brands should consider the implications of this study and develop branding strategies that incorporate the use of appropriate music in the promotion of their products. Nations are uniquely well equipped to this, as they have centuries of musical heritage to draw upon. The 'wine-aisle experiment' demonstrates how the COO effect can be subtly, yet immensely effectively, incorporated into marketing communications. Few, if any, of the numerous national wine promotional campaigns run by various nations over recent years have incorporated a sonic-branding dimension. Future campaigns that do so can thus expect to reap first-mover advantage.

Academic Perspective

True North

Stephen Brown
*Professor of Marketing Research, University of Ulster,
Northern Ireland*

How do you brand a nation whose nation state-status is debatable? How do you brand a nation whose USP – the single thing it is world famous for – is a taboo topic for its inhabitants? How do you look to the future when the past is obscuring the view?

Such are the dilemmas facing Northern Ireland at the dawn of the twenty-first century. Nominally, an integral part of the UK, but subject to a long-standing territorial claim by the Republic of Ireland, an adjacent sovereign state, Northern Ireland is neither one thing nor the other. Is it Irish or British or both? Or something else entirely? Indeed, if the country cannot make up its mind where it is at, how does it expect to sell itself successfully to visitors, investors or the wider international community?

There is of course an obvious solution. In keeping with established marketing principles of differentiation, positioning, mind-share and suchlike, Northern Ireland should emphasize its particularly distinctive attributes.

The only problem is that, in most people's minds, Northern Ireland is irrevocably associated with bombs, bullets, riots, race hate, terrorist attacks, paramilitary associations, religious conflict and an all-pervasive ethos of lawlessness. These are not the kind of things you boast about, much less use as part of a nation-branding strategy. Granted, man's inhumanity to man has spawned many experience marketing attractions, from guided tours of Auschwitz to Madame Tussauds Chamber of Horrors, but basing a nation-branding strategy on 30 years of human suffering is understandably unacceptable to the residents of Northern Ireland, many of whom have lost loved ones in the conflict.

Faced with this seemingly impossible marketing situation, the official response is to evade, or rather avoid, the situation. The story Northern Ireland tells about itself is a combination of 'don't mention the war' and 'whatever you do, don't allude to our orthogonal national identities'. Like many economically depressed, socially deprived regions, Northern Ireland portrays itself as the place to be, a country on the up, a lively, vibrant locale full of arts festivals, fancy restaurants, welcoming pubs, glorious countryside, glittering shopping malls, exclusive night clubs and 24-h party people. The complete opposite, in short, of what most outsiders imagine it to be.

Interestingly, the darker side of the Northern Ireland nation brand does get a look in, albeit in a decidedly displaced form. Central to Northern Ireland's future branding strategy is RMS *Titanic*, the ill-fated luxury liner that hit an iceberg on its maiden voyage to New York in April 1912 and sank with the loss of 1500 lives. *Titanic* was built in Belfast and, as the centenary of the sinking approaches, the iconic liner is being celebrated as never before. A multi-billion pound property development on the site of the old shipyard and slipway is the centrepiece of this Titanic-themed venture, though the final form it will take remains to be seen.

Many marketers might be amazed that the greatest new brand failure in history – greater even than the Edsel debacle or New Coke calamity – is the narrative upon which brand Northern Ireland is being built. But viewed in a strictly symbolic sense, and given the lack of meaningful marketing alternatives, it makes a modicum of sense.

Northern Ireland, then, is sending out mixed messages, seriously mixed-up messages. That might not be a bad thing, however. It is increasingly recognized that, in a world of ambi-brands, the old Ries and Trout idea of one-word-one-brand positioning strategies no longer passes muster. There is more to Volvo than 'safety'. There is more to Guinness than 'fortitude'. There is more to Brazil than 'carnival'. There is more to Kenya than 'safari'. Nation-branding strategies are moving beyond hackneyed stereotypes, and it is arguable that ambivalent images of Northern Ireland –riot-torn, *Titanic*-loving, party people! – are singularly appropriate in today's paradoxical postmodern milieu. The only thing that remains to be settled is the timing of the annual deckchair rearranging ceremony.

*****

■ An alternative lexicon for nation branding?

The words 'brand' and 'branding' generate mixed responses. For some, the words are innocuous descriptors of elements and practices of the commercial world; for others, the words embody notions of manipulation, deceit and superficiality. It is this book's contention that nation branding is a benign force at the disposal of all nations, but particularly smaller, poorer or otherwise struggling nations, to help them compete effectively on the world stage rather than being trampled upon by more powerful rivals. 'Nation branding' is an imperfect term, as the activities involved in nation branding transcend conventional views of branding as merely marketing hype for everyday products. The activation of diaspora networks, the coordination of diverse government agencies and debate on national identity are all part of nation branding yet are far removed from the conventional view of branding's domain. Other terms that may at some point in the future supplant the term 'nation branding' include 'reputation management', 'competitive identity', 'public diplomacy' and so on.

■ Soft power and public diplomacy

The concept of 'soft power' needs to infuse nation-branding strategy. Soft power has been defined as 'the ability to get what you want by attracting and persuading others to adopt your goals. It differs from hard power, the ability to use the carrots and sticks of economic and military might to make others follow your will' [19]. Internally, the relevance of soft power is that nation-branding strategy can only succeed if it is voluntarily endorsed and agreed upon by a critical mass of stakeholders [20]. Coordinating bodies need to be established that do not impose obligations onto the nation-brand stakeholders, but which identify potential synergies between the different stakeholders and act as a catalyst to help realise these synergies.

The notion of 'public diplomacy' is another concept that governments may increasingly turn to in their nation-branding efforts. Public diplomacy includes 'the cultivation by governments of public opinion in other countries' [21], and a key way in which this is done is through the promotion of cultural programmes. It has been argued, for example, that 'culture is increasingly recognised as the national brand par excellence, the source of both amity and discord in a world marked by infinite variety' [22]. The critical role of culture in nation branding has been discussed in Chapters 3, 5 and 6.

■ Nation branding as a driver of sustainable development and competitive parity

In his academic perspective (Chapter 2), Professor Dipak Pant has shown how a sustainable development agenda can form the foundation of a nation-brand strategy, particularly for nations that are challenged by geographic remoteness, lack of access to foreign markets and so on. By highlighting their performance on environmental stewardship indexes such as the ESI, countries can seek to leverage their nation-brand through high levels of performance across a wide range of sustainability metrics. The practice of nation branding can thus help nations to achieve competitive parity in cases where they do not possess the resources or the favourable locations of competing nations; nation branding may be viewed in this light as the ultimate expression of soft power.

■ Summary

As more and more nations turn to the techniques of nation branding, and as nation branding begins to gain academic, practitioner and government recognition as an important phenomenon, a proliferation of new approaches, tactics and strategies should occur. Policymakers at a national level will become more aware of the power of branding to help achieve national goals, and there will be increasing understanding of the need for nations to manage their reputations rather than passively endure the malign and humiliating effects of persistent, outdated national stereotypes. Perhaps the key lesson for nations to learn is the need to coordinate their nation-branding efforts. Without such coordination, a country's nation-branding strategy will stagnate and the nation's image will drift, almost certainly in a negative direction. The concept and practice of nation branding is not, as its detractors claim, cultural commodification; it is quite the opposite, in that nation branding aspires to allow cultural diversity to flourish and to enable all nations, regardless of size or power, to compete effectively on the global stage.

■ References

1. Ambler, T. (2006) Mastering the metrics. *The Marketer*, 24, May, pp. 22–23.
2. Stewart, G. (2006) Can reputations be 'Managed'? *The Geneva Papers*, **31**, 480–499.
3. Anderson, C. (2006) *The Long Tail: How Endless Choice Is Creating Unlimited Demand*, Random House Business Books, UK.
4. Mortimer, R. (2006) Chris Anderson on smashing hits. *Brand Strategy*, March, p. 17.

5. Kirby, J. and Marsden, P. (eds.) (2005) *Connected Marketing: The Viral, Buzz and Word of Mouth Revolution*, Butterworth-Heinemann, UK.

6. Armstrong, S. (2006) Bloggers for hire. *New Statesman*, August, pp. 26–27.

7. Burmann, C. and Zeplin, S. (2005) Building brand commitment: A behavioural approach to internal brand management. *Journal of Brand Management*, **12**, 4, 279–300.

8. Sartain, L. (2005) Branding from the inside out at Yahoo!: HR's role as brand builder. *Human Resource Management*, **44**, 1, 89–93.

9. Jackson, D.M. (2003) *Sonic Branding: An Introduction*, Palgrave Macmillan, UK.

10. Mortimer, R. (2005) Sonic branding: Branding the perfect pitch. *Brand Strategy*, February, p. 24.

11. Treasure, J. (2007) Sound: the uncharted territory. *Brand Strategy*, March, pp. 32–33.

12. Arnold, S. (2005) That Jingle is Part of Your Brand, *Broadcasting & Cable*, January 24, p. 78.

13. Alpert, J.I. and Alpert, M.I. (1990) Music influences on mood and purchase intentions. *Psychology and Marketing*, **7**, 2, 109–133.

14. Herrington, J.D. and Capella, L.M. (1996) Effects of music in service environments: a field study. *Journal of Services Marketing*, **10**, 2, 26–41.

15. Milliman, R.E. (1982) Using background music to affect the behaviour of supermarket shoppers. *Journal of Marketing*, **46**, Summer, 86–91.

16. Roballey, T.C., McGreevy, C., Rongo, R.R., Schwantes, M.L., Steger, P.J., Wininger, M.A., and Gardner, E.B. (1985) The effect of music on eating behaviour. *Bulletin of the Psychonomic Society*, **23**, 3, 221–222.

17. McElrea, H. and Standing, L. (1992) Fast music causes fast drinking. *Perceptual and Motor Skills*, **75**, 362.

18. North, A.C., Hargreaves, D.J., and McKendrick, J. (1999) The influence of in-store music on wine selections. *Journal of Applied Psychology*, **84**, 271–276.

19. Nye, J.S., Jr. (2003) Propaganda isn't the way: Soft power. *The International Herald Tribune*, January 10.

20. Anholt, S. (2007) *Competitive Identity: The New Brand Management for Nations, Cities and Regions*, Palgrave Macmillan, UK.

21. What is public diplomacy? http://www.publicdiplomacy.org (accessed 19/03/07).

22. Brown, J. (2005) Should the piper be paid? Three schools of thought on culture and foreign policy during the Cold War. *Place Branding*, **1**, 4, 420–423.

Glossary

CBBE	=	Customer-based brand equity
CETSCALE	=	Consumer ethnocentric tendency scale
COO	=	Country-of-origin
CPPI	=	Contextualized product-place image
CRM	=	Customer relationship management
CSR	=	Corporate social responsibility
EFI	=	Environmental Footprint Index
ESI	=	Environmental Sustainability Index
EVI	=	Environmental Vulnerability Index
IMC	=	Integrated marketing communications
FATF	=	Financial Action Task Force
FMCG	=	Fast-moving consumer goods
NBEQ	=	Nation-brand equity
NBI	=	Nation Brands Index
NFC	=	Need for cognition
OECD	=	Organisation for Economic Cooperation and Development
PCI	=	Product-country image
PDO	=	Protected Designation of Origin
PLC	=	Product life cycle
PSC brand	=	Product, service, or corporate brand
TLA	=	Technologically less advanced (countries)
TMA	=	Technologically more advanced (countries)
USP	=	Unique selling proposition
WEF	=	World Economic Forum

Index